I0729644

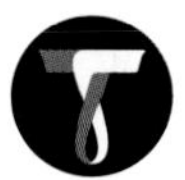 TROPE PUBLISHING Co.

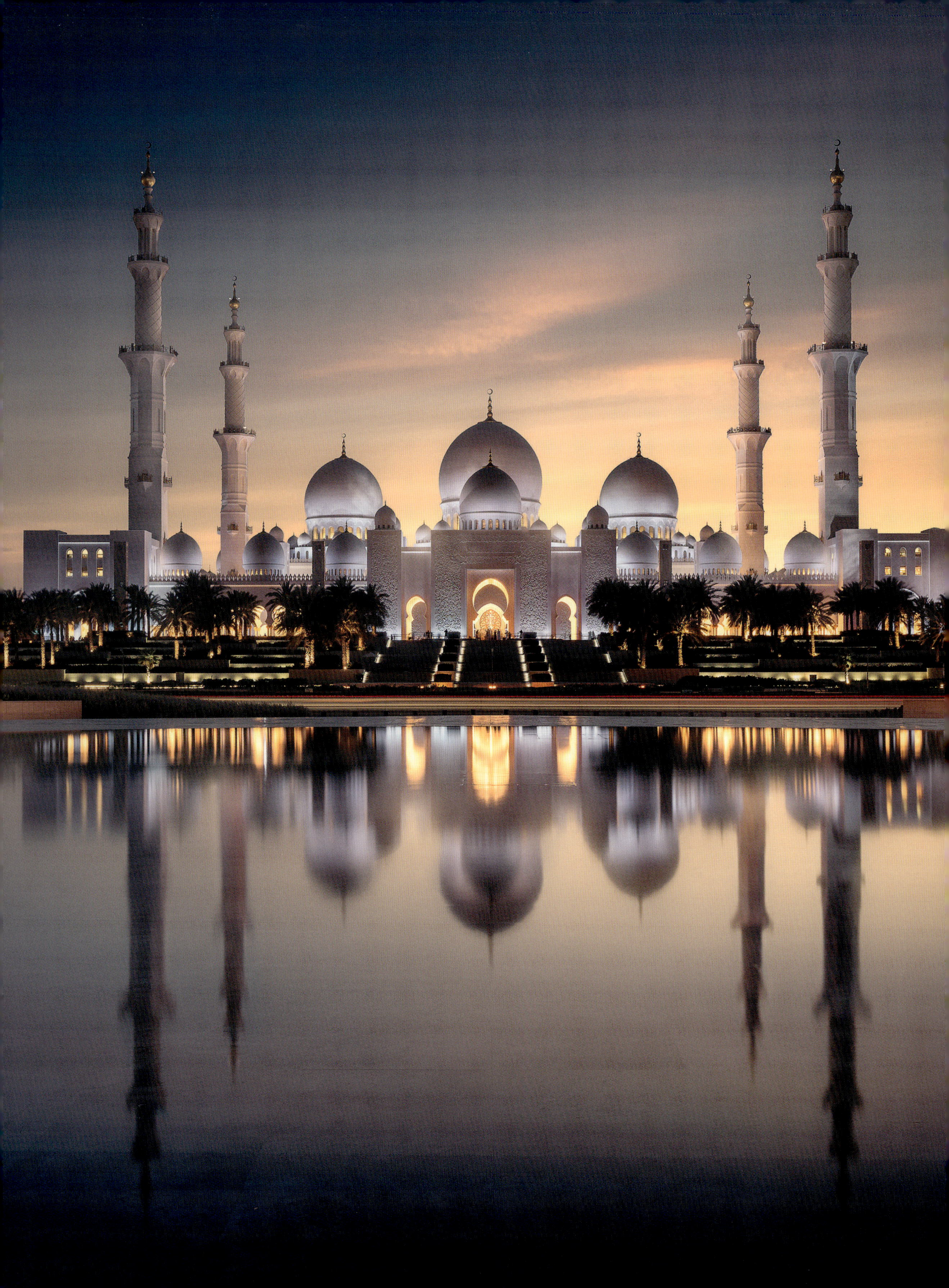

TRAVEL PHOTOGRAPHY
THROUGH THE LENS
OF MINDZEYE

WONDER
AROUND
EVERY
CORNER

MICHAEL SIDOFSKY

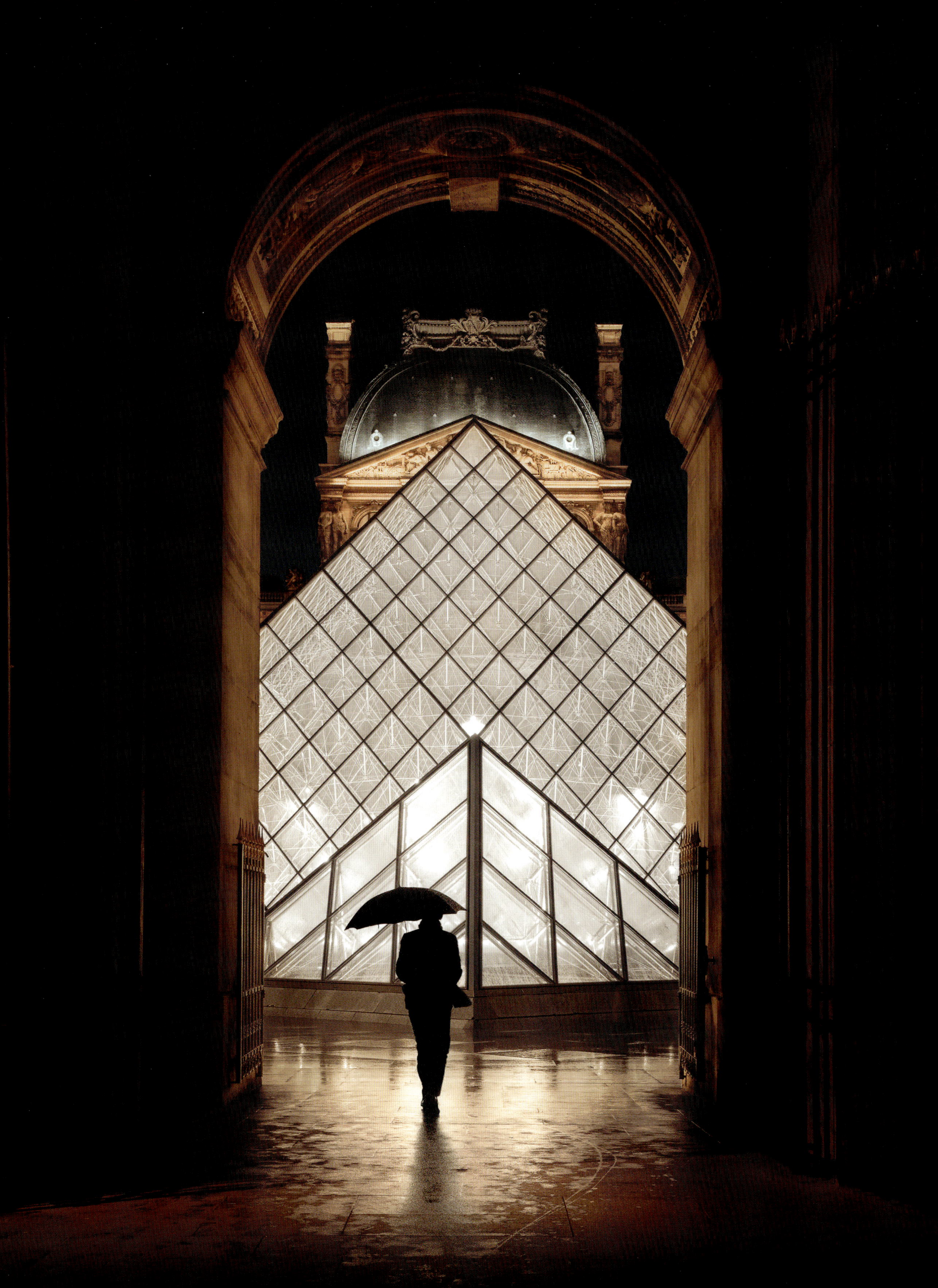

Beauty can be found everywhere whether we notice it or not. It surrounds us at all times and exists in the most obscure places. It's present when we're out for a simple walk, wandering the halls of an old museum, and even waiting in an overcrowded train station. Wonders exist outside of epic destinations like the Taj Mahal or the Roman Colosseum — in fact, they are often hiding in plain sight. They are found in the deserted alley we pass by every day or in the deteriorating building sitting on the corner of a busy street.

Beauty is complex and layered. What defines it has less to do with the bigger picture and everything to do with the smaller components that create it. From the shapes present, the colors, the lighting, the lines, the angles, even the weather and the time of day — all of these details build an atmosphere before our eyes, adding depth to the places and things we typically deem unappealing.

Beauty is subjective yet expansive, and I look forward to uncovering its many layers each time I load my camera. Before I take a photo, I set the scene in my mind's eye, then trust my instincts, skills, and the location to ignite the magic.

Like many photographers today, I began my journey by shooting on my phone. My hometown of Toronto was my muse, and I took pictures on the streets that I traveled regularly on my walk home from work. I considered the task a hobby and a good excuse to get outside but what I didn't expect was to fall in love with the art so quickly. With that love, I began to take my craft more seriously. I upgraded my phone to a DSLR camera and despite the transition being a challenge, I was determined to learn all I could to hone my skills. I spent my free time watching tutorials and reading books and blogs with information about camera settings and post-processing techniques. I was a sponge, soaking up every bit of knowledge available.

After a year of shooting Toronto and using it as practice grounds, I finally decided to broaden my eye. From New York City, the California coast, Chicago, Paris, and Barcelona, I spent two years exploring and becoming inspired by the world and its allure. Those years proved to be transformational, and I knew then that photography was something I wanted to do for the rest of my life.

With time I was able to formulate my purpose. Taking photos was my way of preserving memories and creating art out of my experiences. After building an online presence, I knew I wanted to share my perspective of these various cities and the landscapes surrounding them. I wanted to provide a unique and emotive portrayal people could connect with. To be successful, I needed to develop my own style.

The more comfortable and confident I became, the more my style began to shape on its own. I acquired techniques, abandoned those that didn't fit, and even created some of my own that, together, created the "painterly" style I've adapted today. My grandfather was an avid impressionist oil painter who had a keen eye for composition, color, and storytelling. His incredible and unique paintings adorned the walls of my childhood home and in many ways, though unbeknownst to me at the time, influenced my style as an artist and photographer. I take a lot of inspiration from his work and the works of the classical masters.

Capturing a new image is addictive. There is a rush during the process and a sense of pride once I complete a new piece I feel passionately about. The pursuit of the perfect photograph drives me to explore more, to take more photos, and it inspired me to create this book.

Though the delicate details of all the marvelous places featured already existed, much goes into capturing them. Sometimes it was as simple as a quick snapshot using manual settings of ISO, Aperture, and Shutter Speed. Other times, I may have adjusted and used long exposures, image bracketing, time-blending, or focus stacking to capture all the elements required to create the ideal image in my mind.

Once the stills are secured, I move to the editing stage. Applications such as Lightroom and Photoshop are involved and between them, I make adjustments to the white balance, exposure, highlights, shadows, blacks/whites, camera lens profile corrections and removal of chromatic aberration. I blend different exposures together if needed, create contrasts throughout the scene, dodge and burn to highlight some areas and darken others. I like to color grade and create subtle glow effects to further enhance the lighting, and finally, apply finishing touches like adjustments to textures and sharpening.

The goal after all these phases, from the moment I see the image in-camera to the editing stage, is to end with a photo that can stand the test of time. Whether 10 years from now or 50, I hope that the photographs in *Wonder Around Every Corner* feel timeless because these wonders are just that.

Michael Sidofsky, aka MINDZEYE

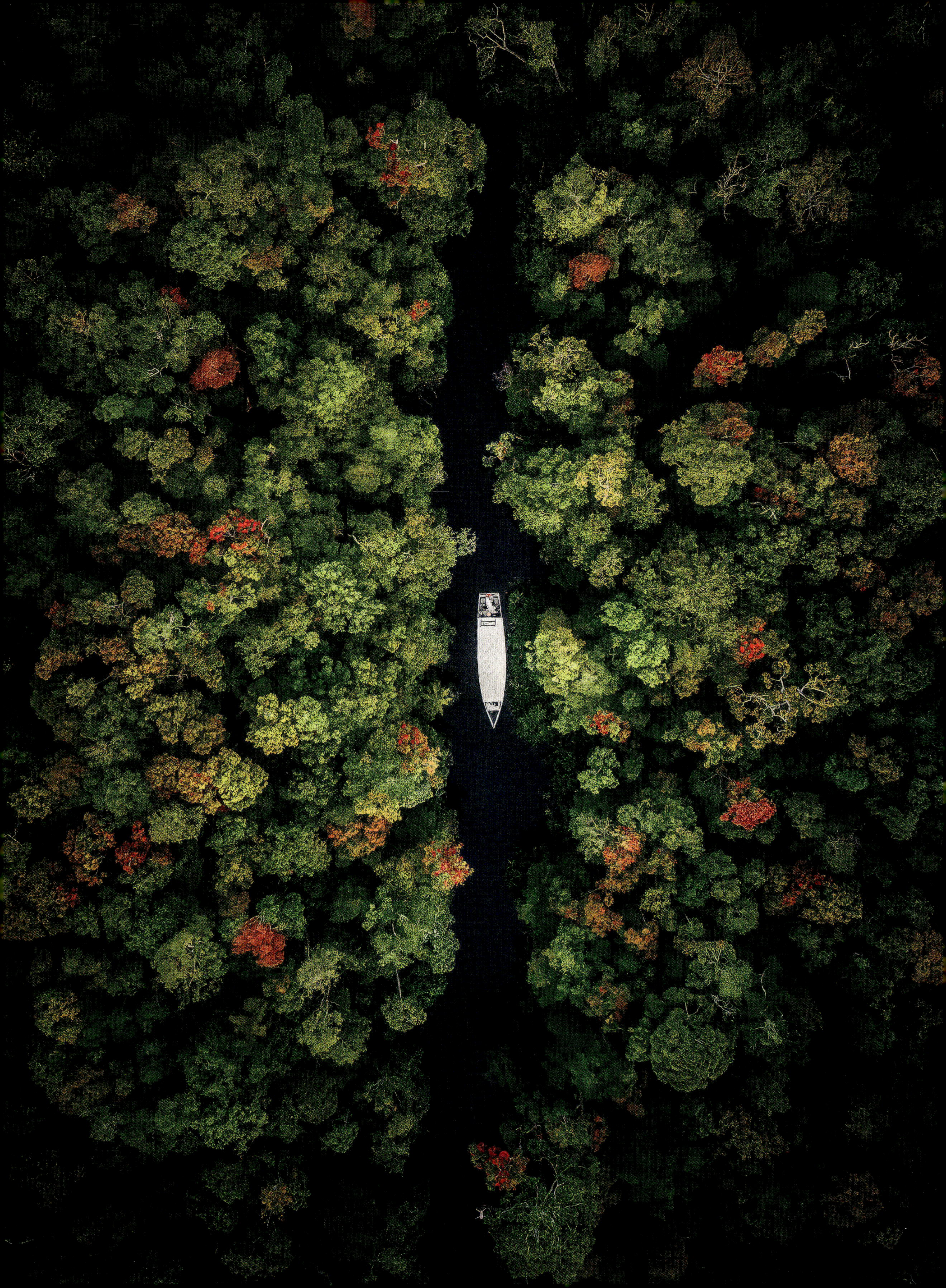

WONDER
AROUND
EVERY
CORNER

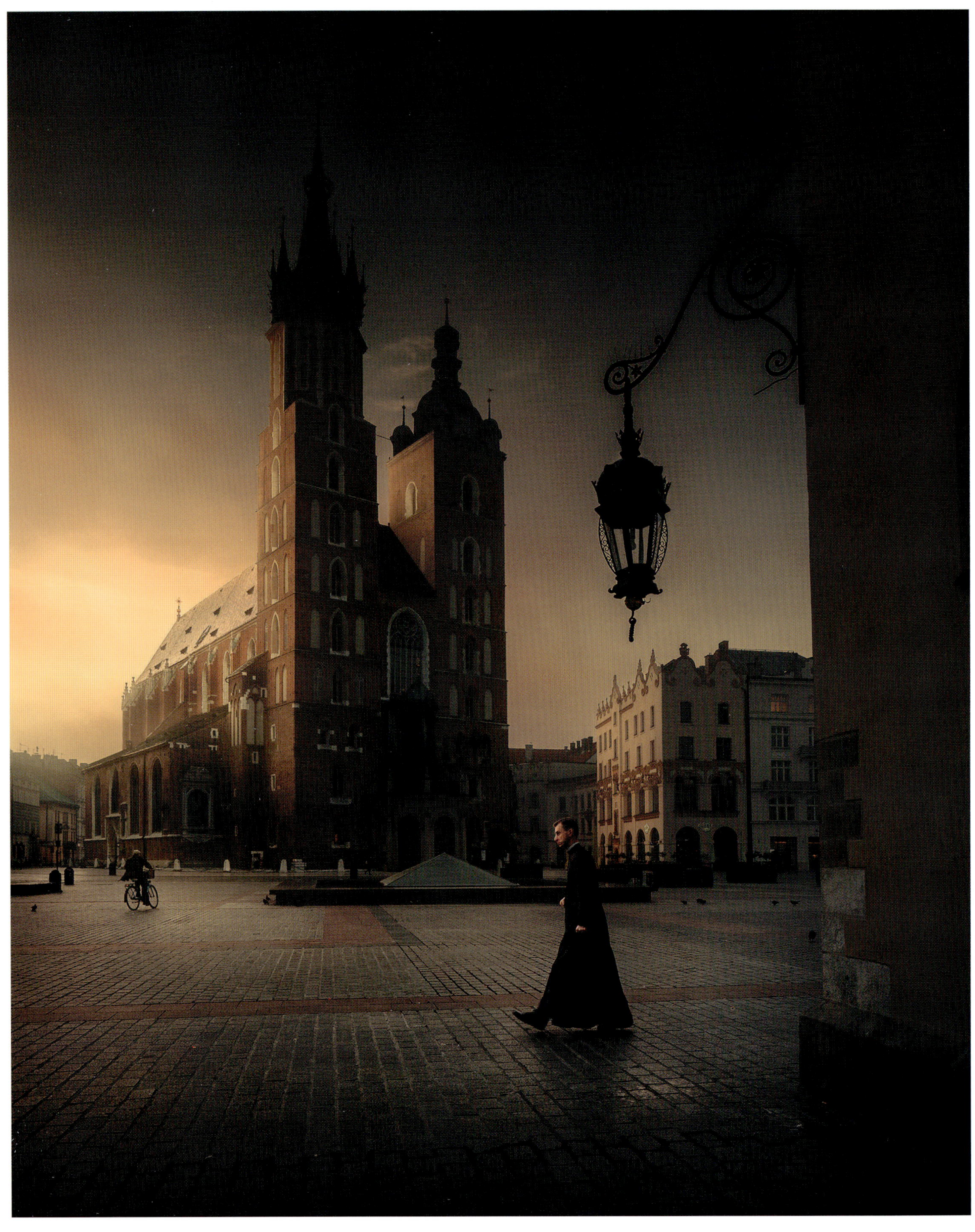

Krakow, Poland

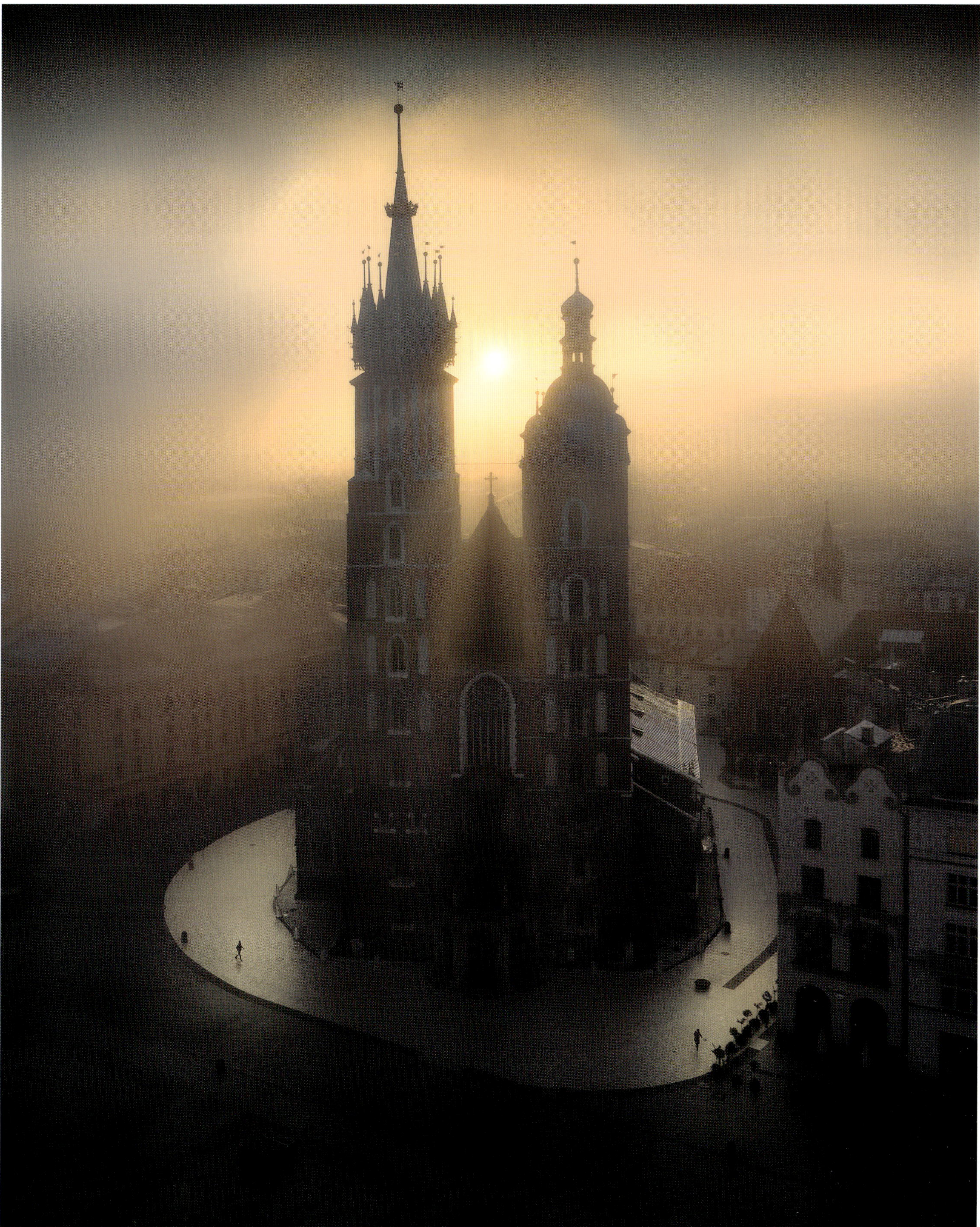

Krakow, Poland

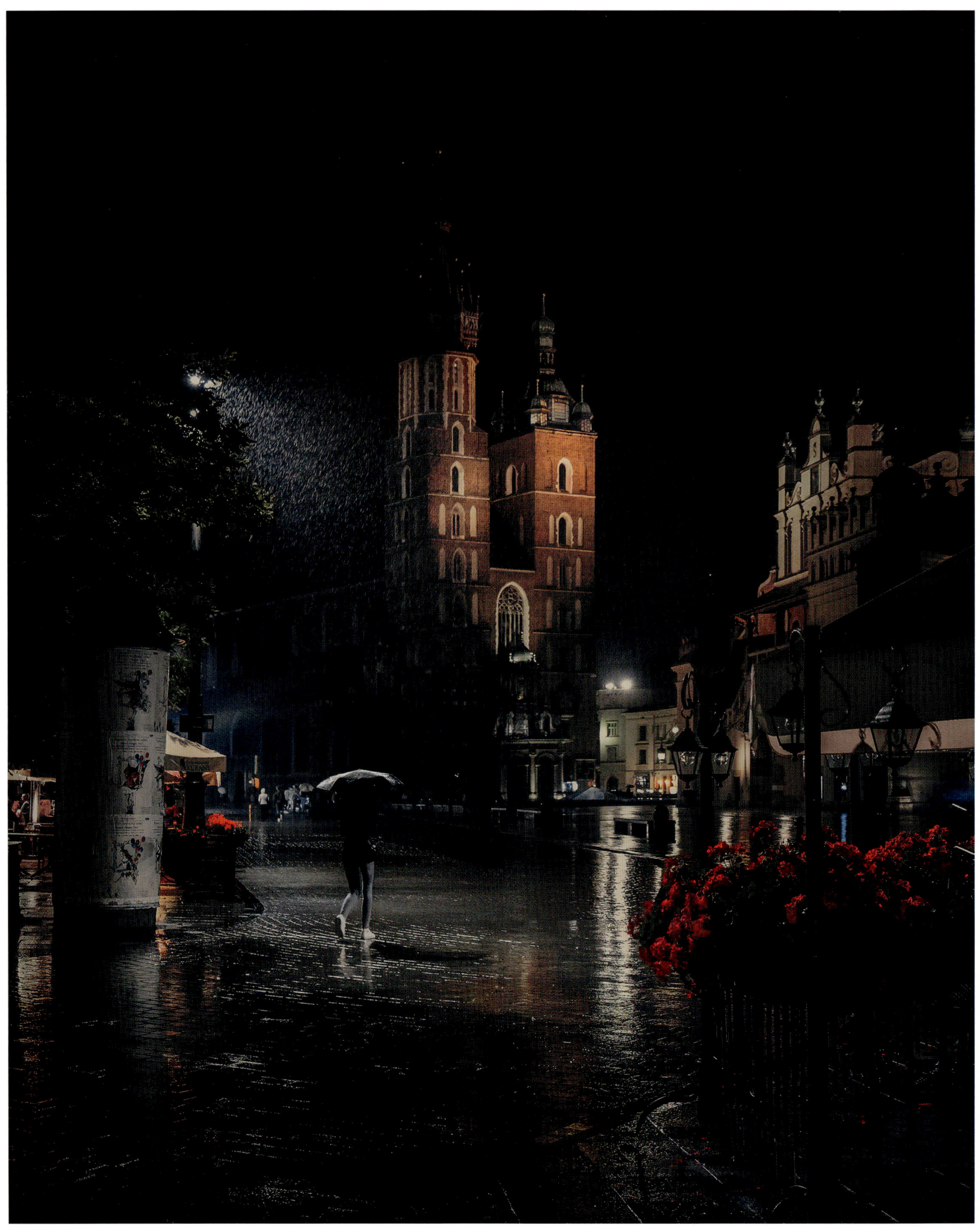

Krakow, Poland

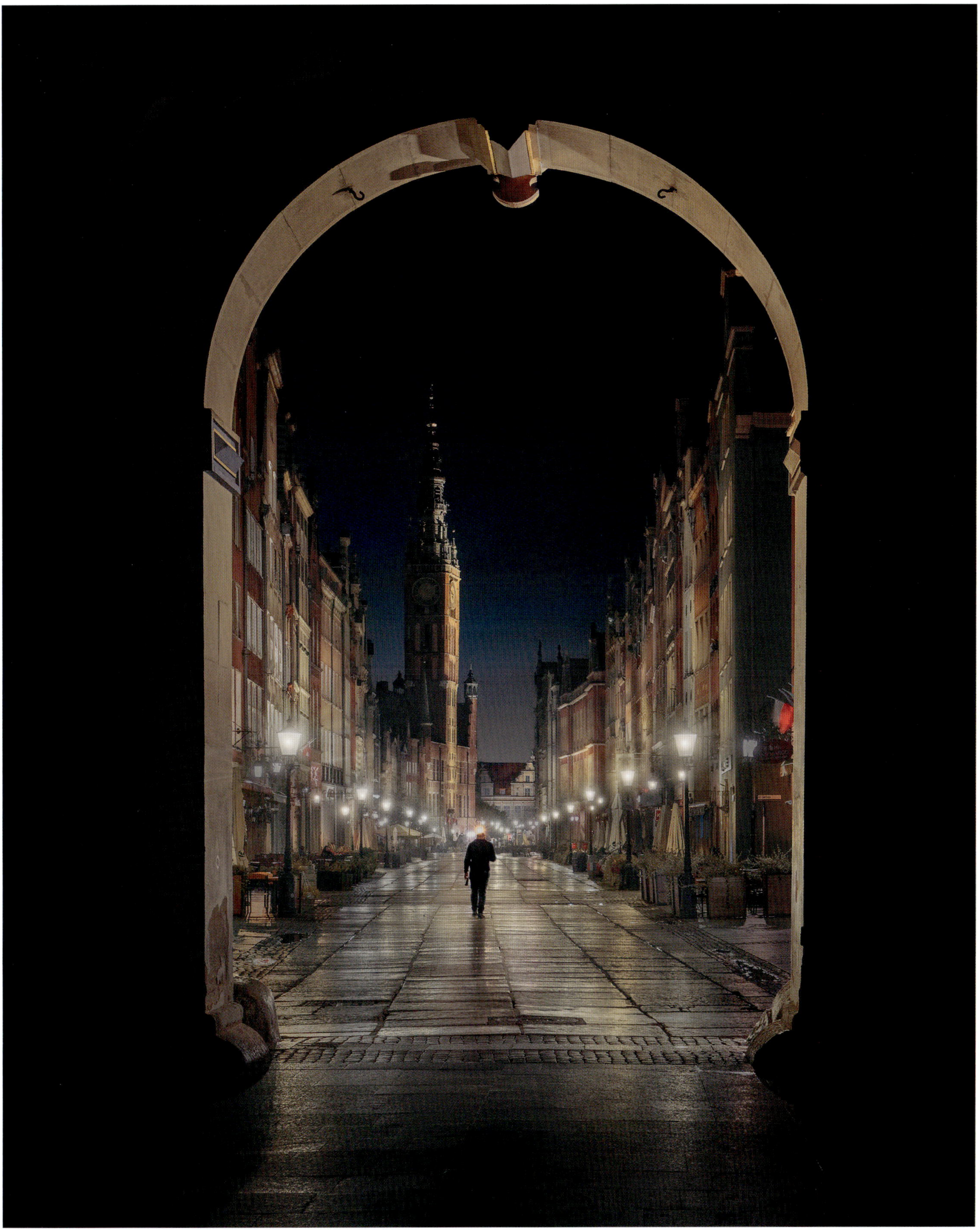

Gdansk, Poland

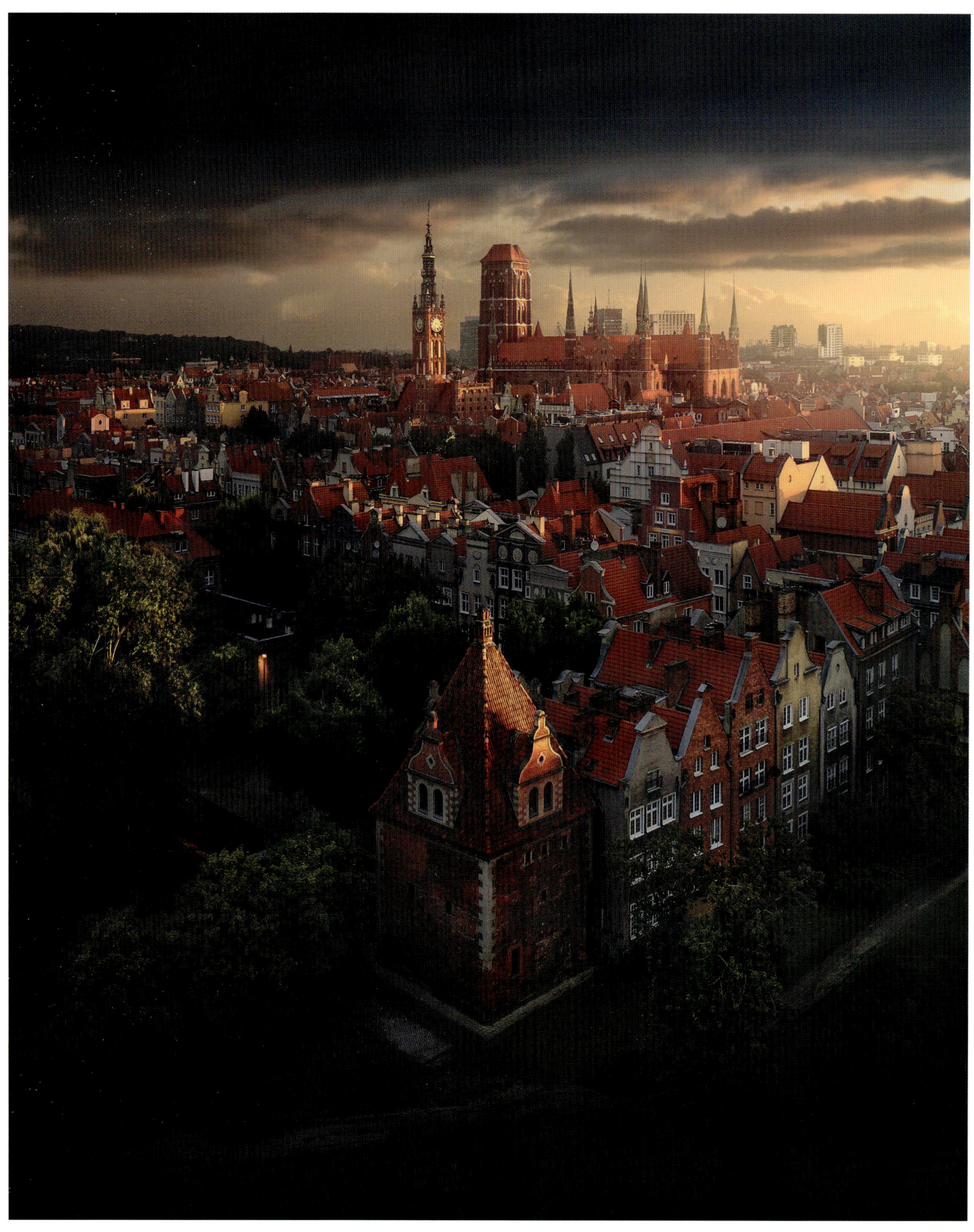

Gdansk, Poland

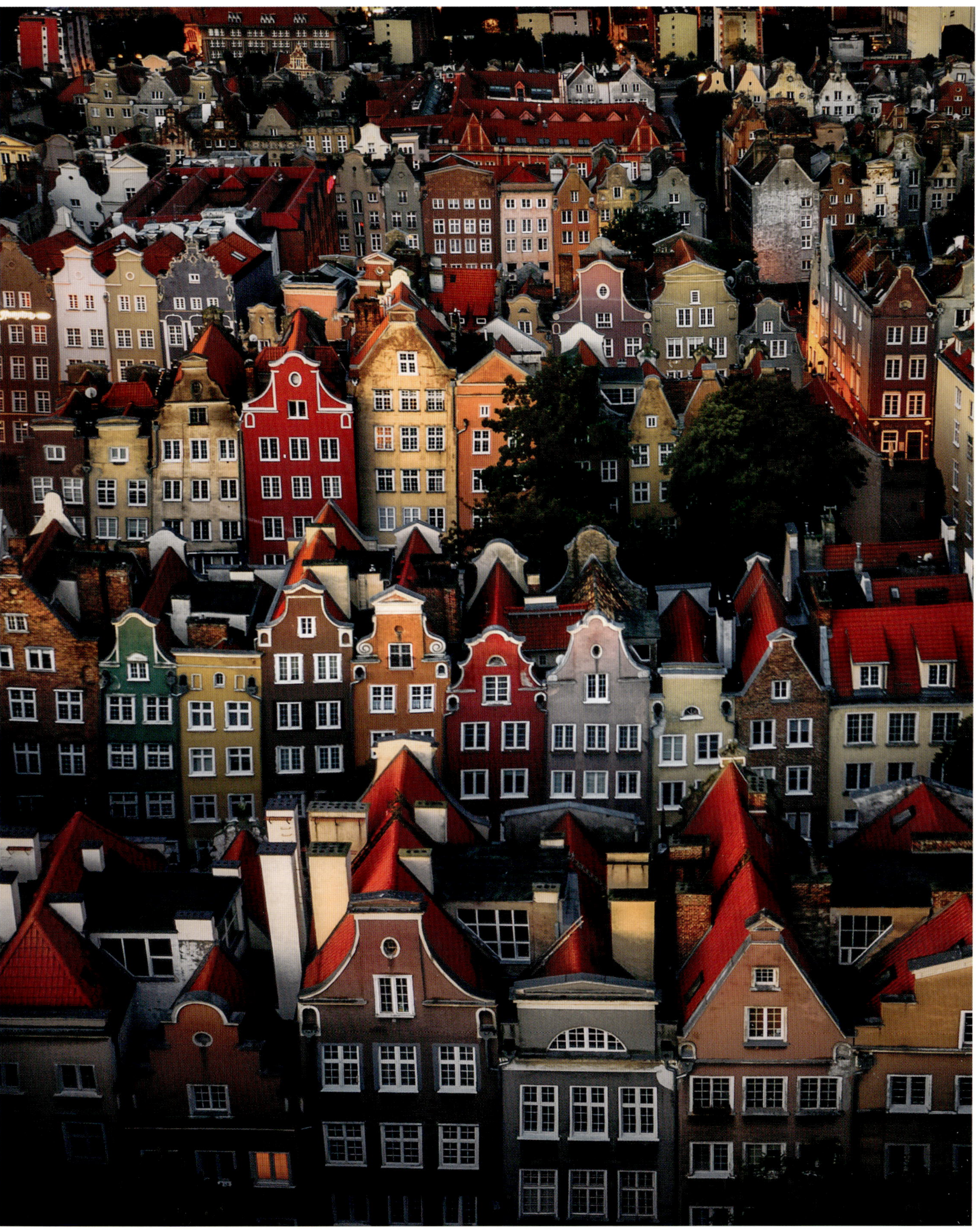

Gdansk, Poland

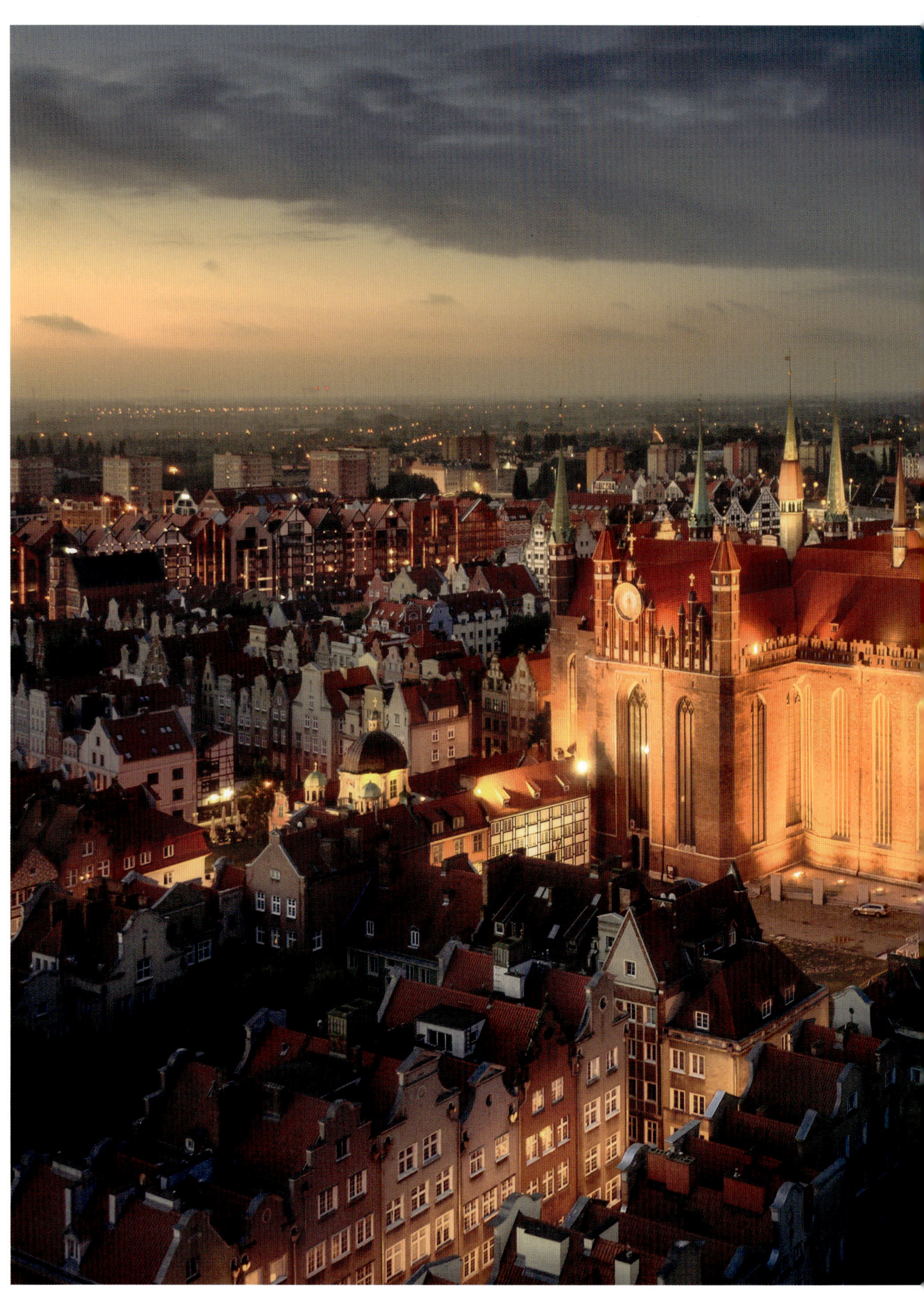

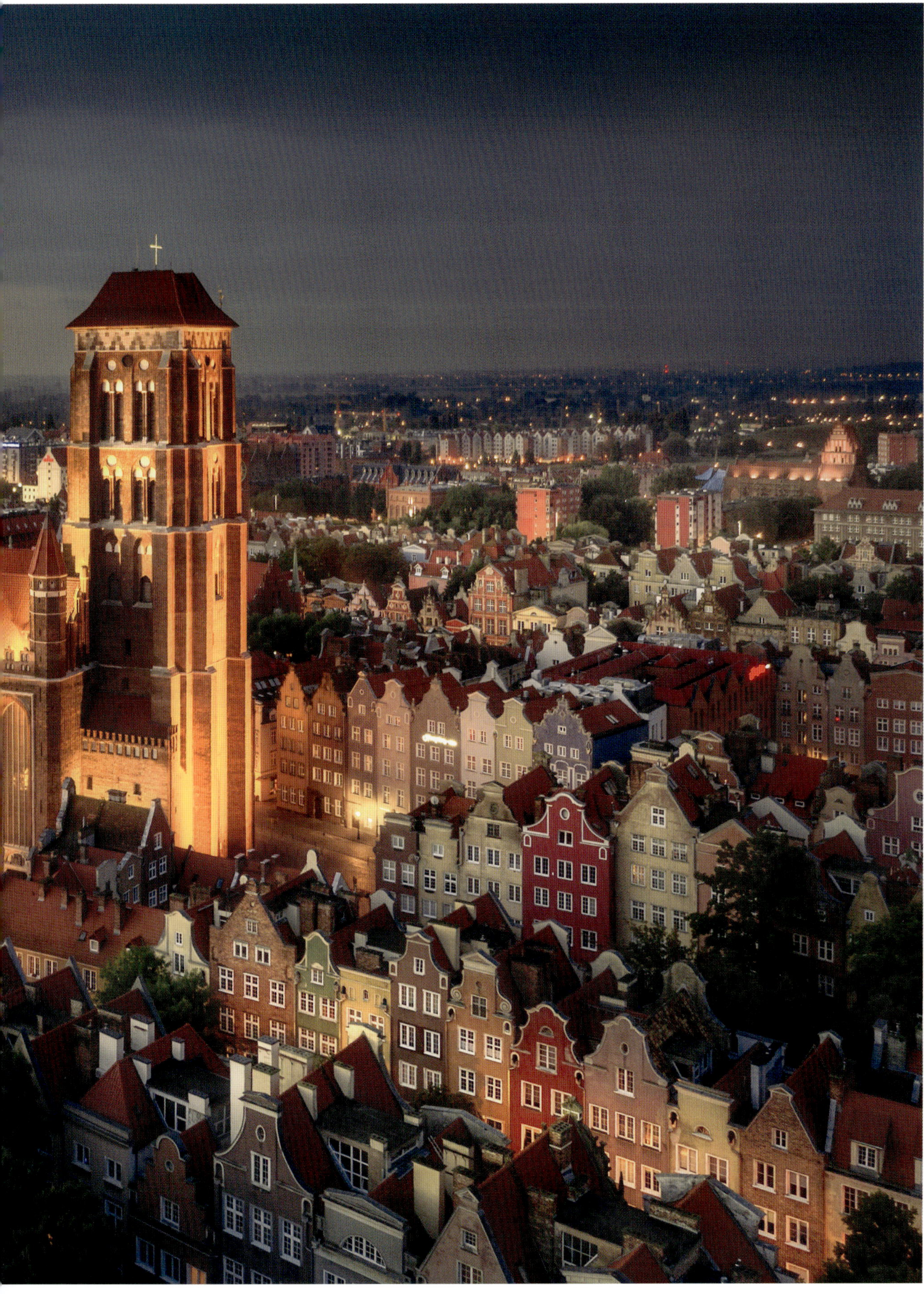

Gdansk, Poland

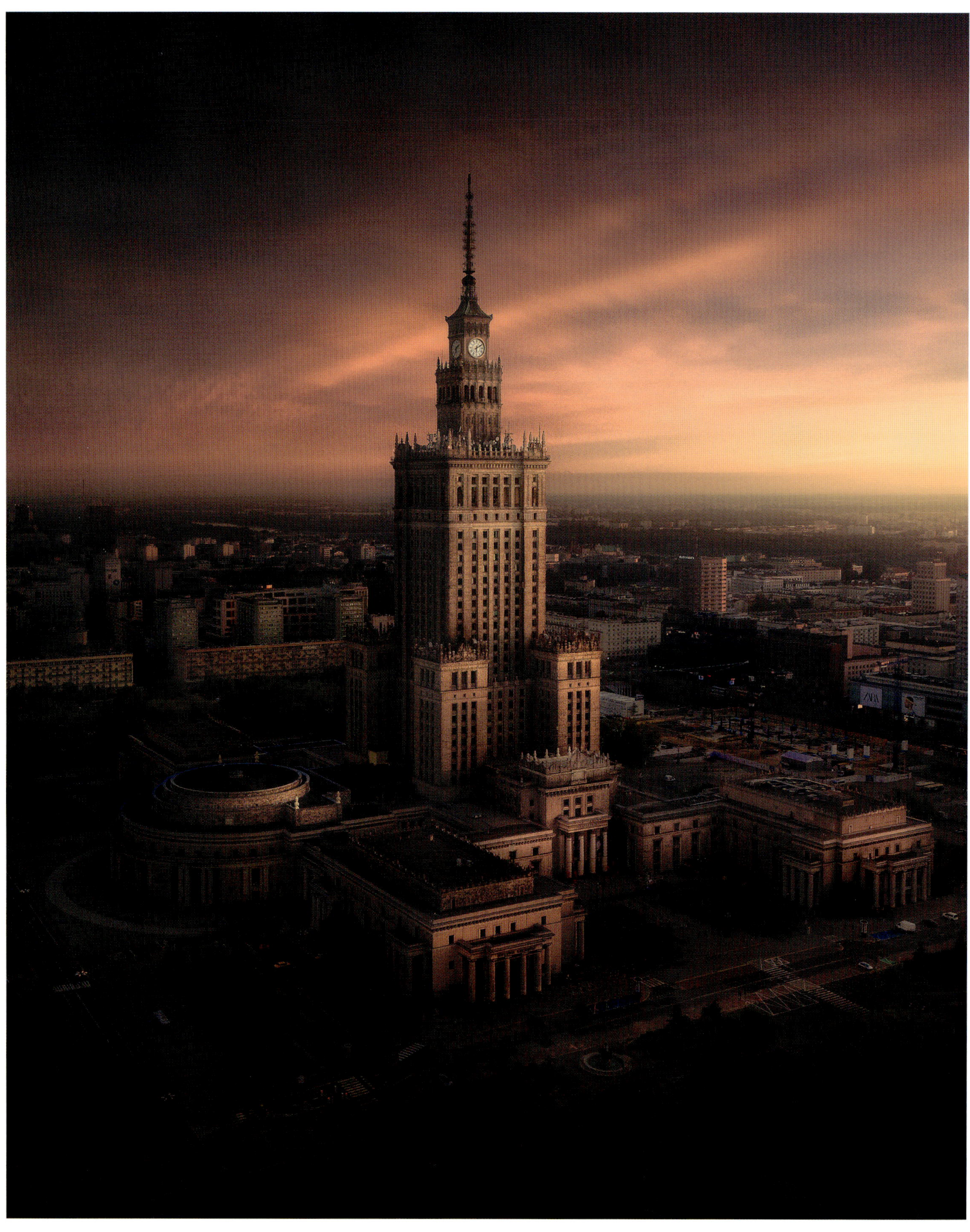

Warsaw, Poland

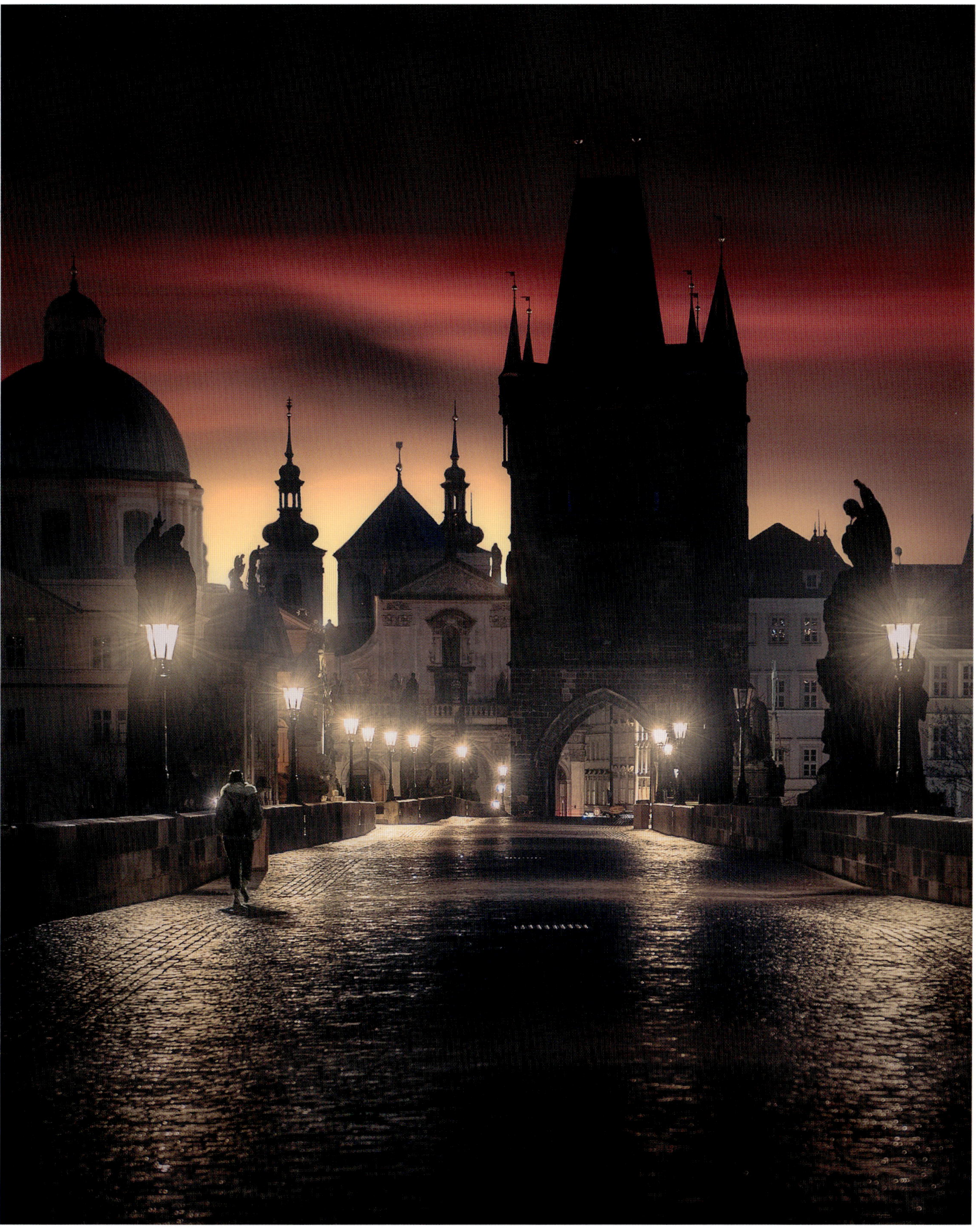

Prague, Czech Republic

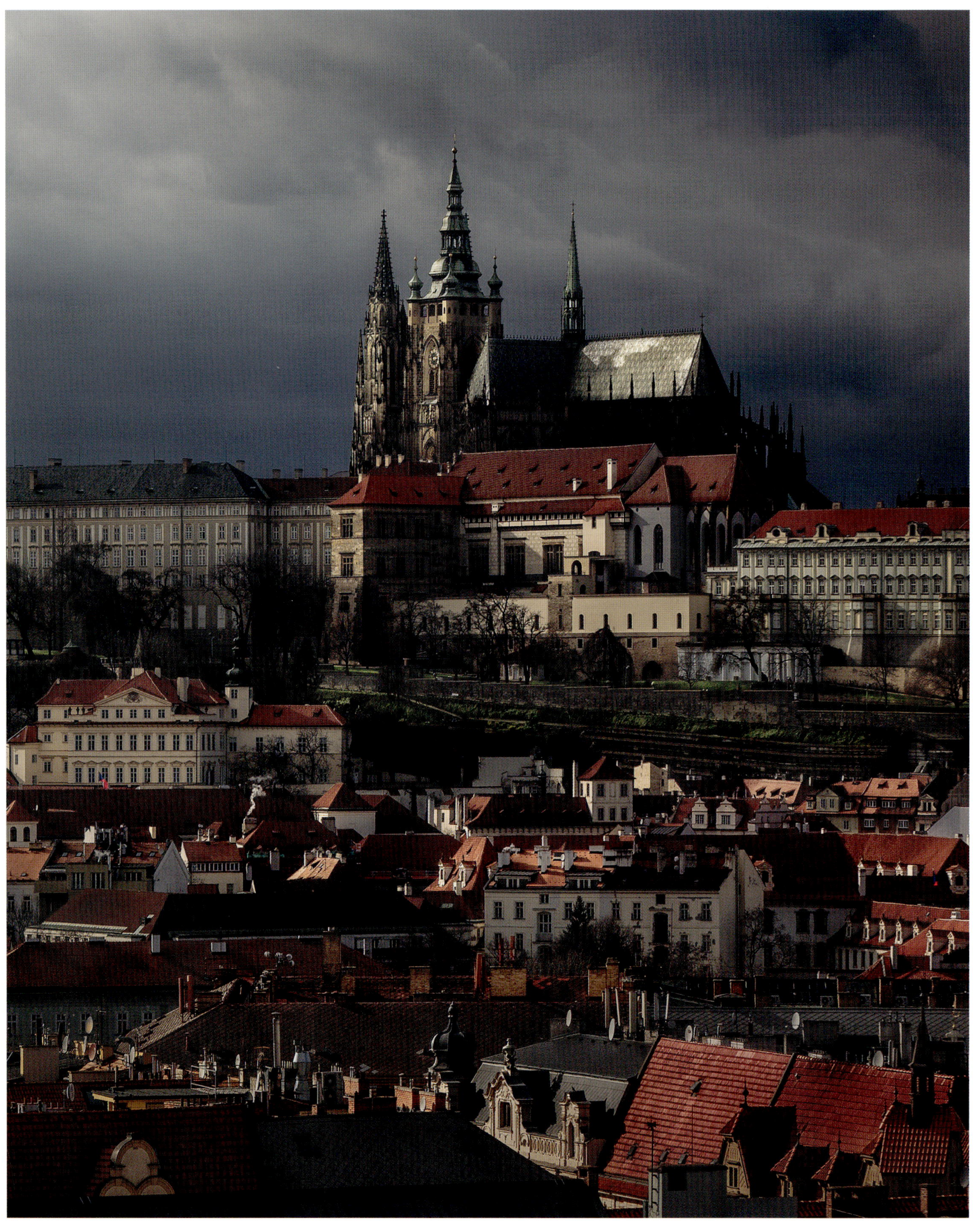

Prague, Czech Republic

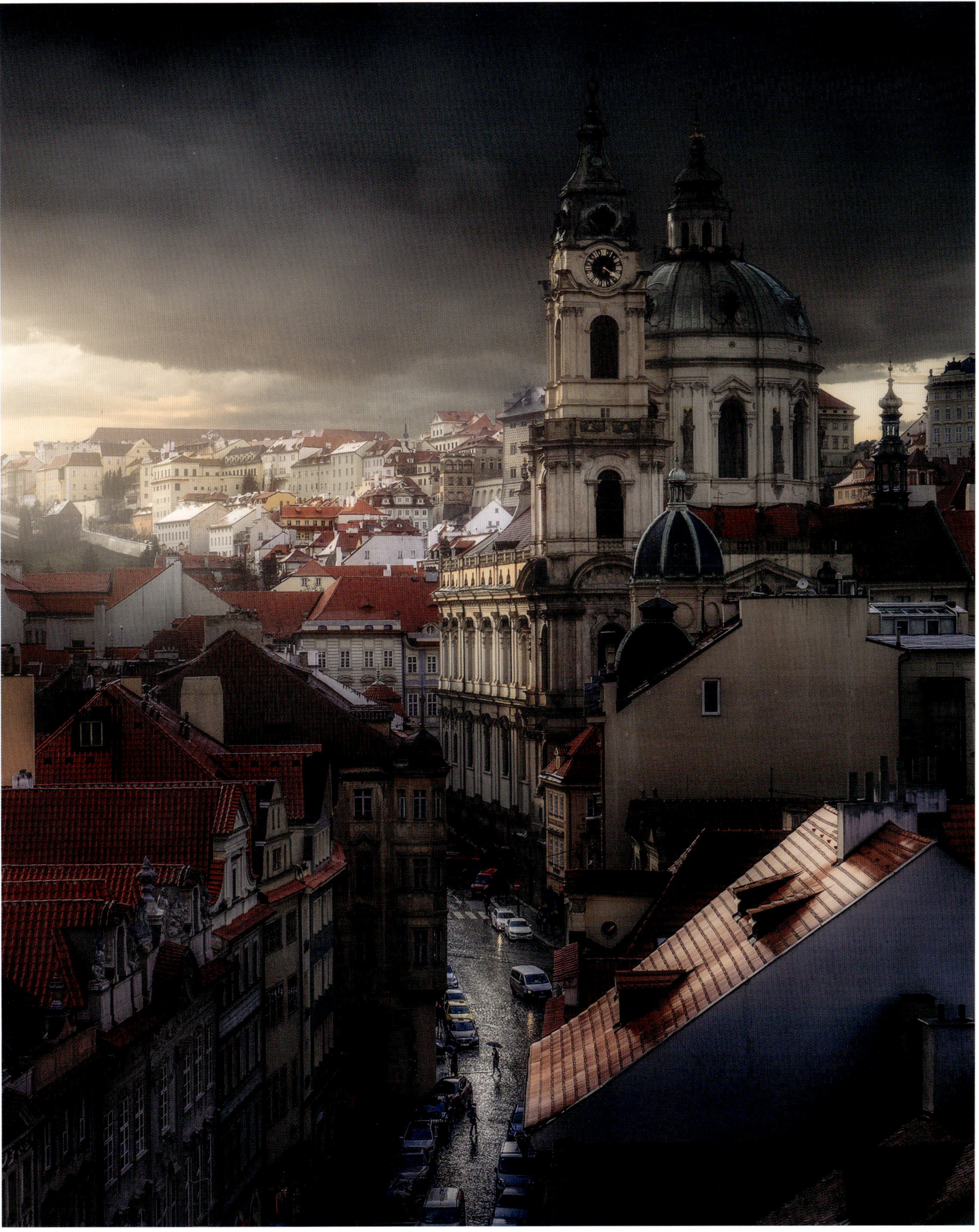

Prague, Czech Republic

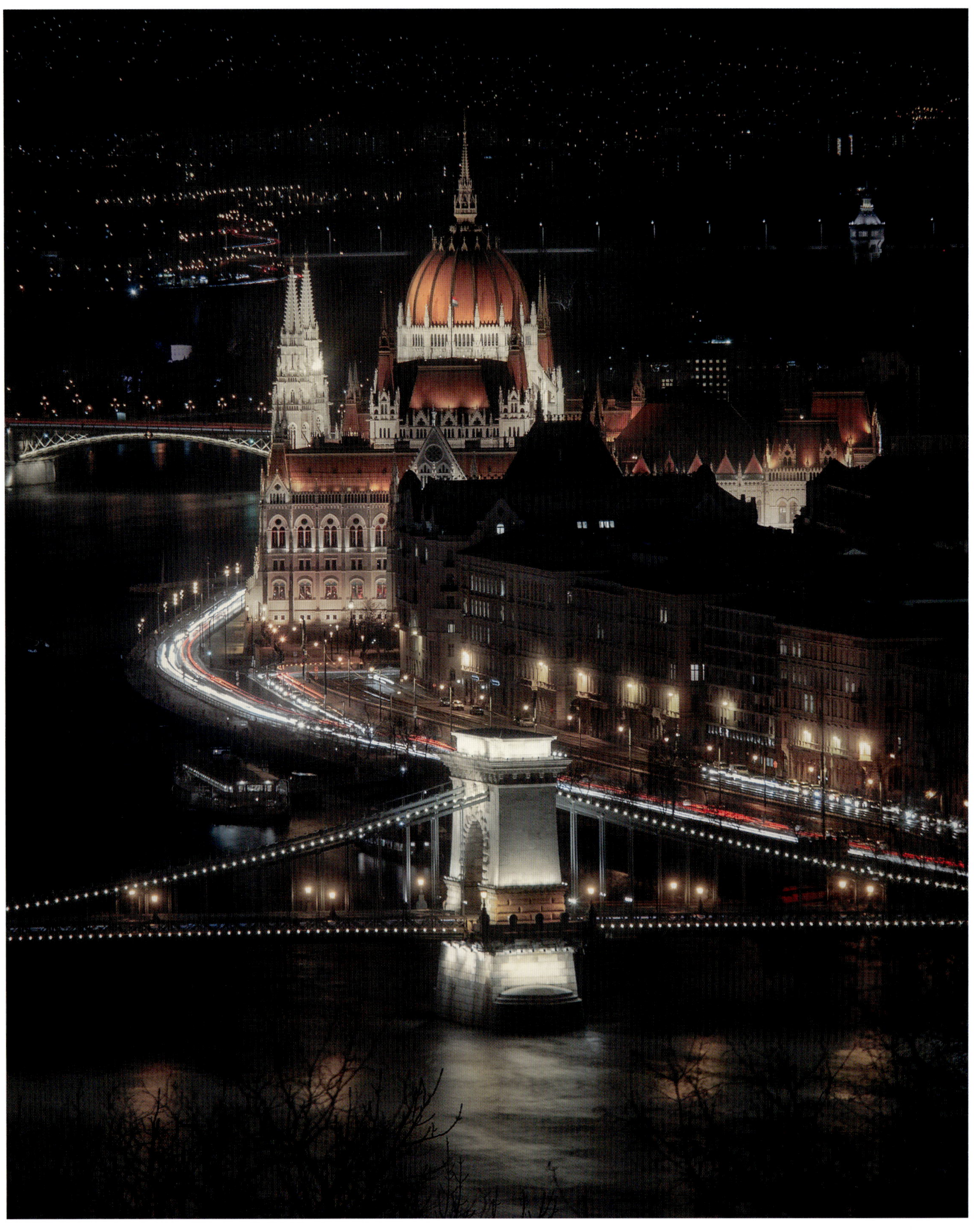

Budapest, Hungary

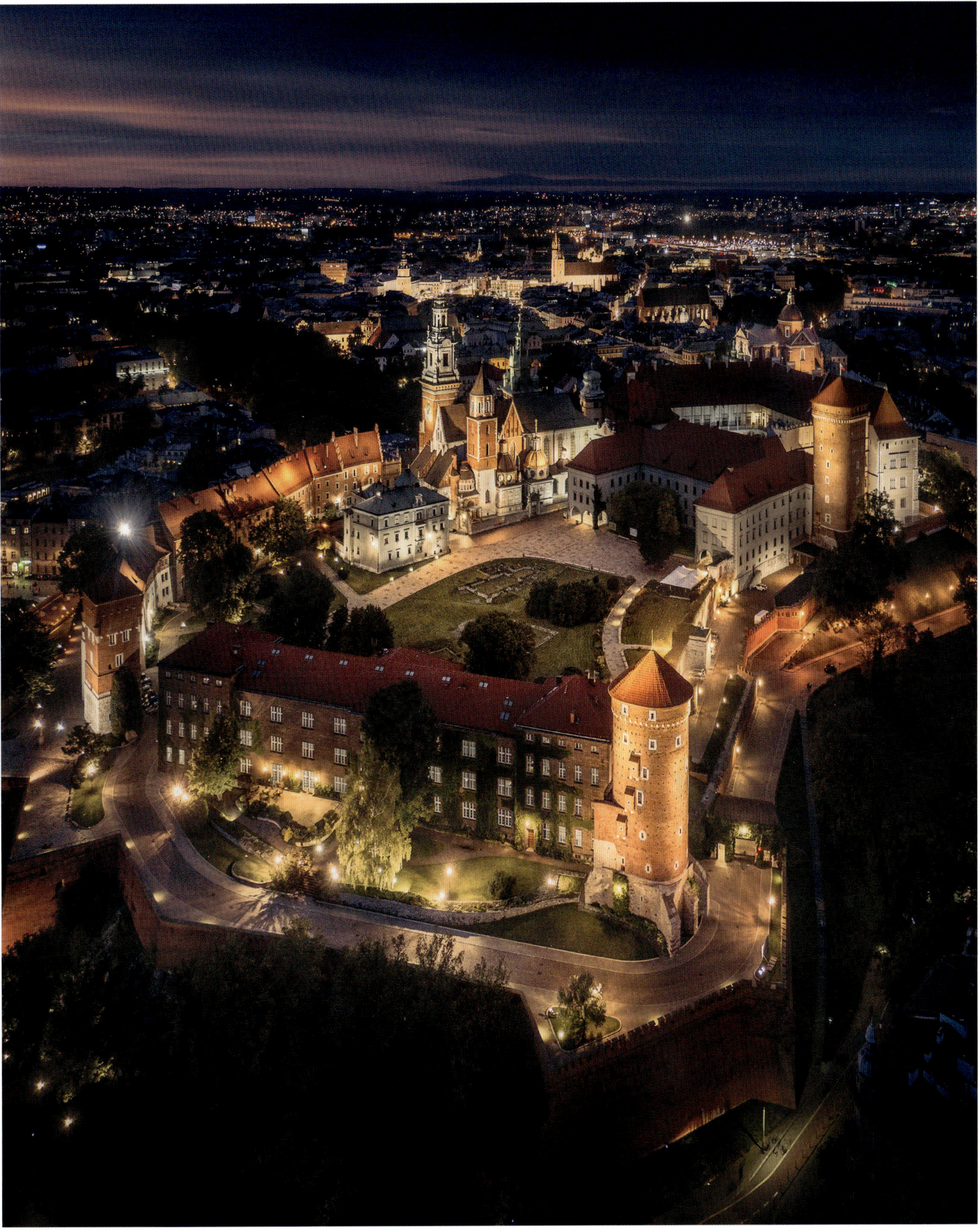

Wawel Royal Castle, Poland

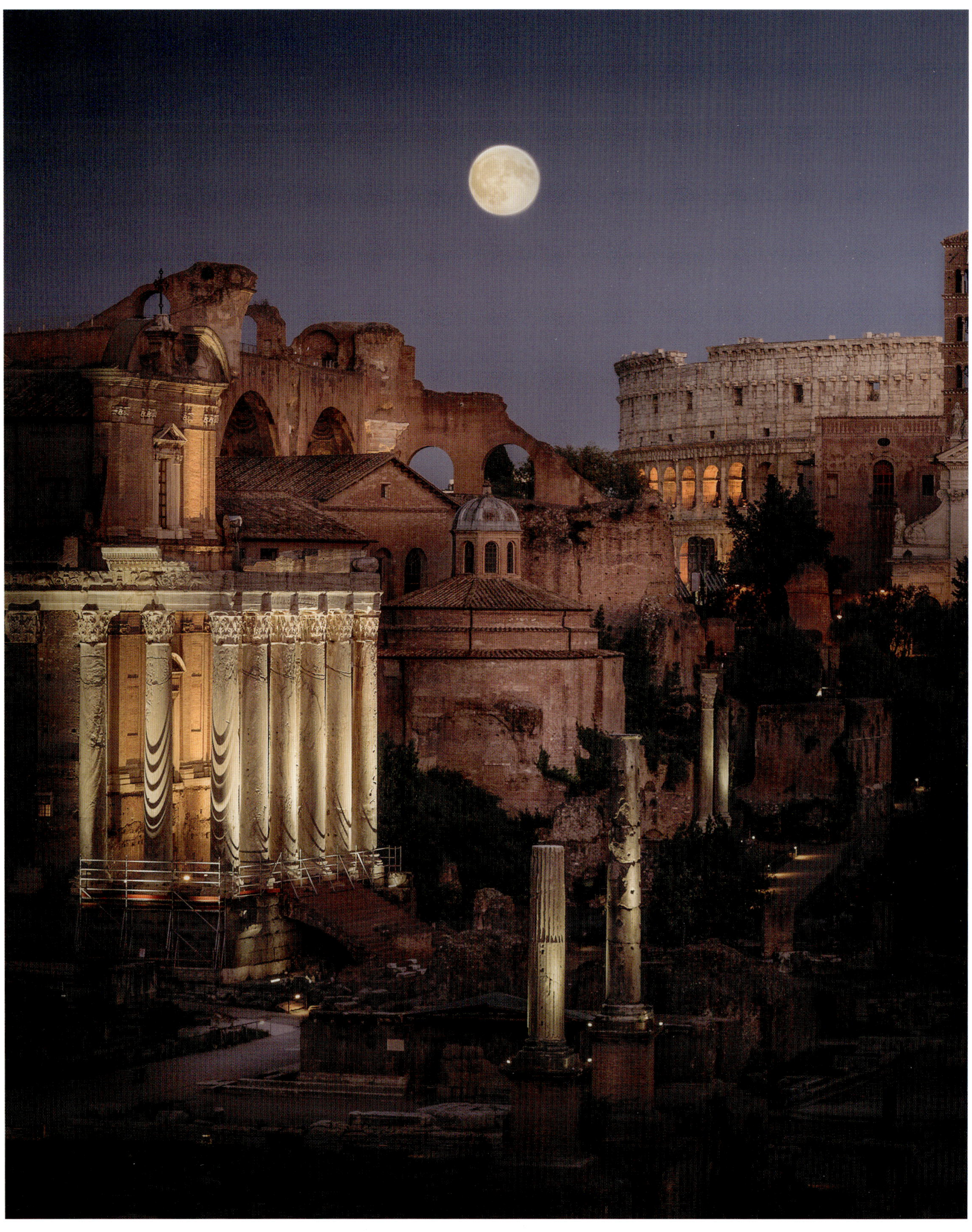

Rome, Italy

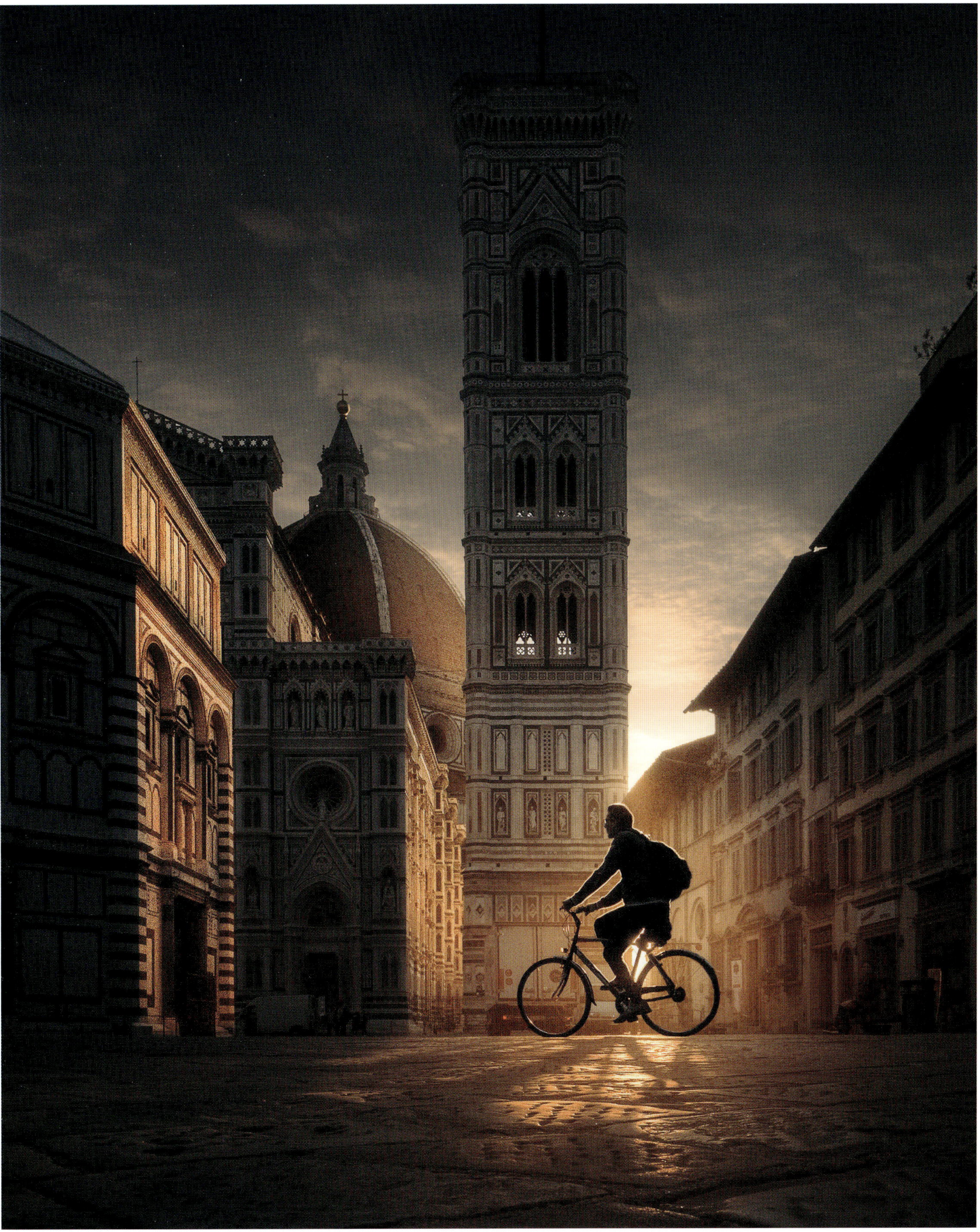

Florence, Italy

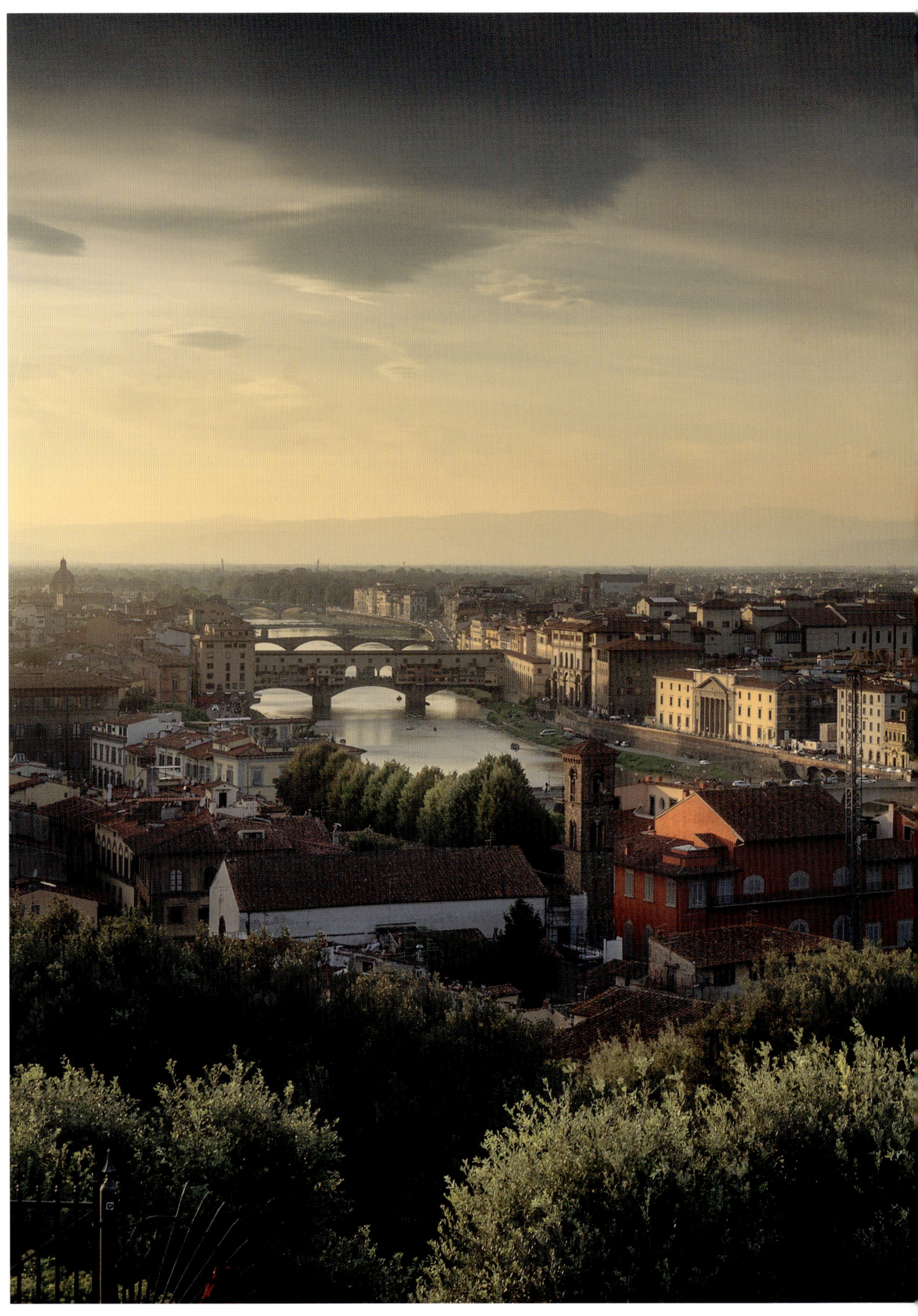

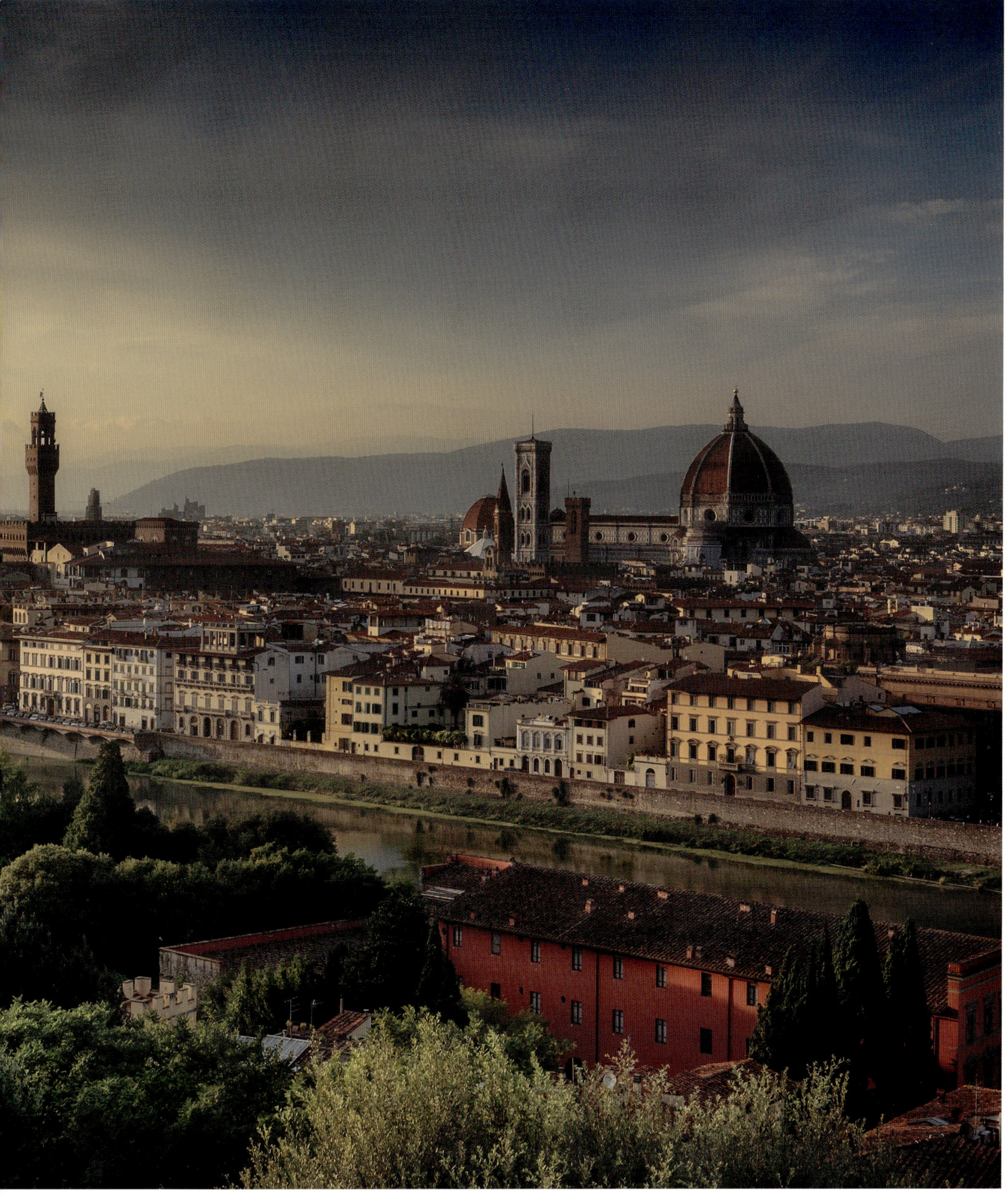

Florence, Italy

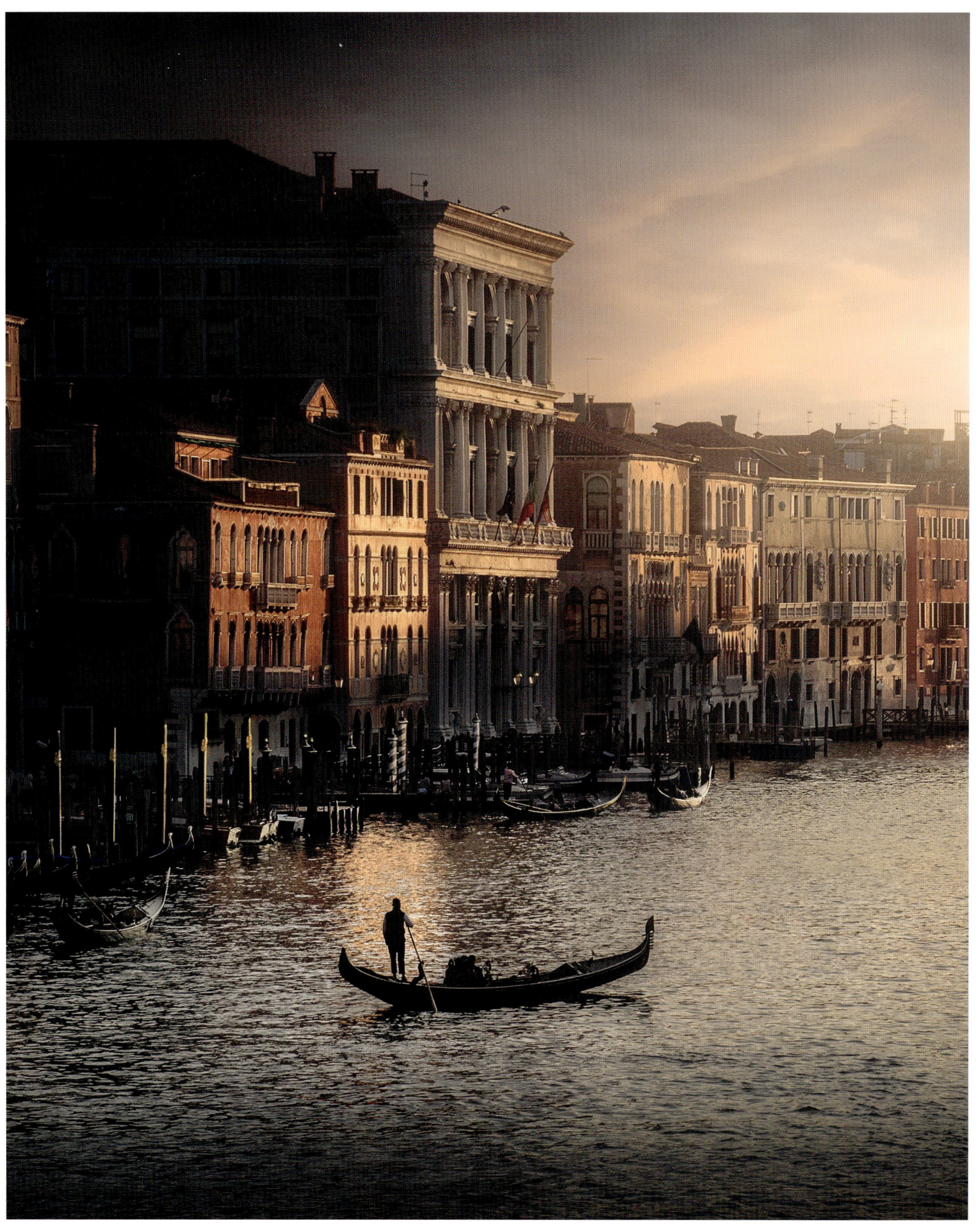

Venice, Italy

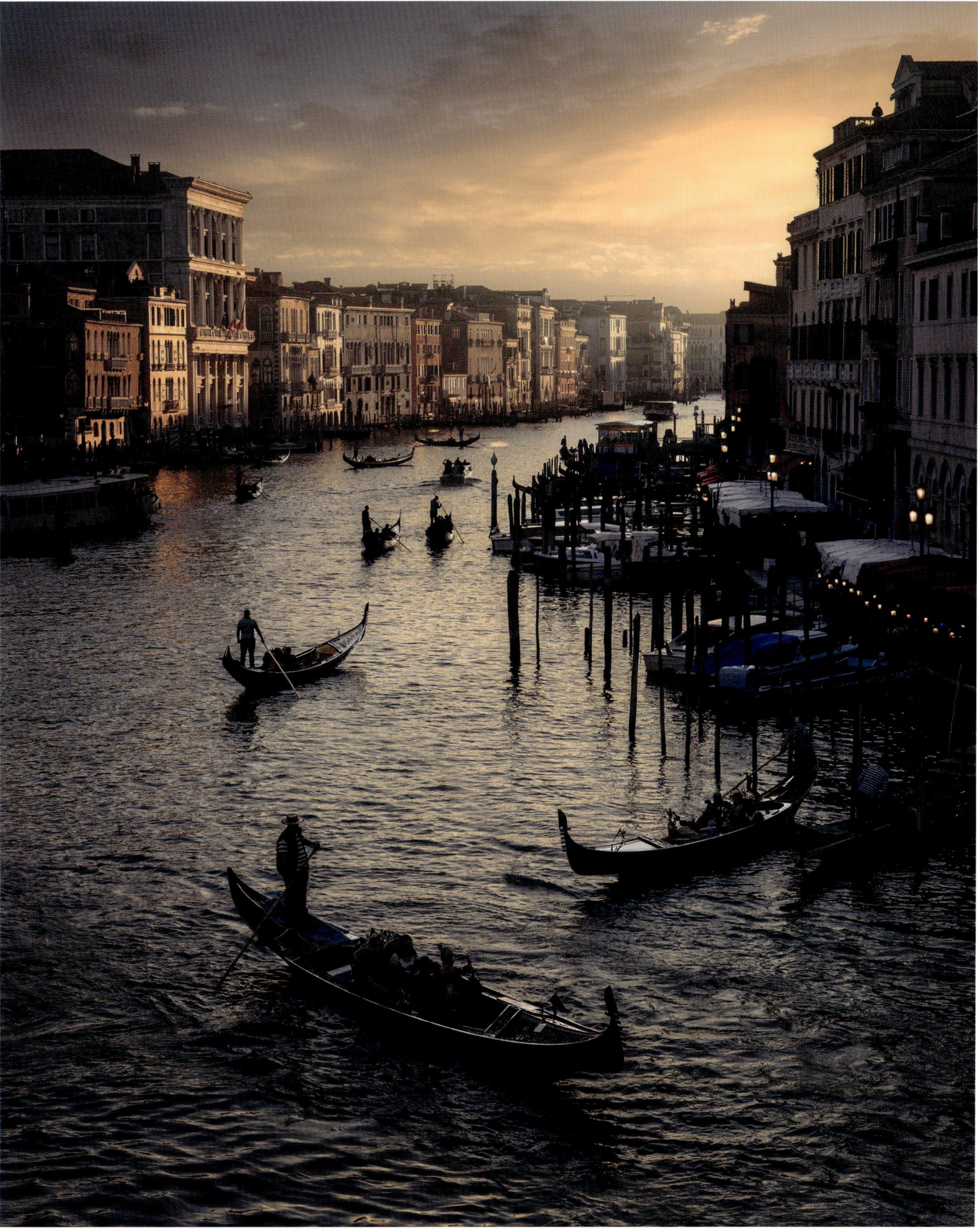

Venice, Italy

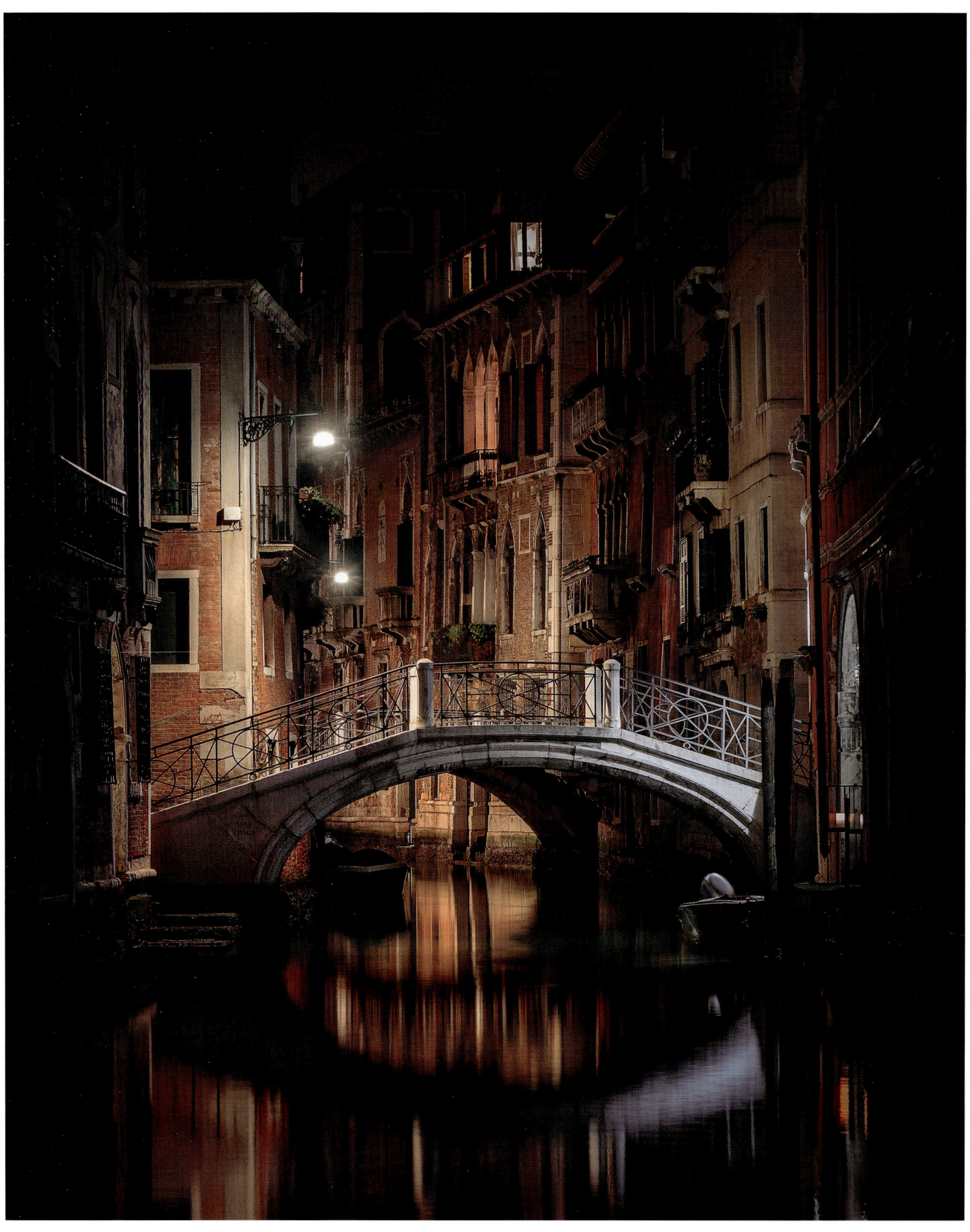

Venice, Italy

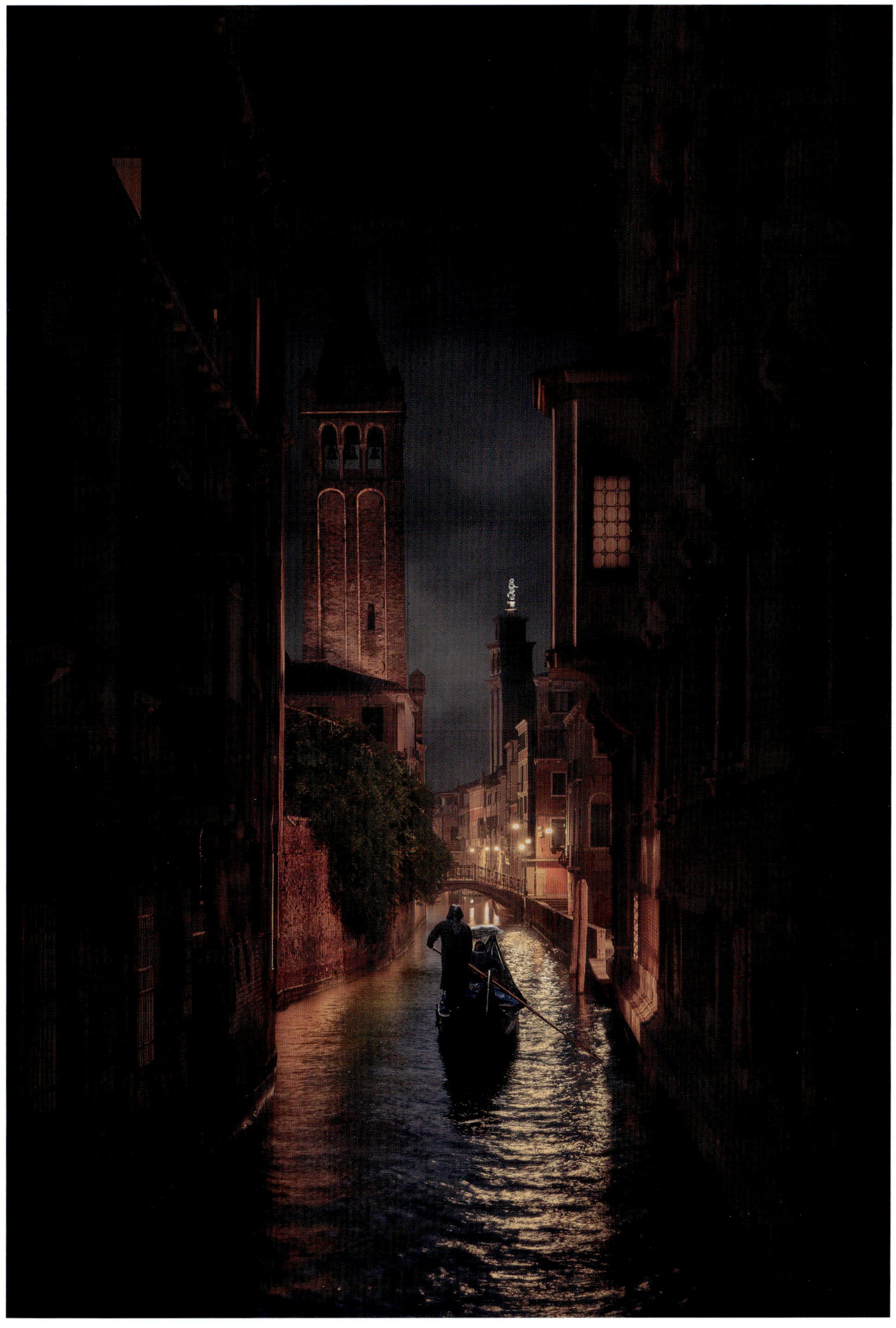

Venice, Italy

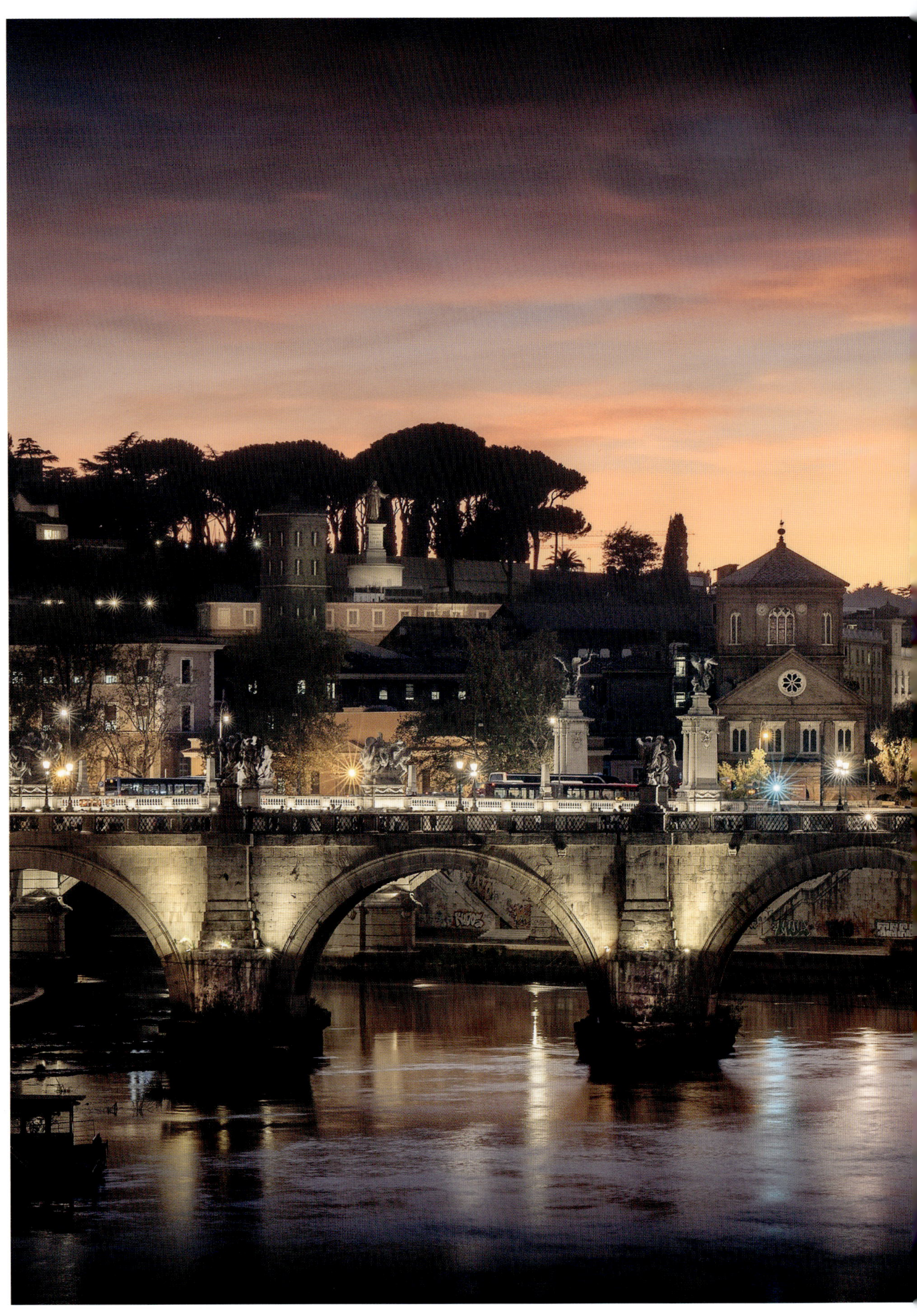

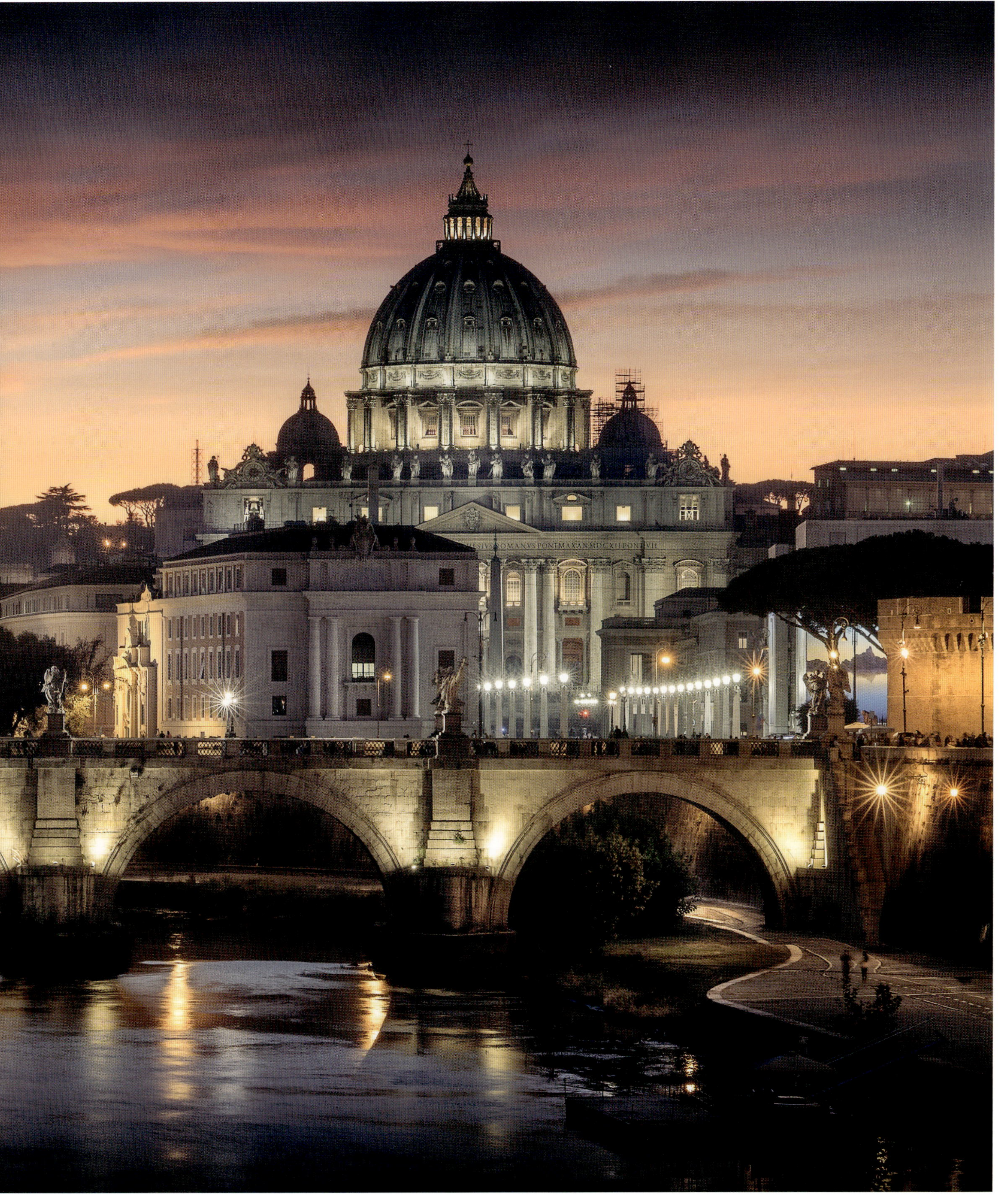

Vatican City

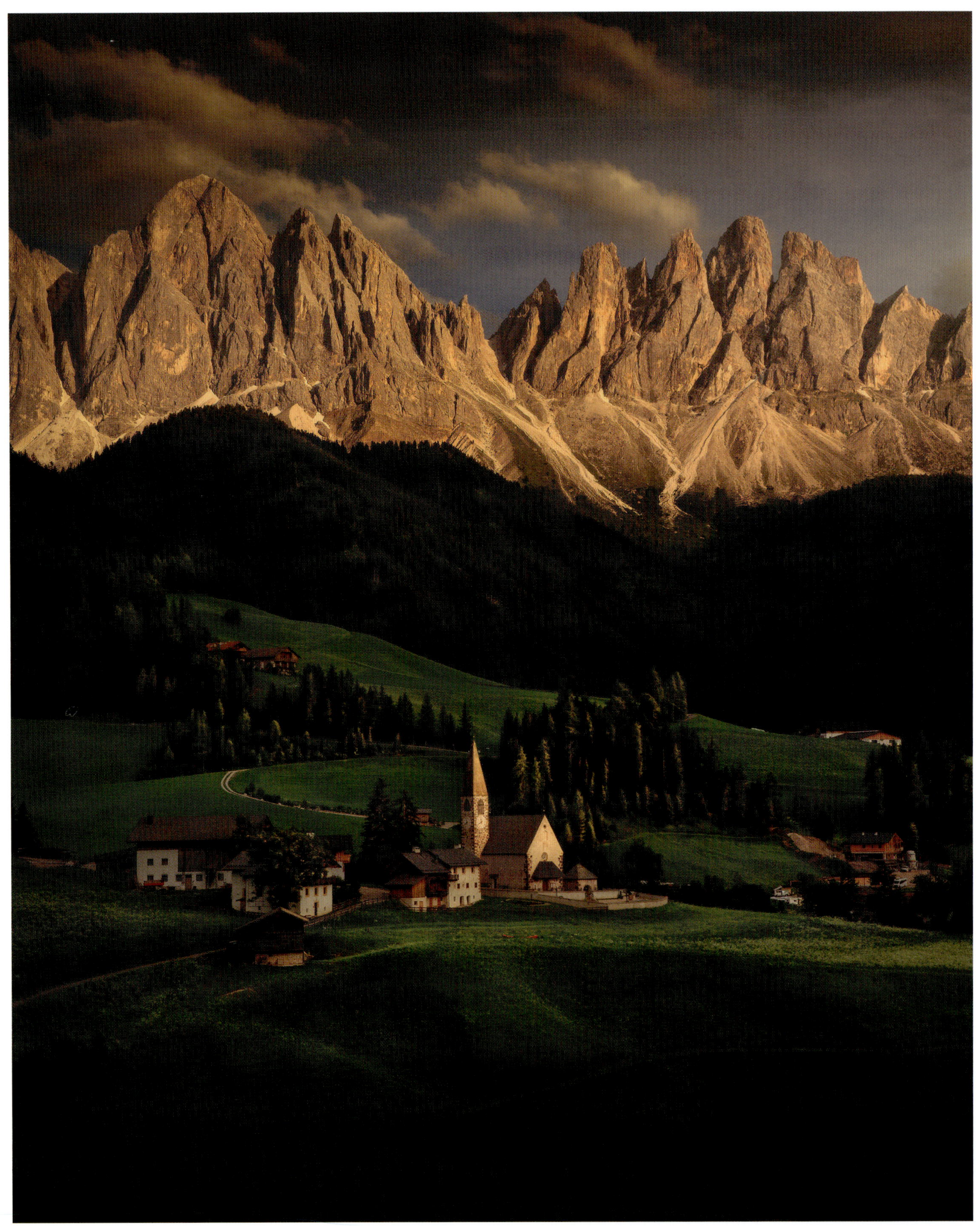

Santa Maddalena, Italy

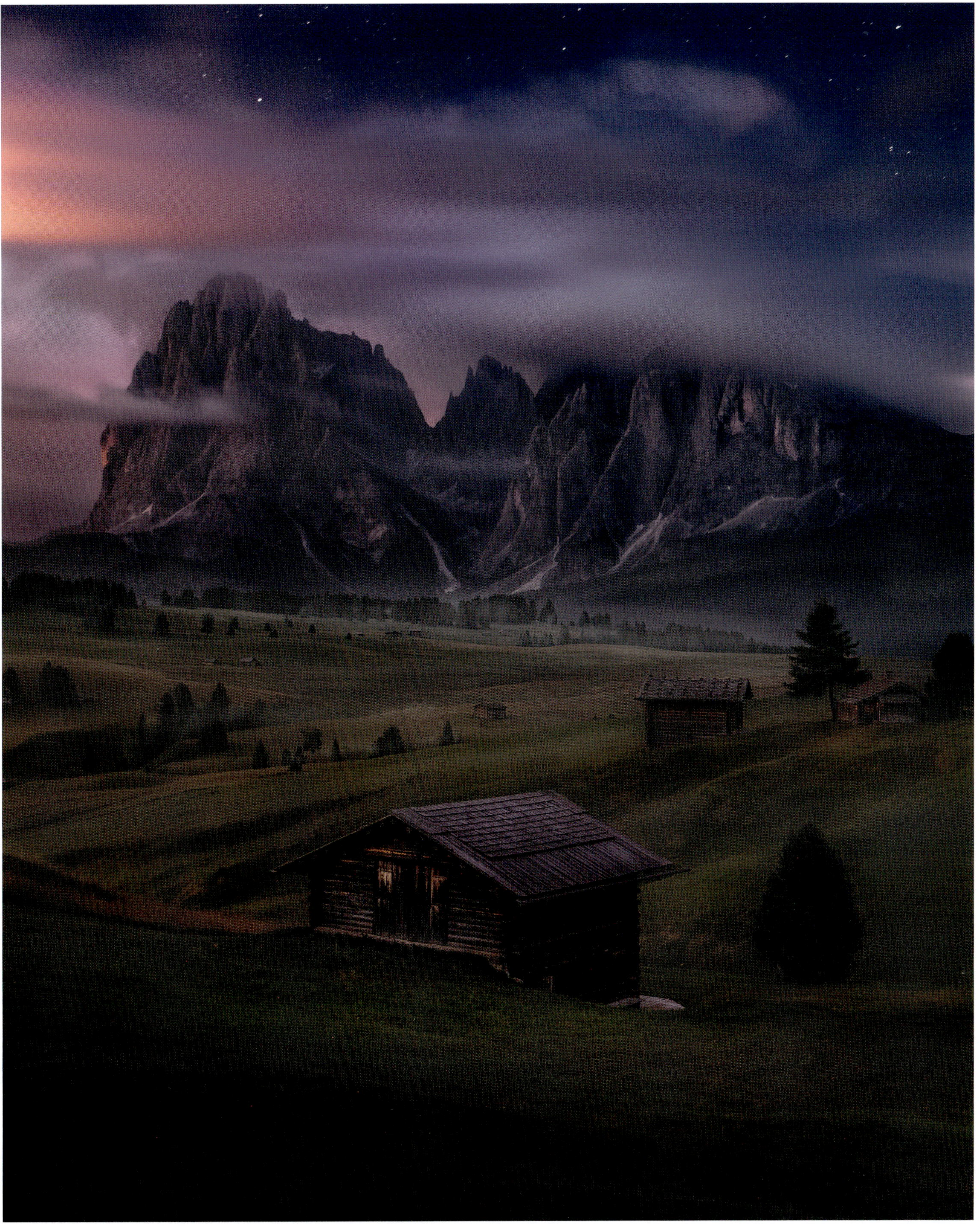

Dolomites, Italy

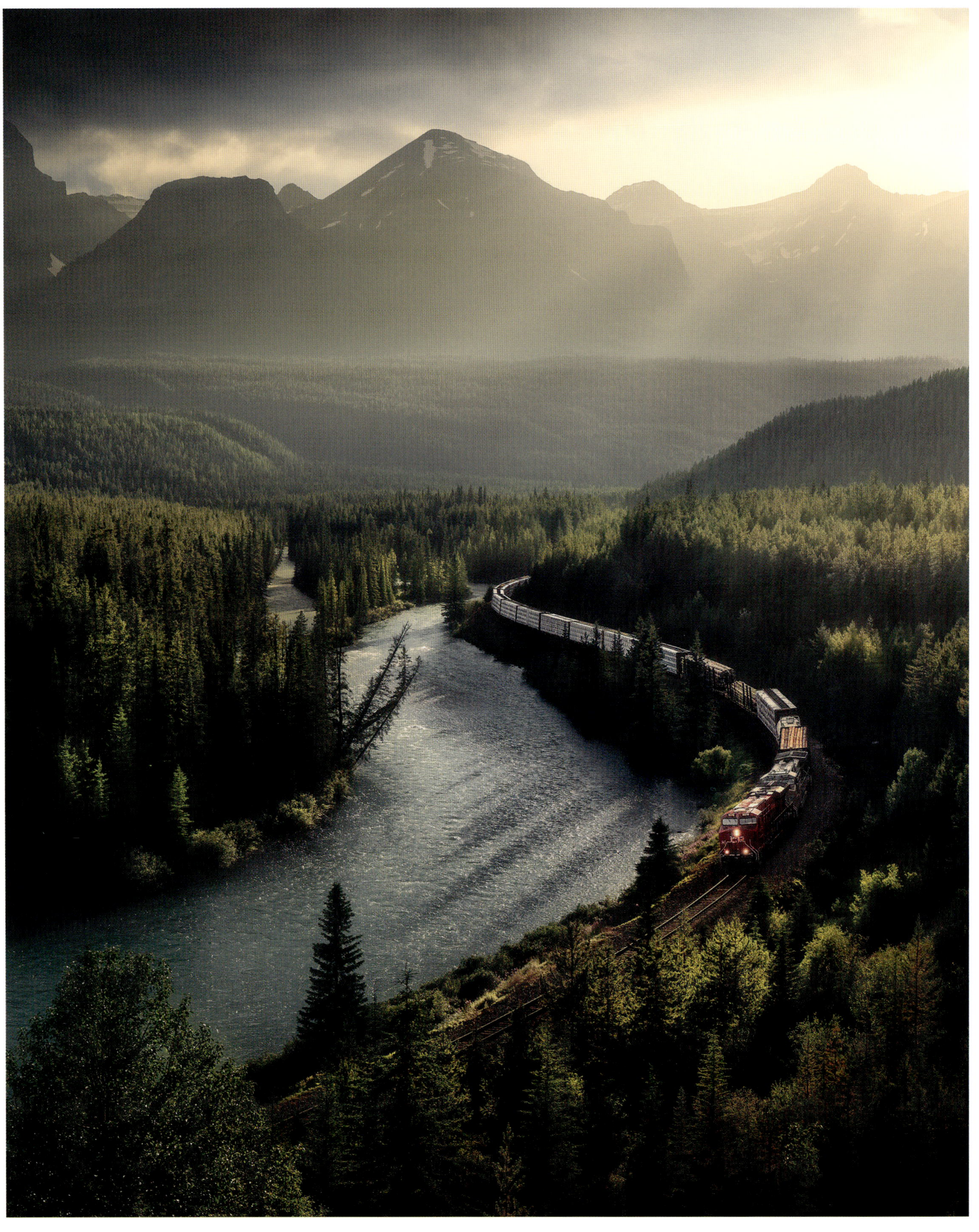

Morant's Curve, Canada

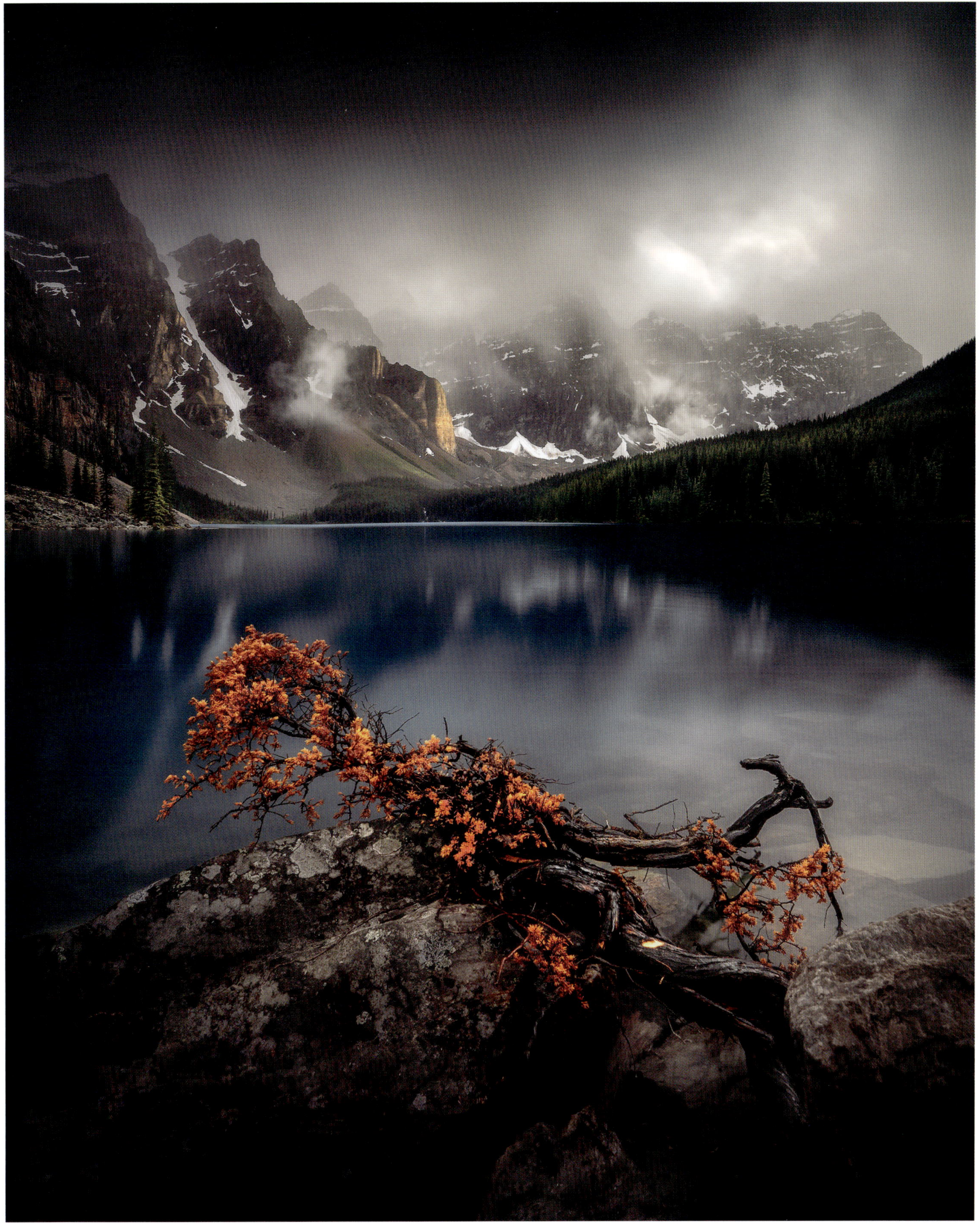

Moraine Lake, Canada

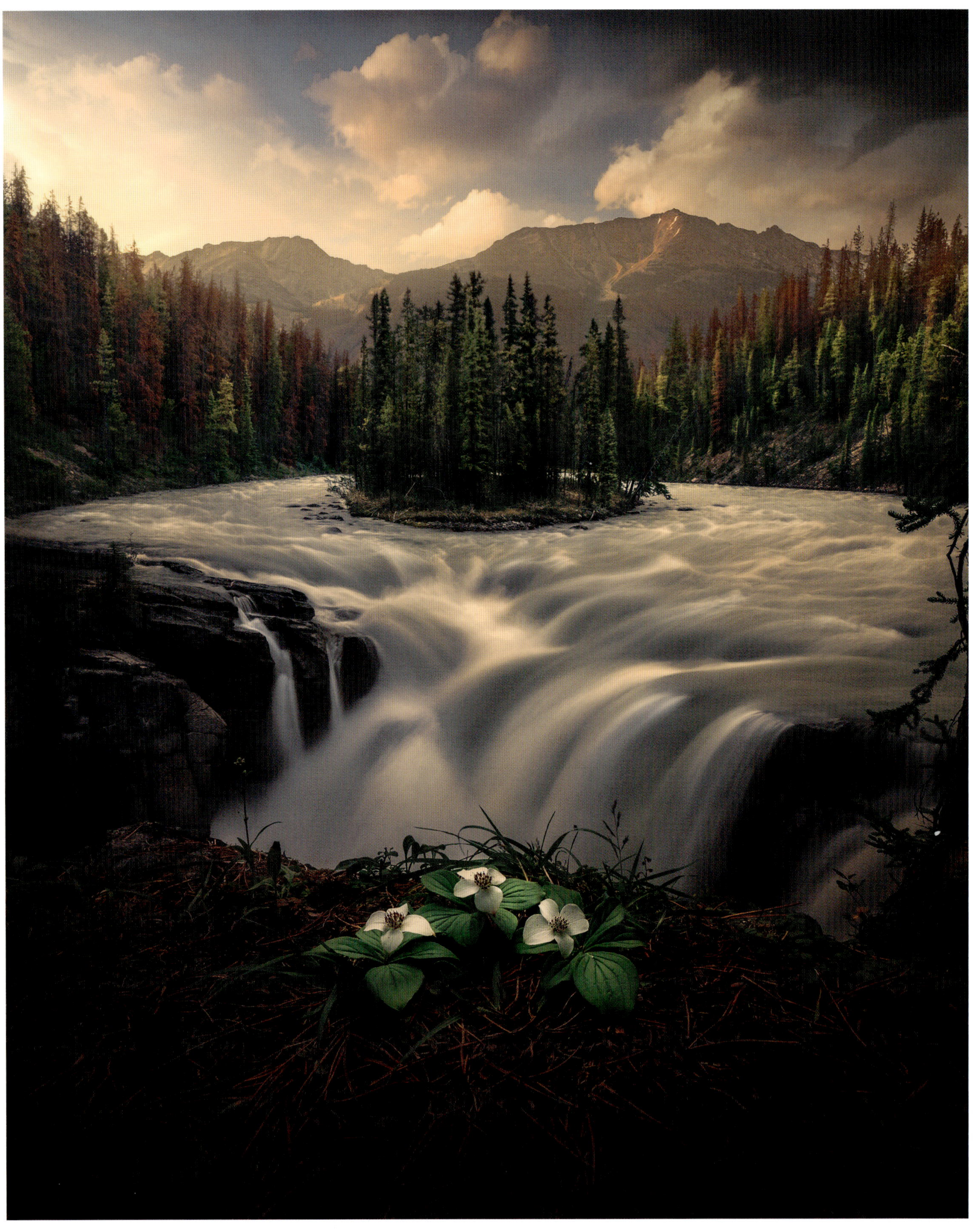

Sunwapta Falls, Canada

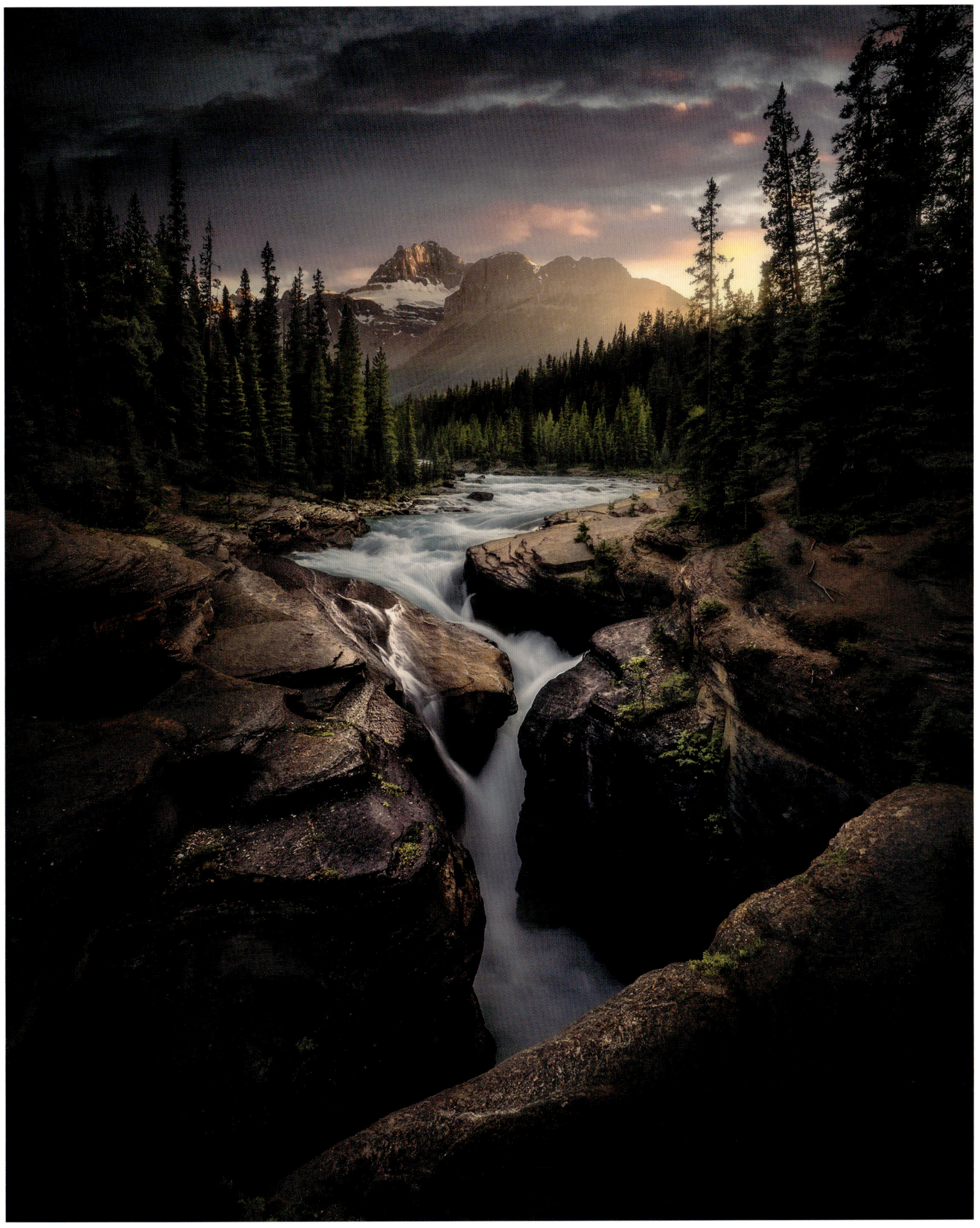

Mistaya Canyon, Canada

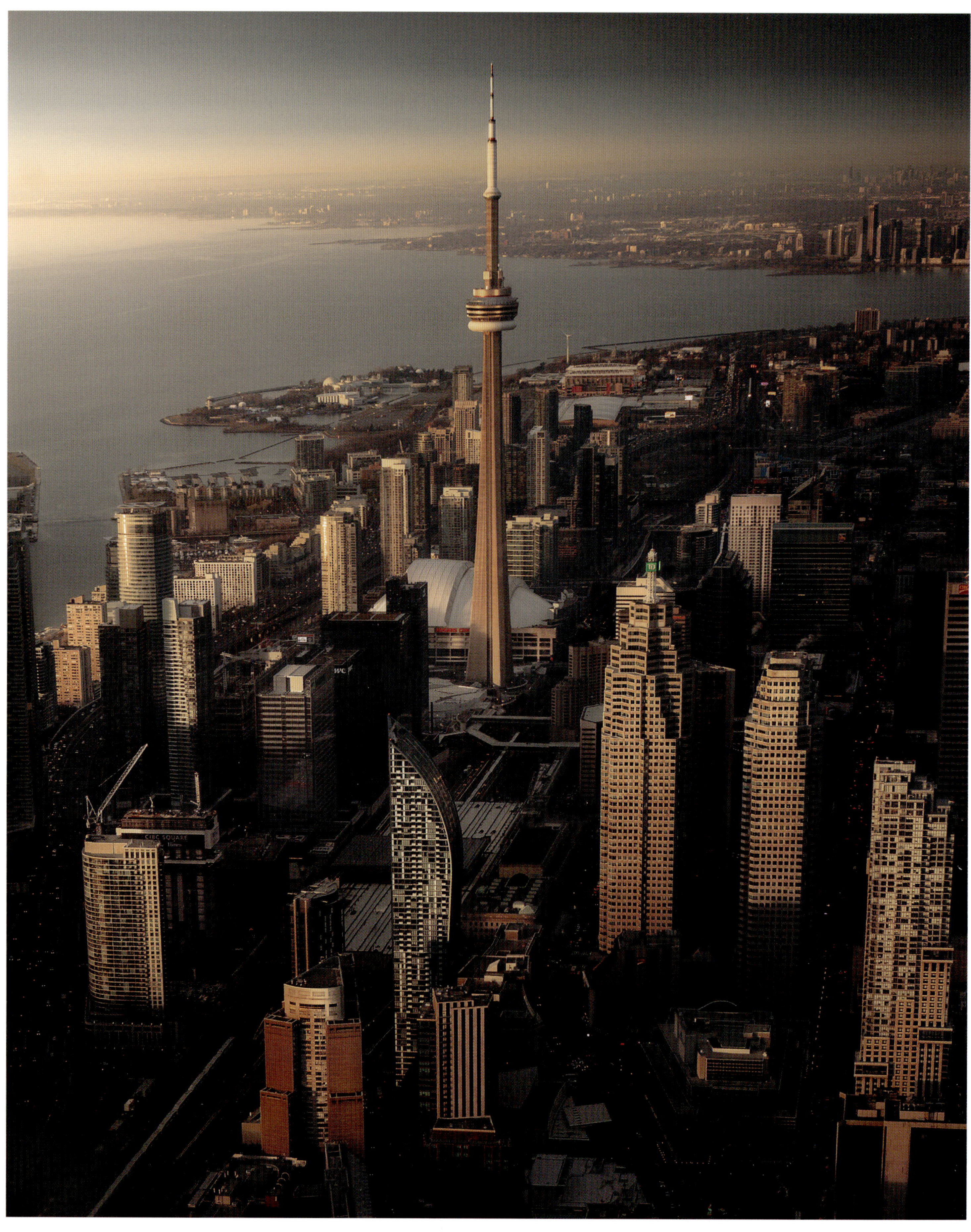

Toronto, Canada

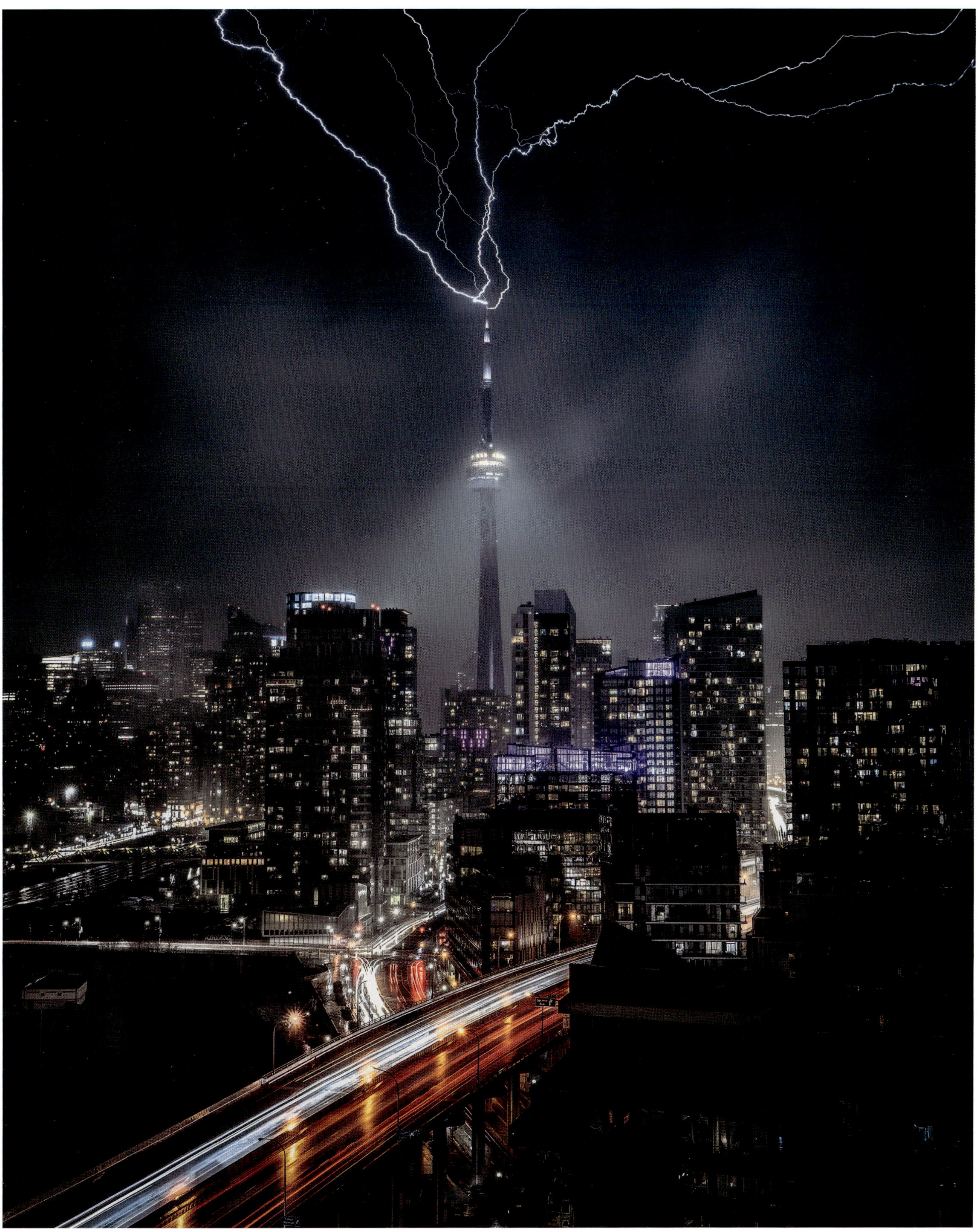

Toronto, Canada

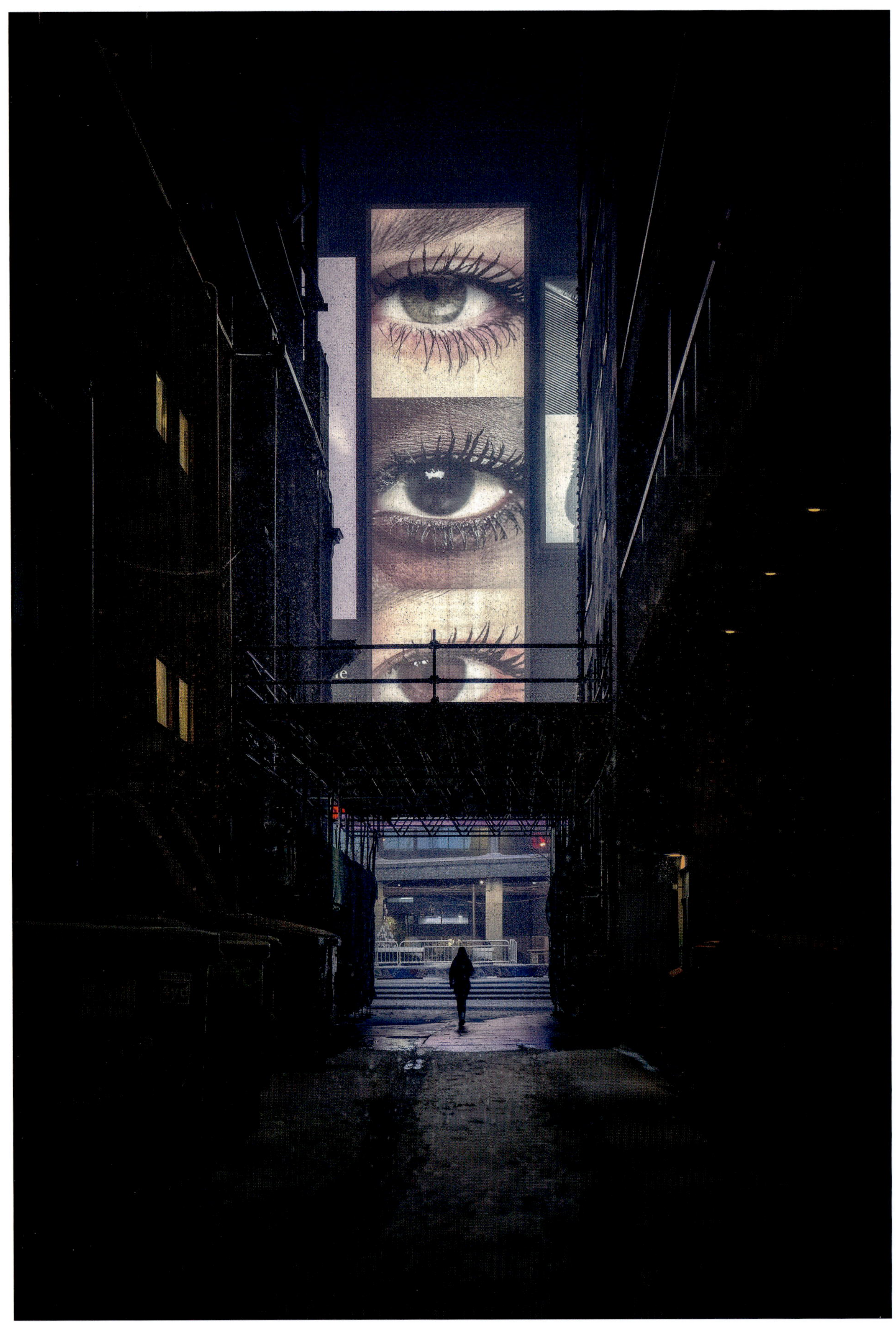

Toronto, Canada

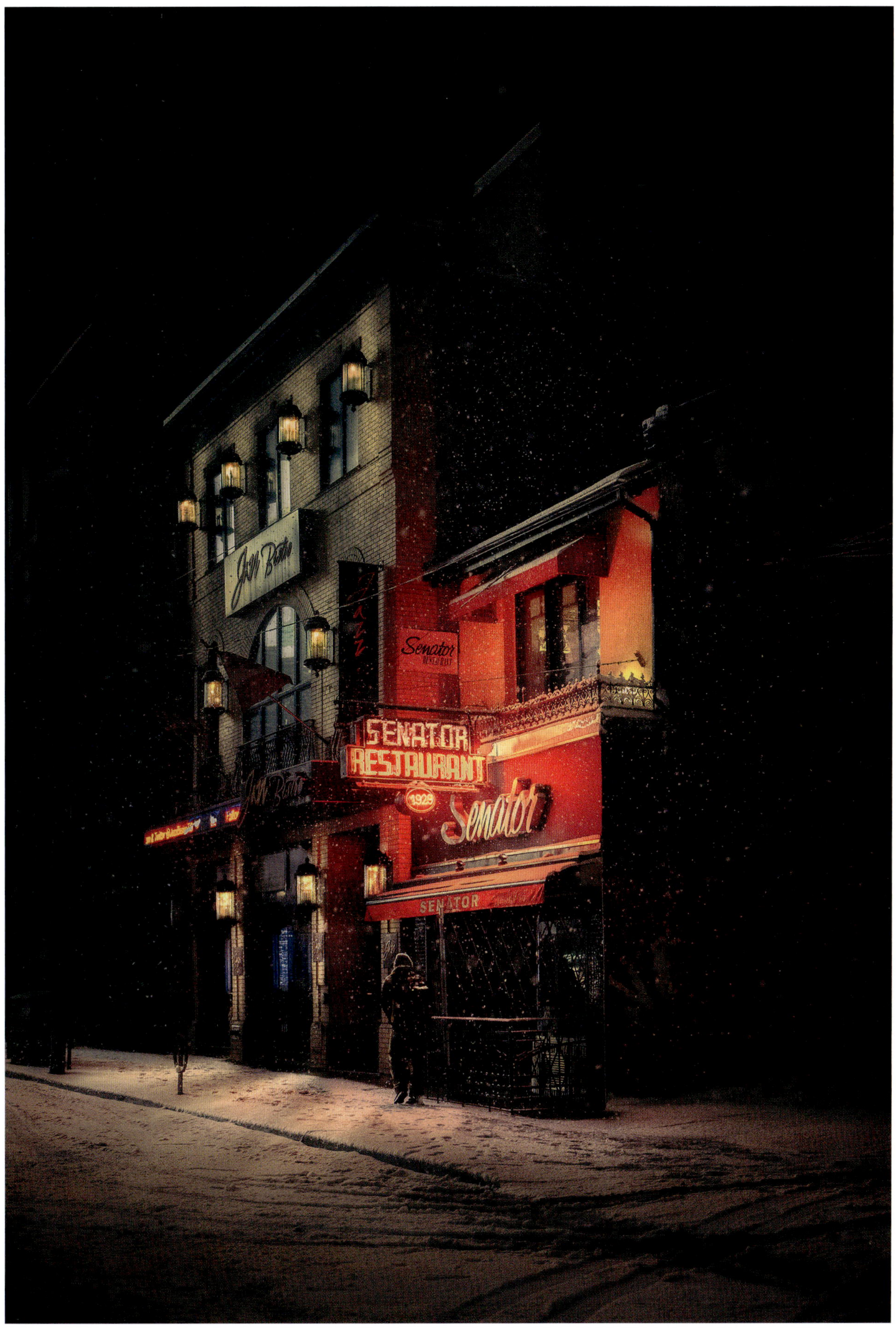

Toronto, Canada

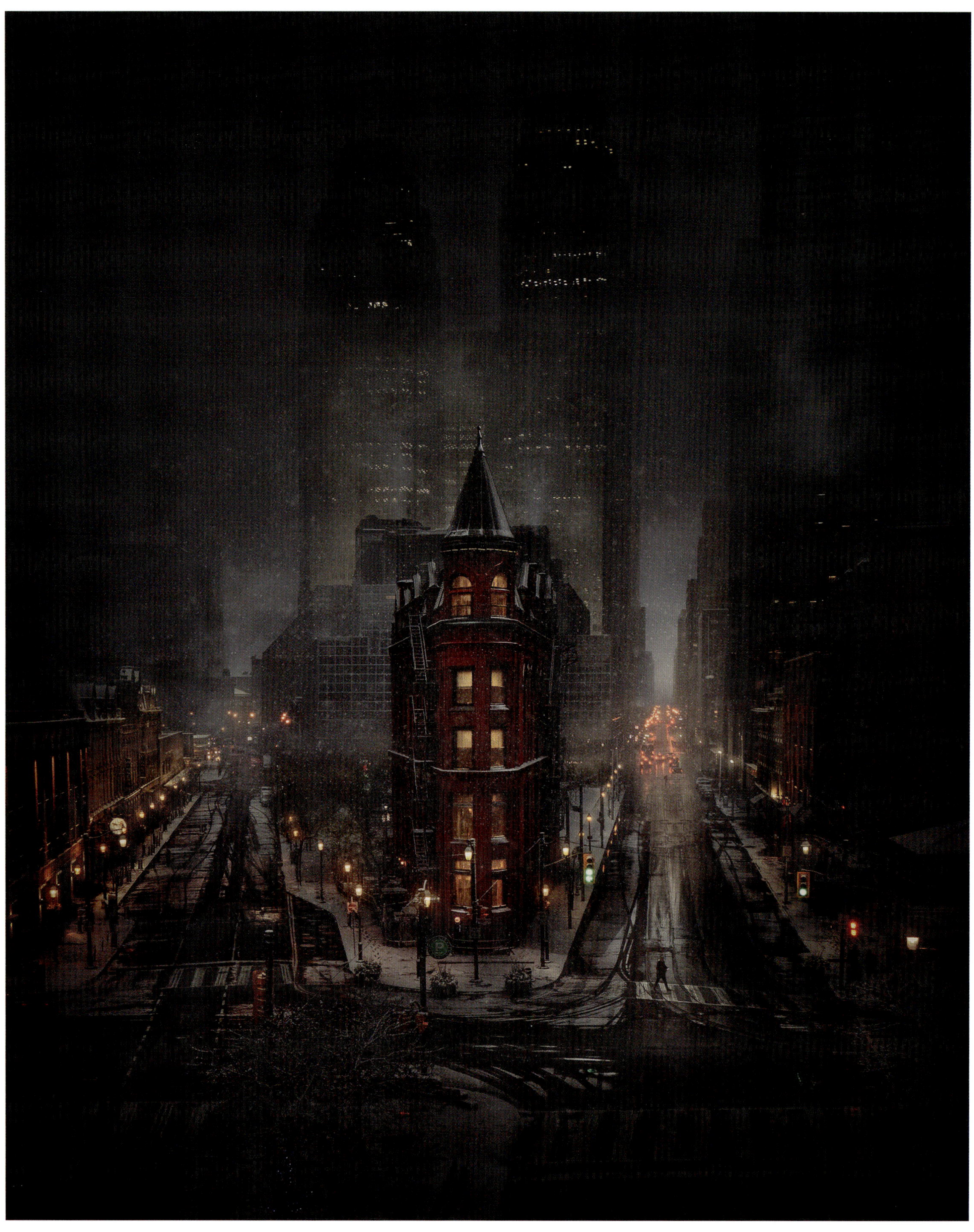

Toronto, Canada

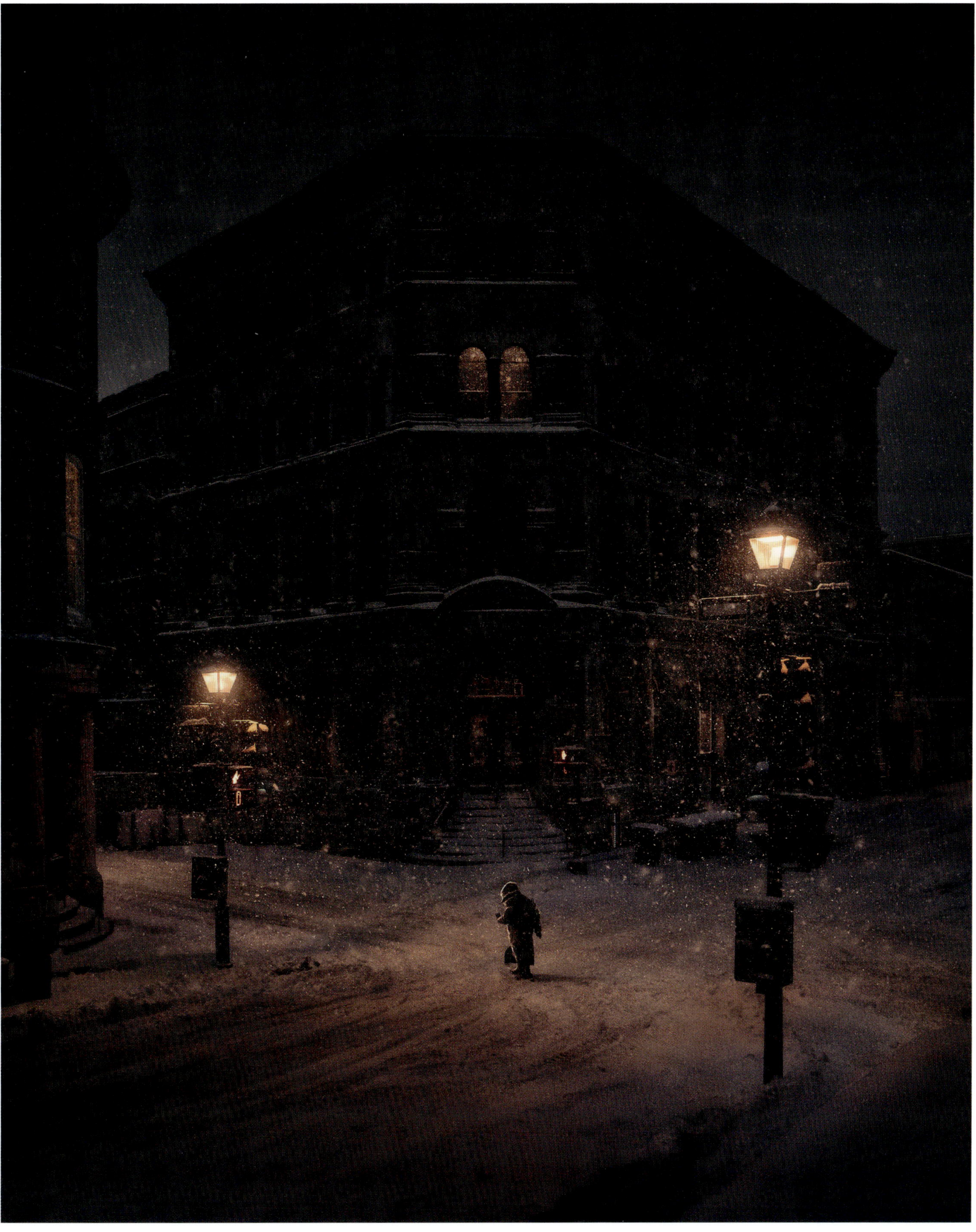

Montreal, Canada

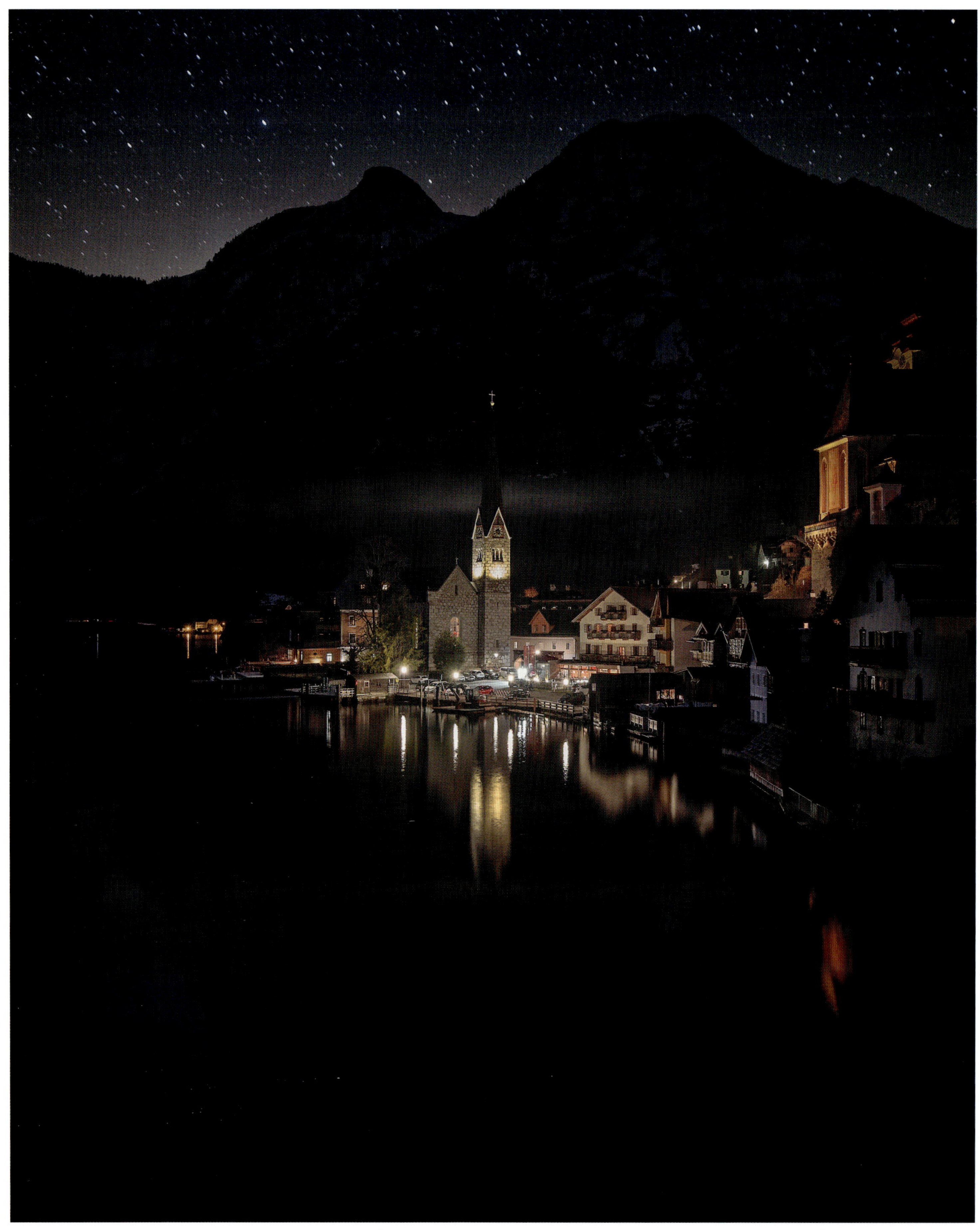

Hallstatt, Austria

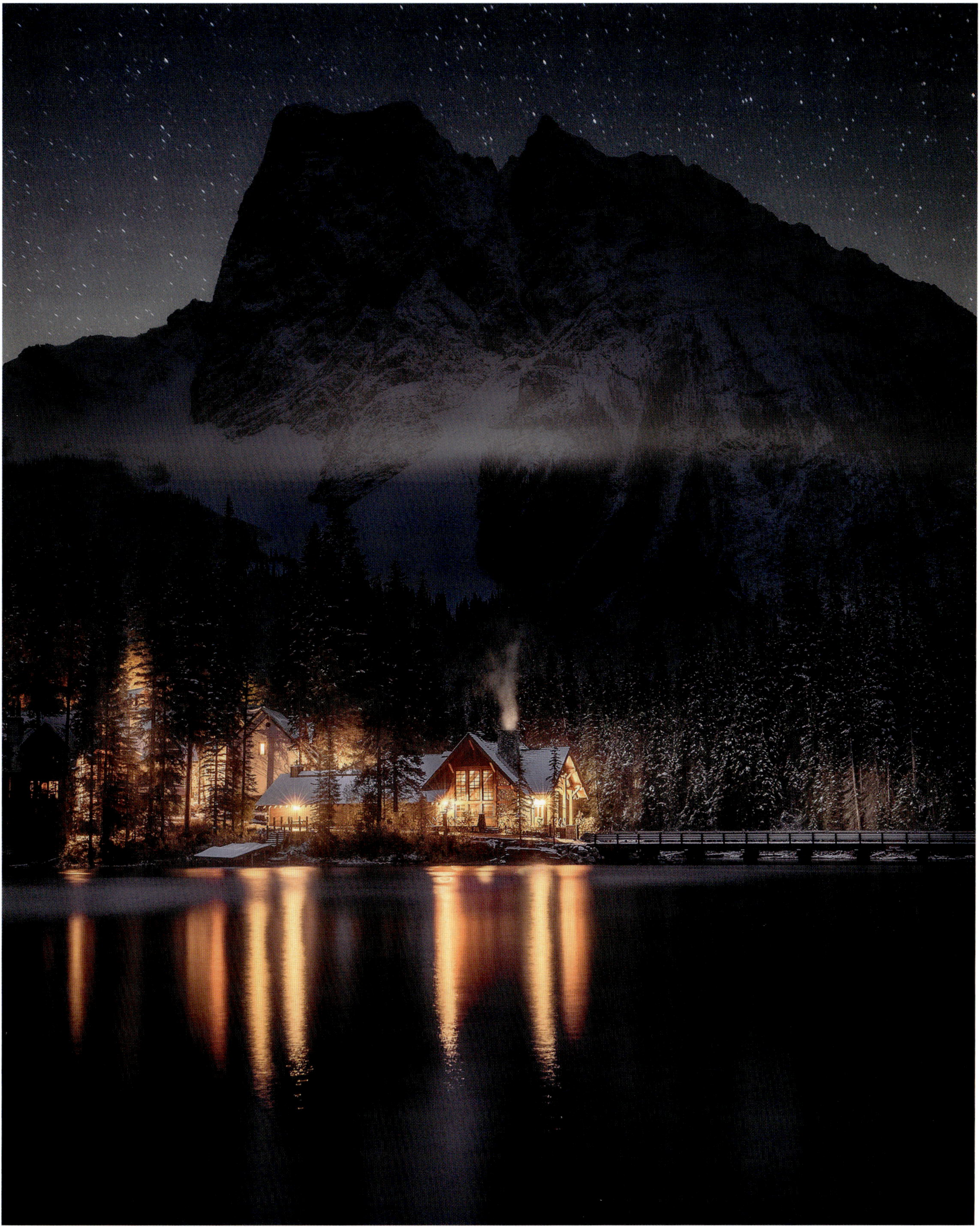

Emerald Lake, Canada

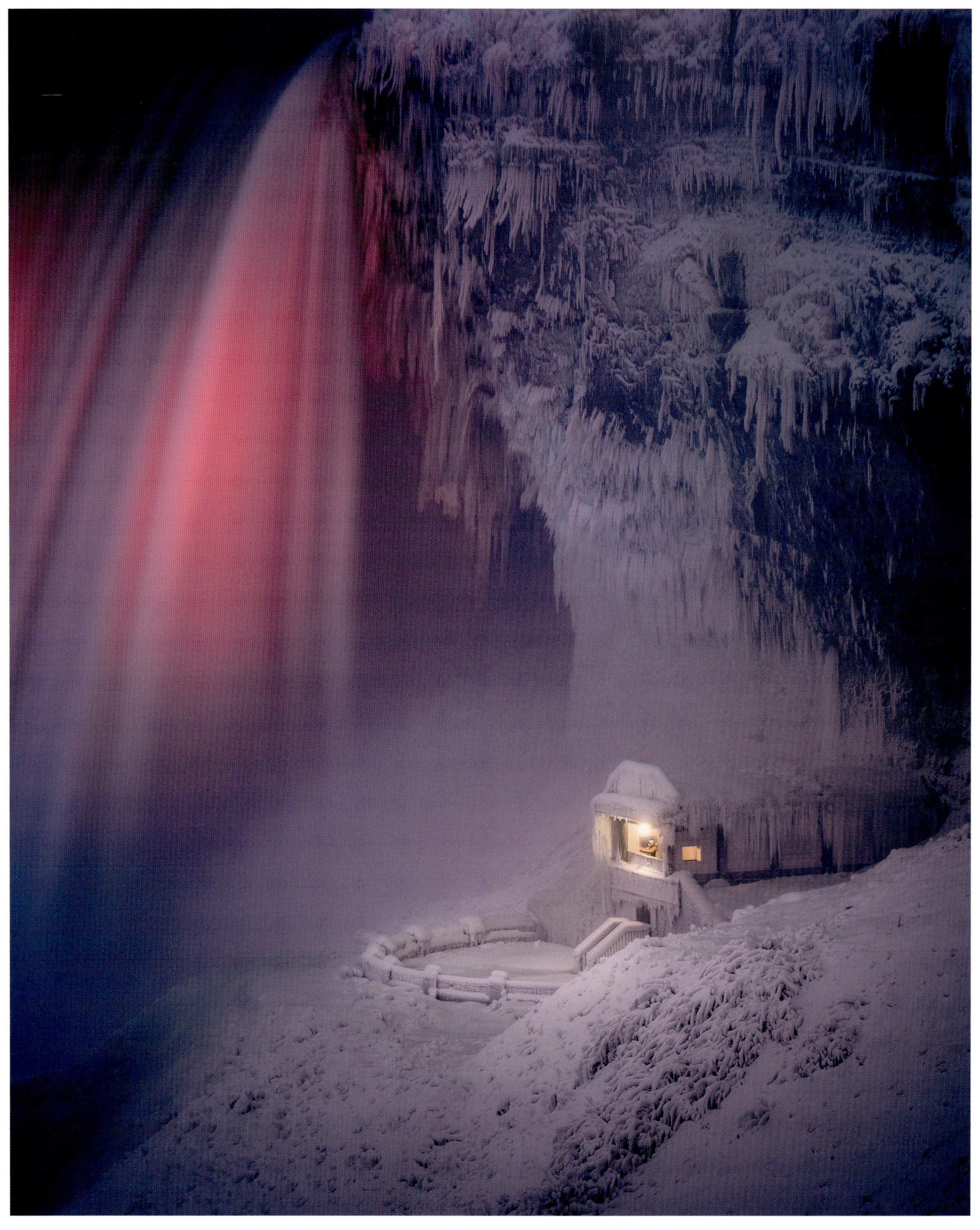

Niagara Falls, Canada

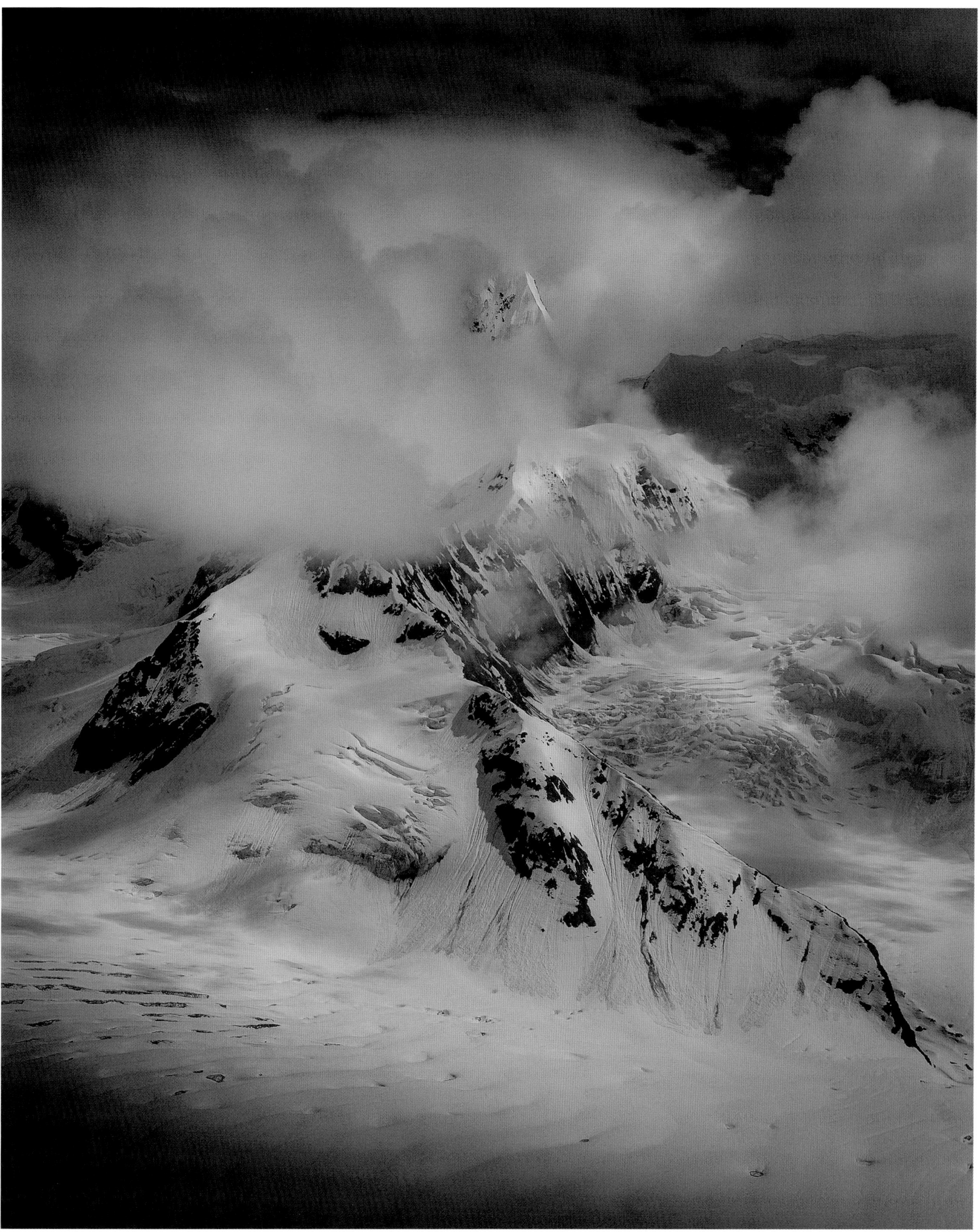

Denali National Park, Alaska, USA

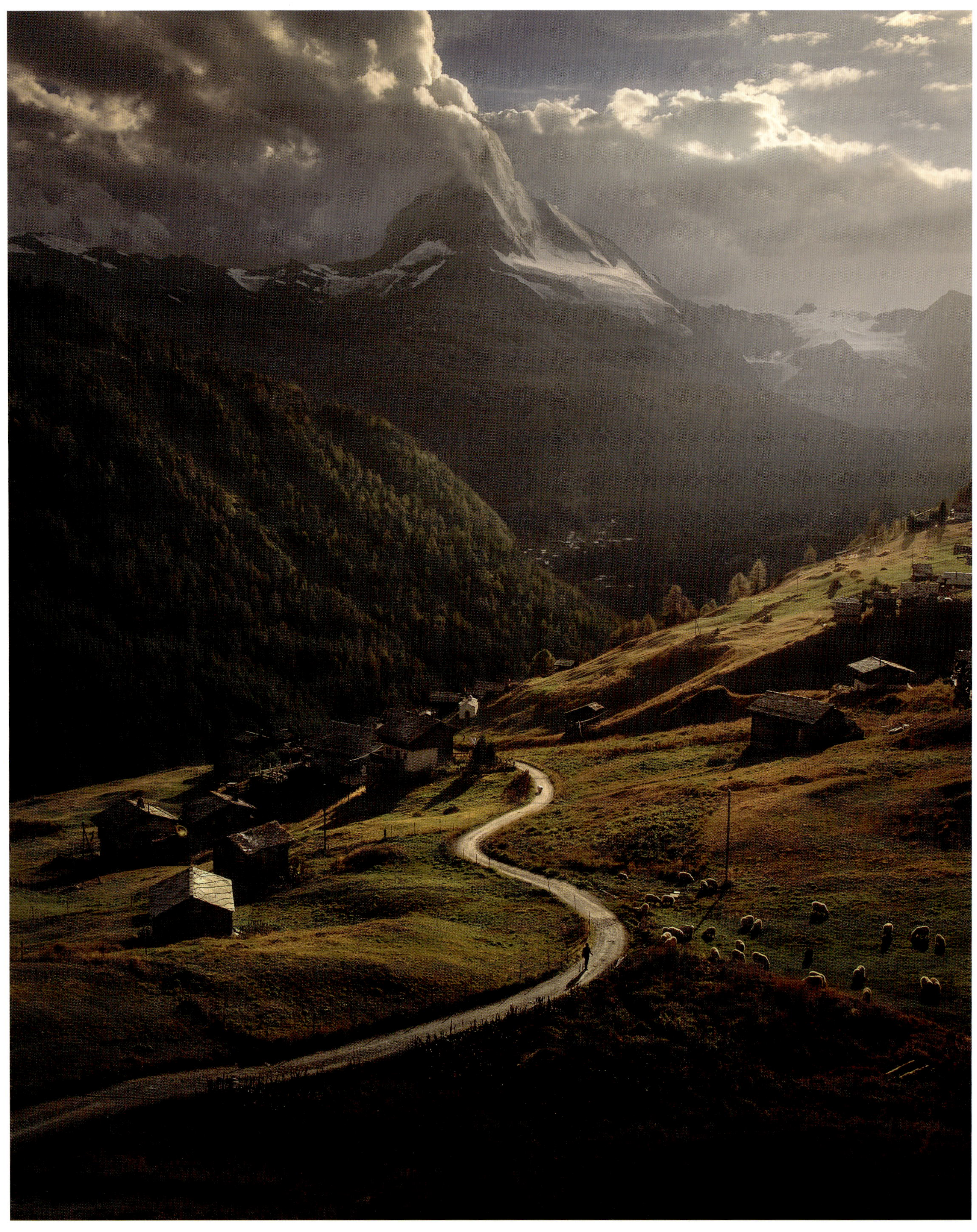

Matterhorn, Switzerland

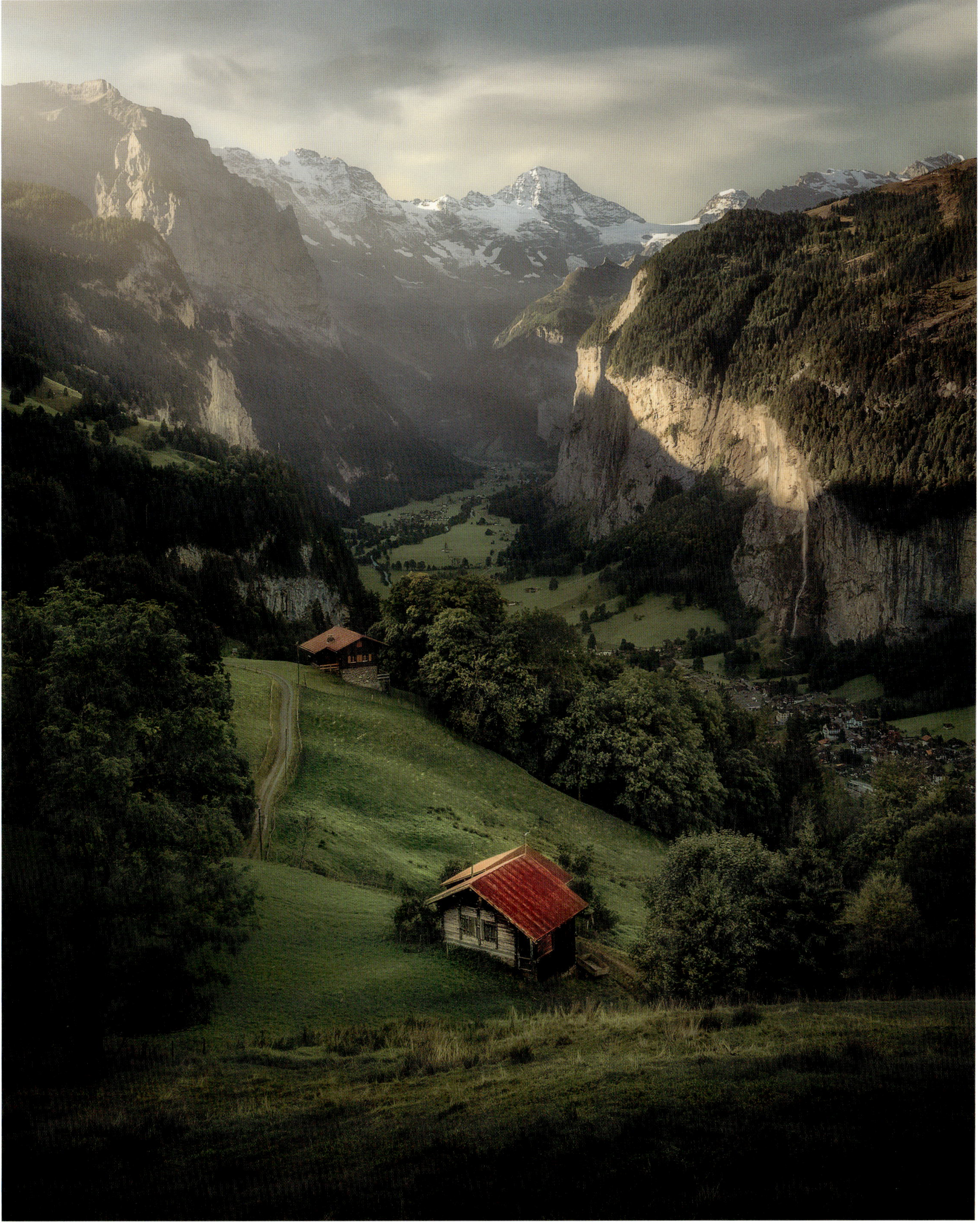

Wengen, Switzerland

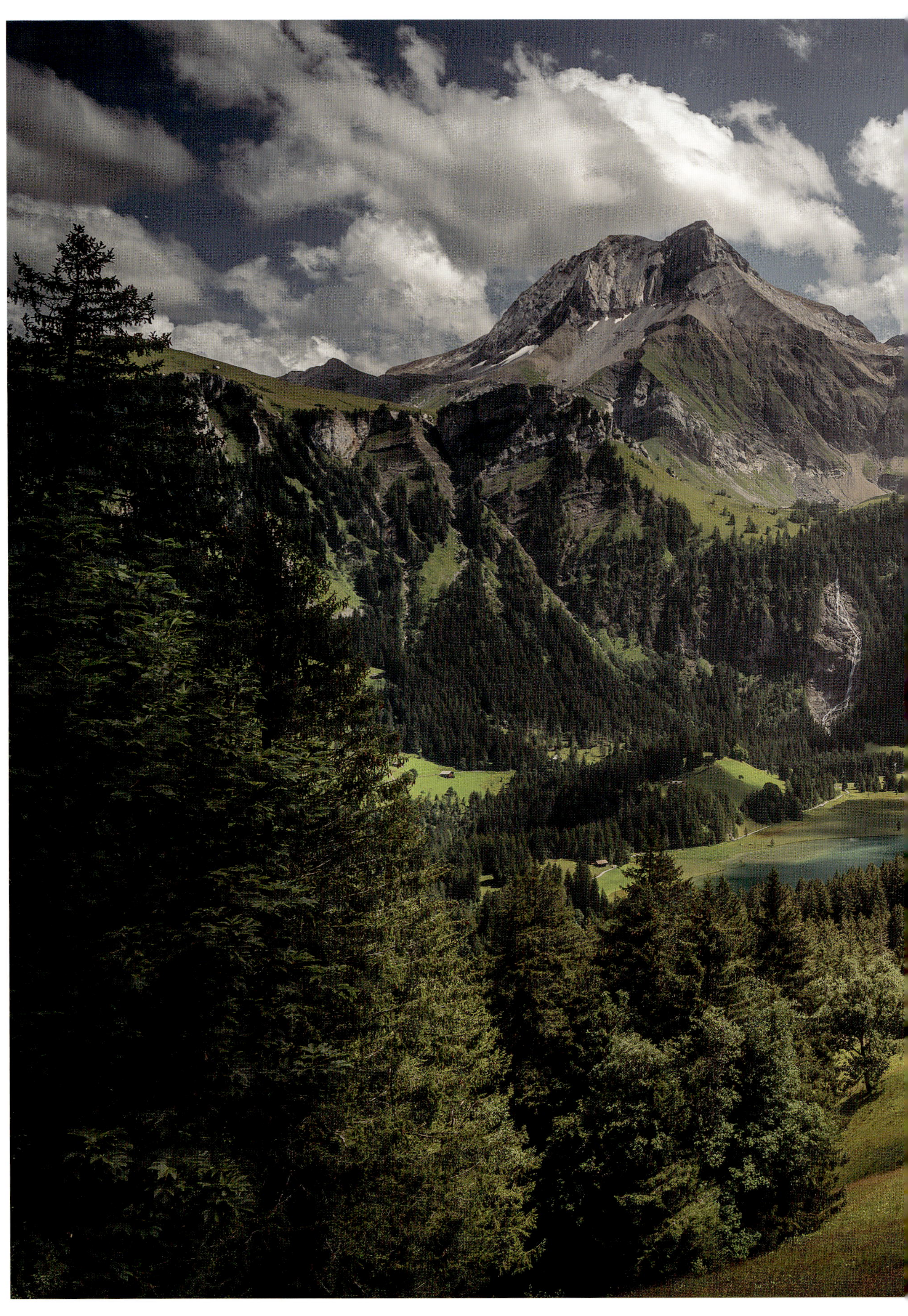

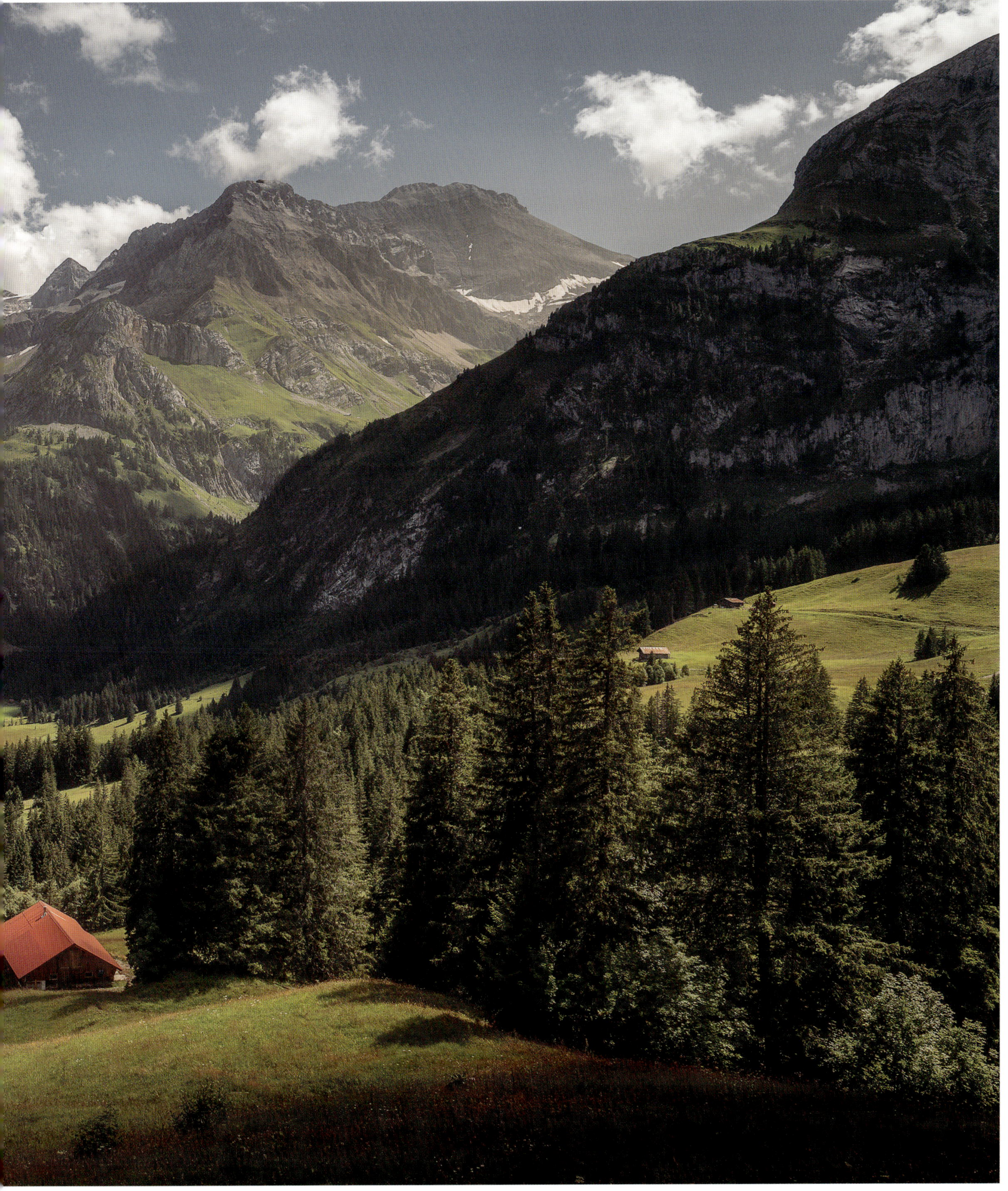

Lauenen, Switzerland

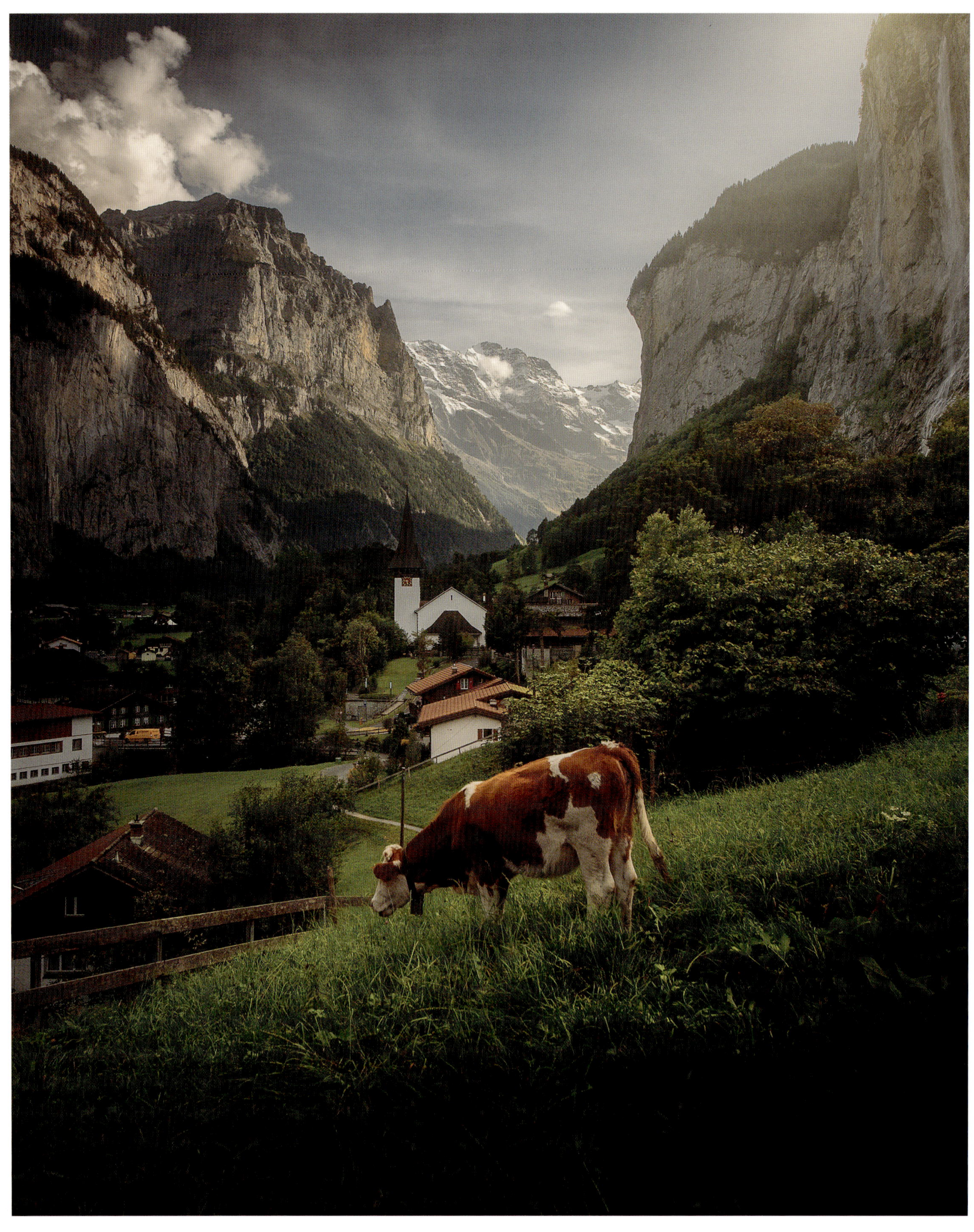

Lauterbrunnen, Switzerland

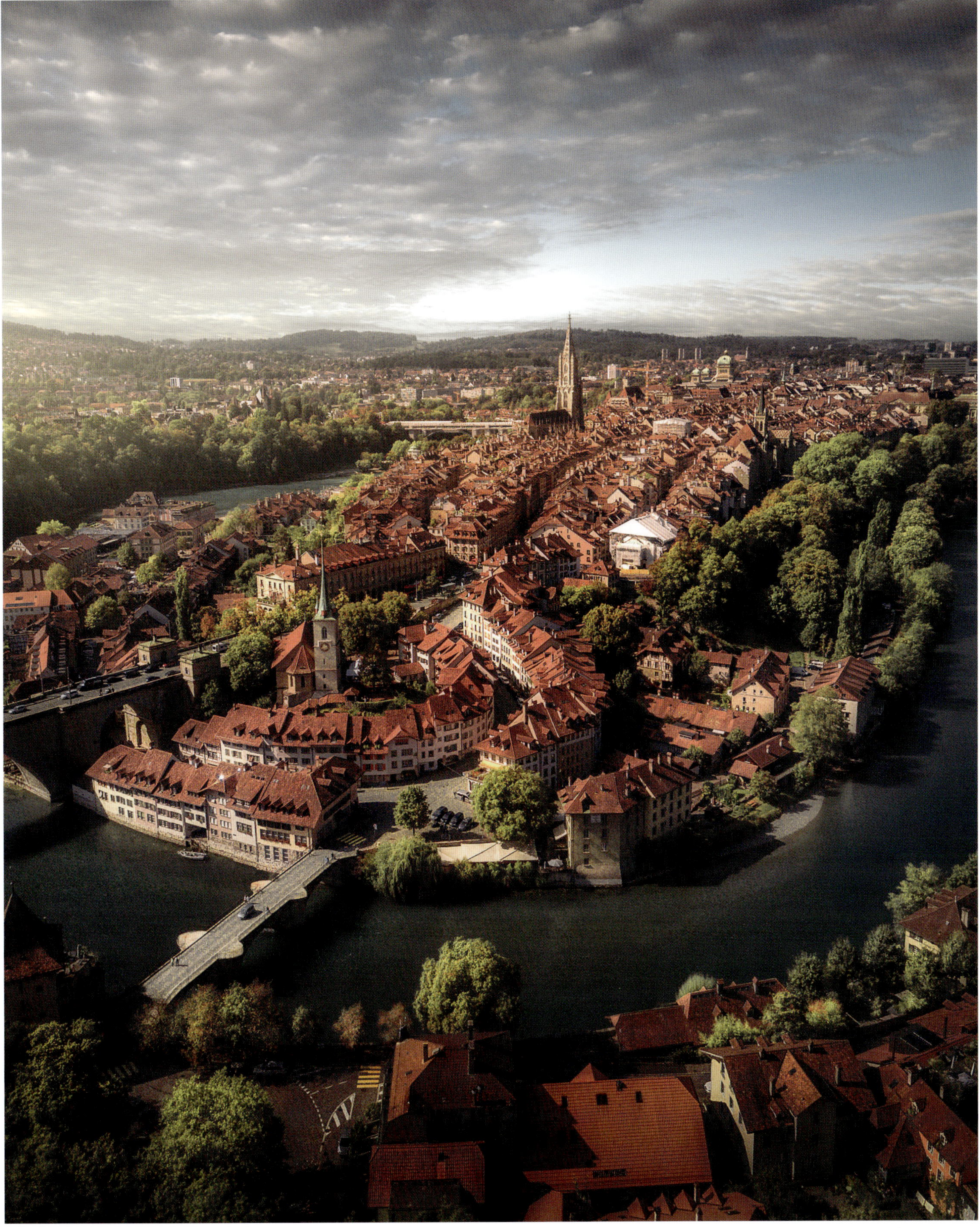

Bern, Switzerland

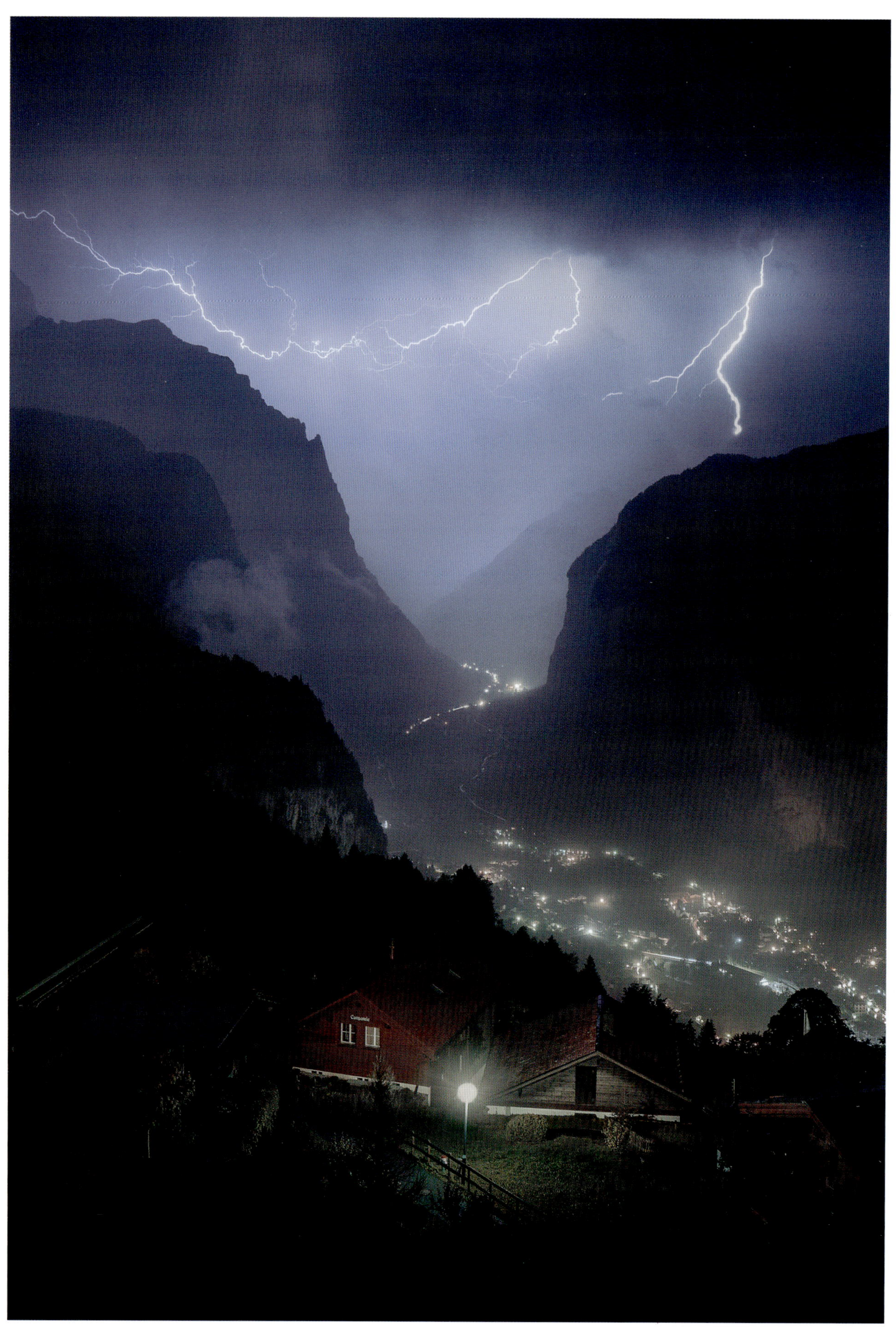

Wengen, Switzerland

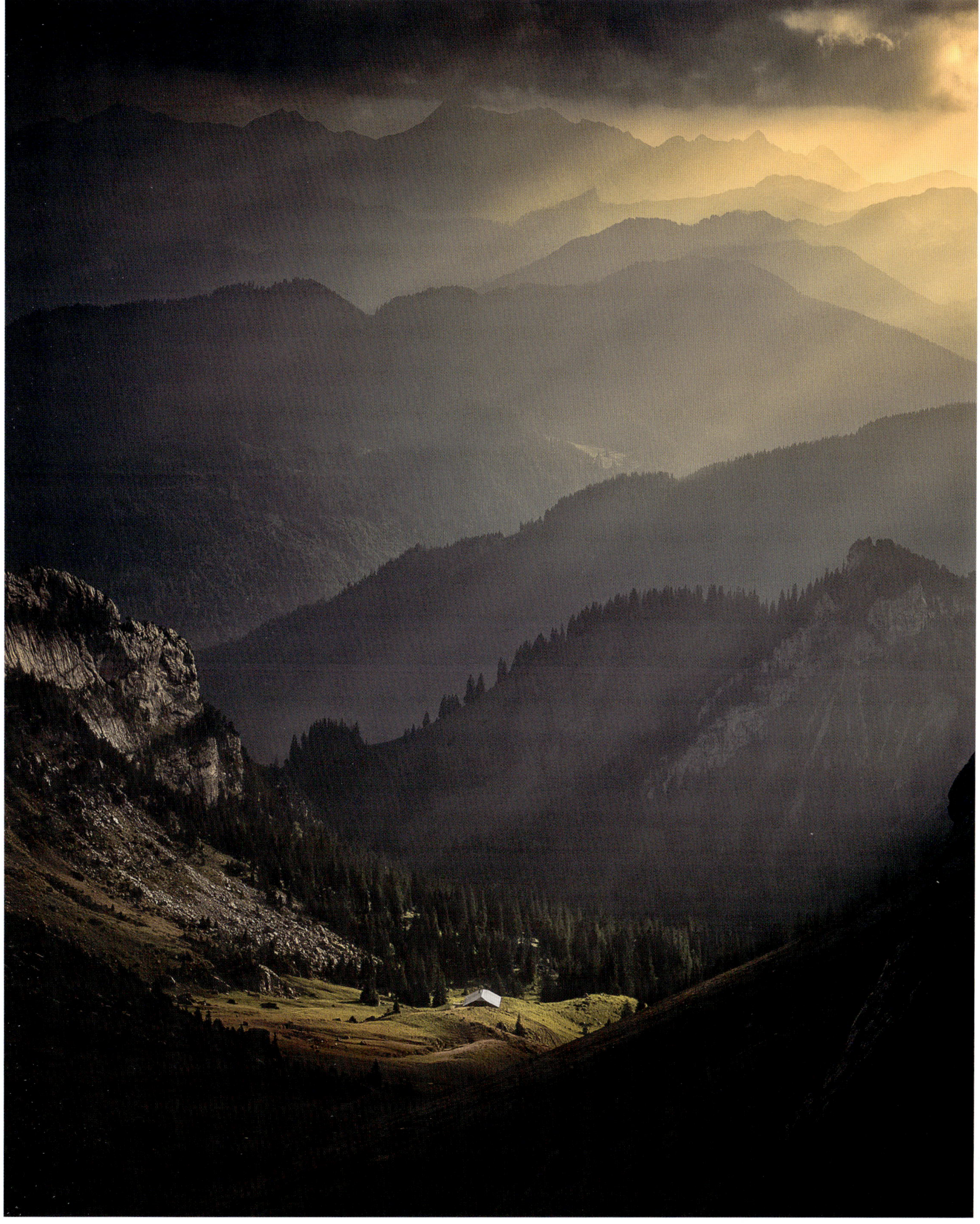

Lucerne, Switzerland

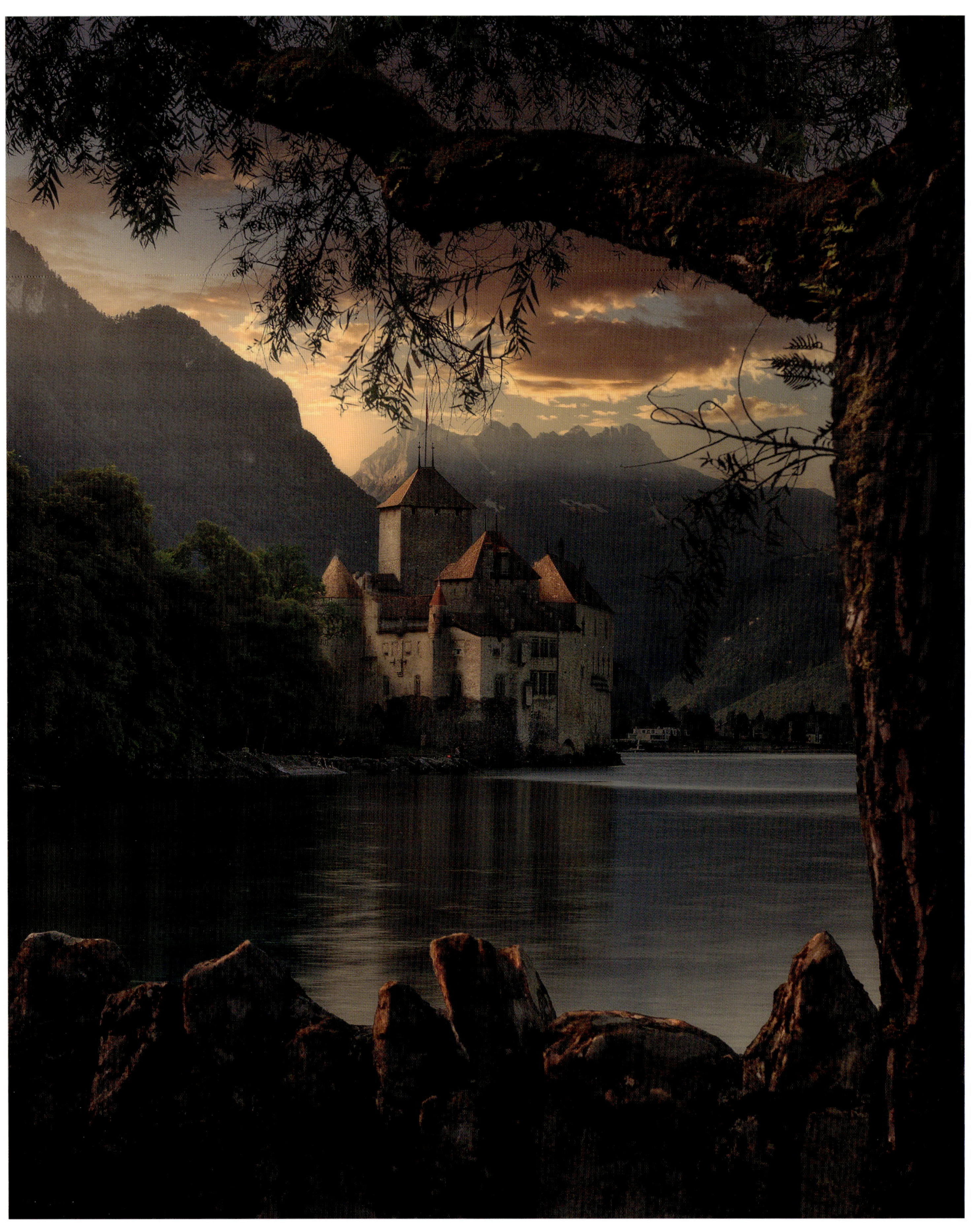

Chateau de Chillon, Switzerland

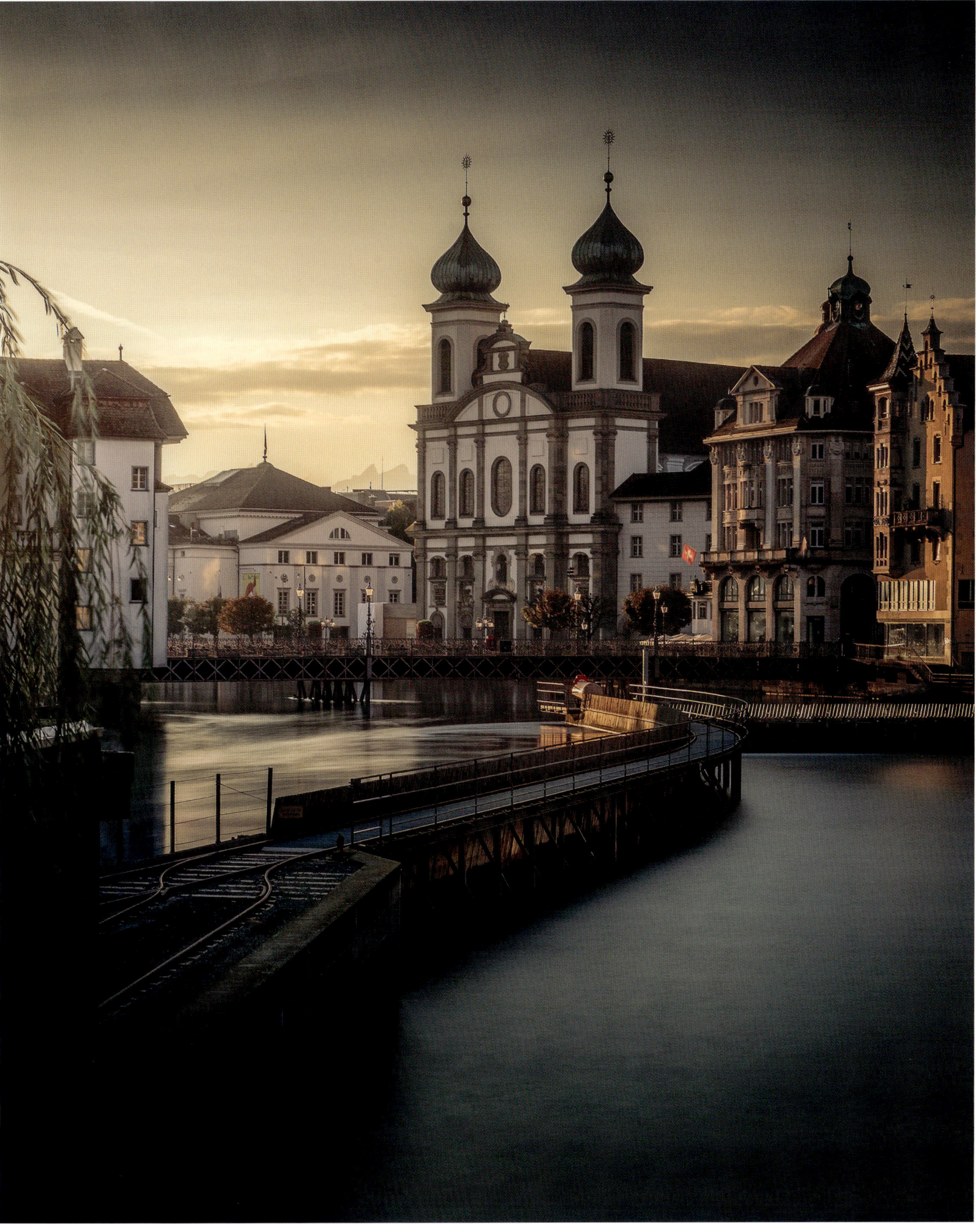

Lucerne, Switzerland

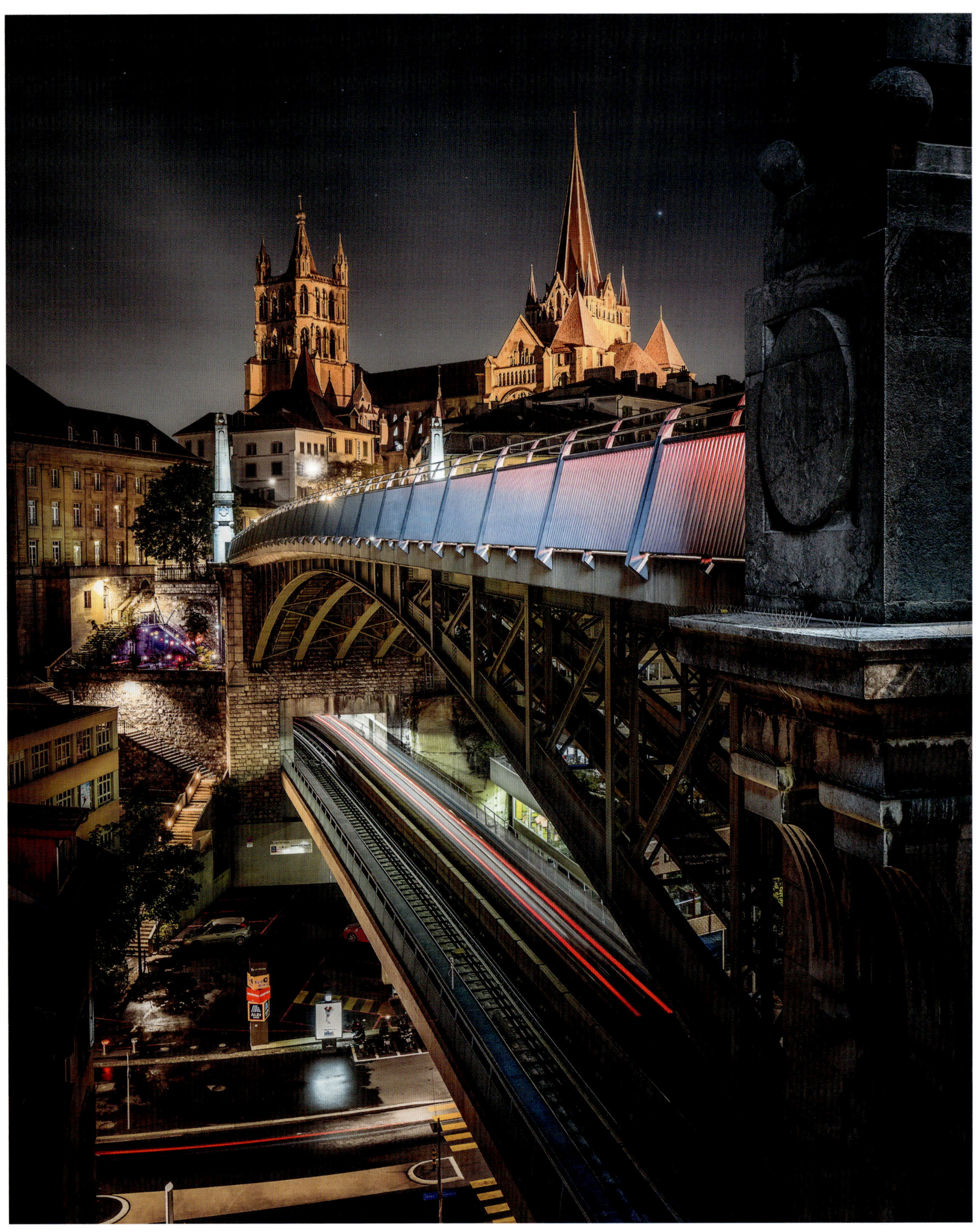

Lausanne, Switzerland

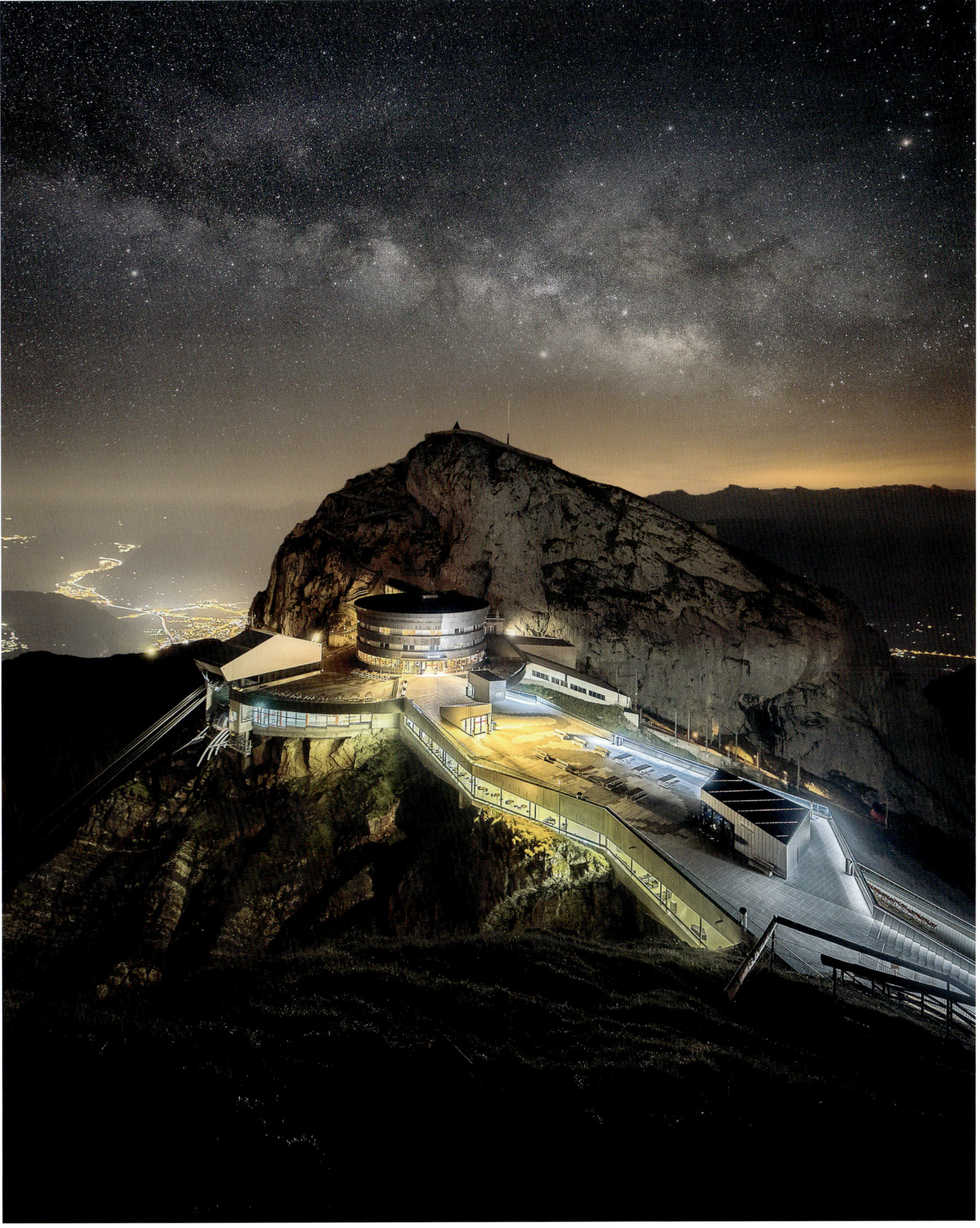

Mount Pilatus, Switzerland

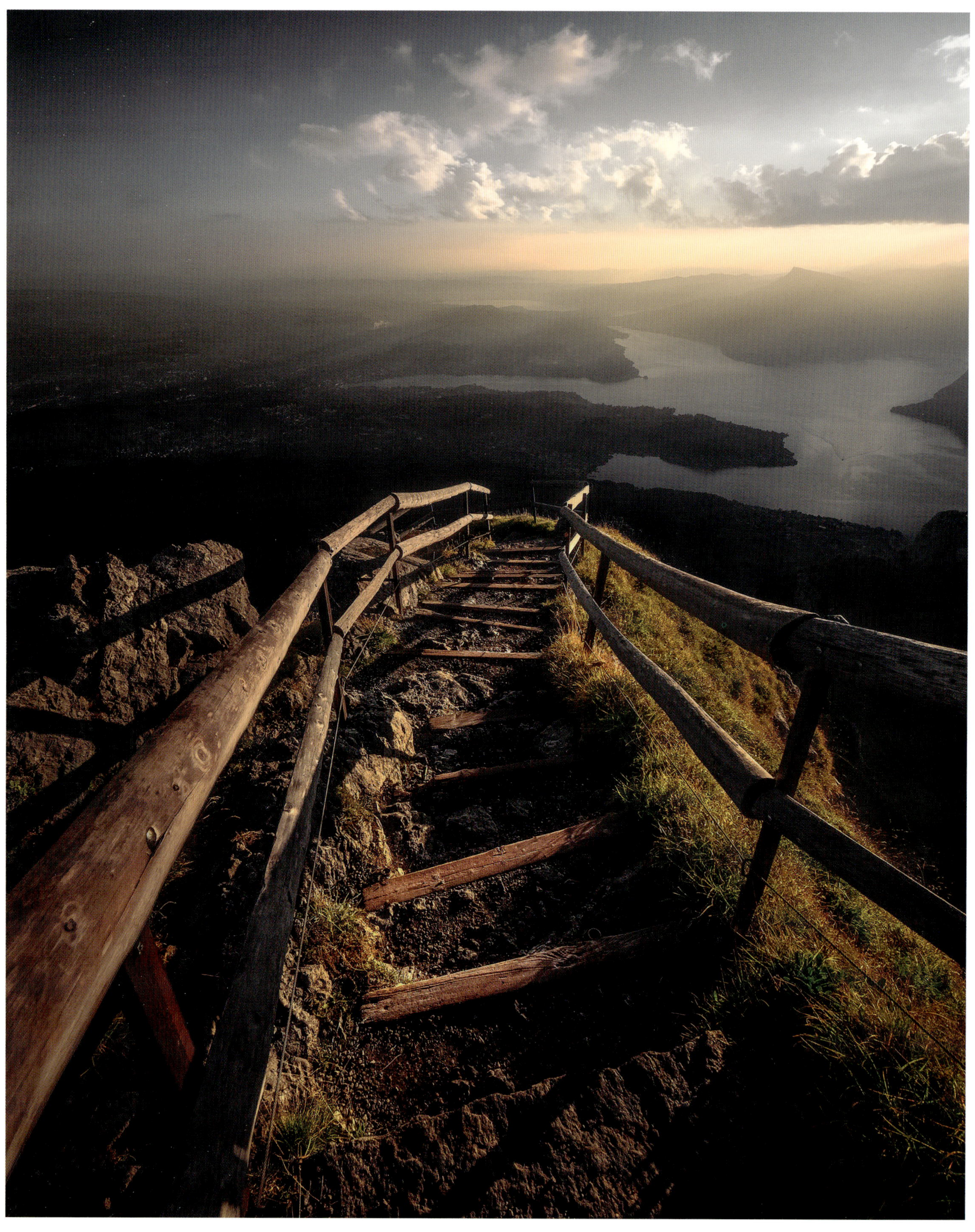

Lucerne, Switzerland

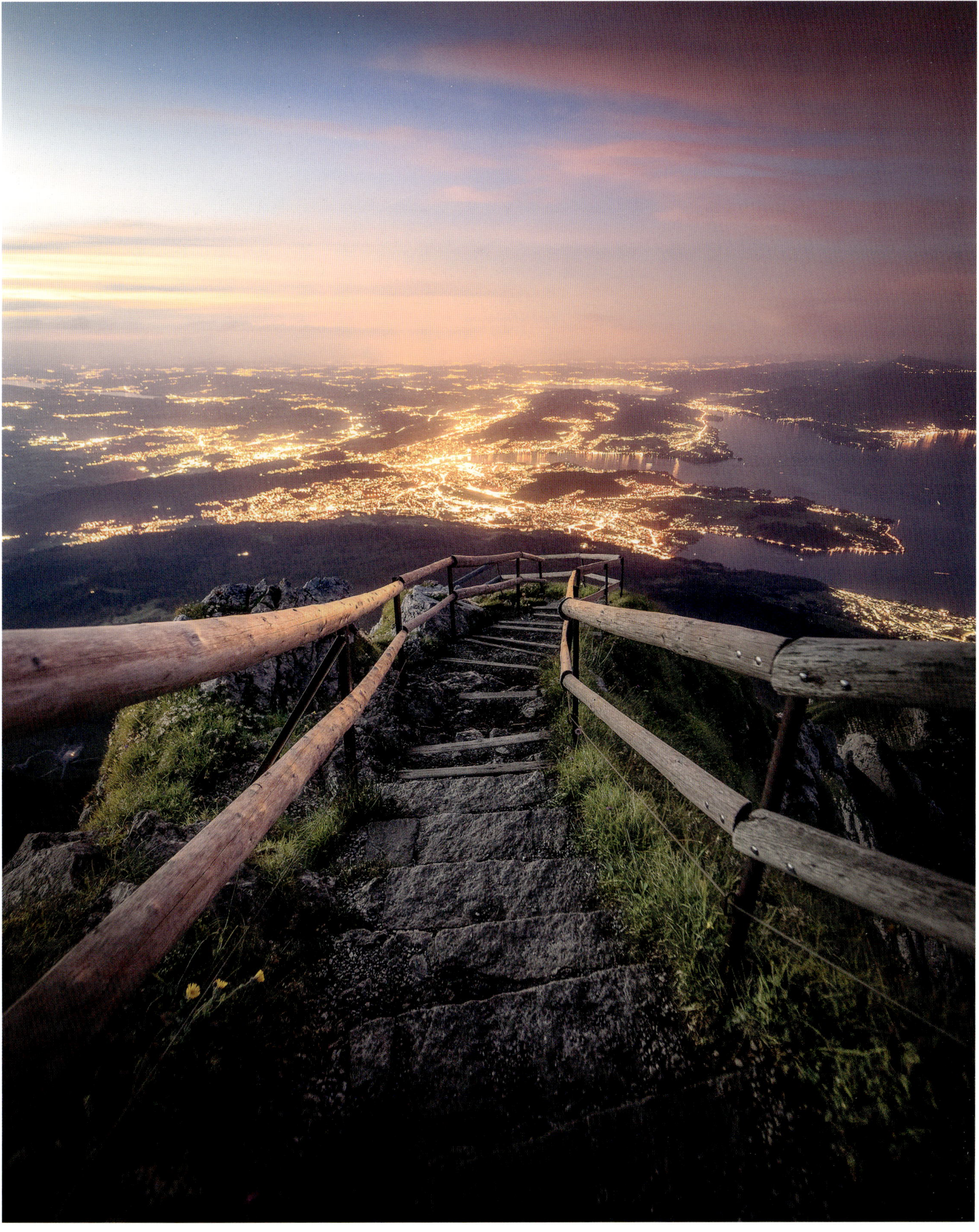

Lucerne, Switzerland

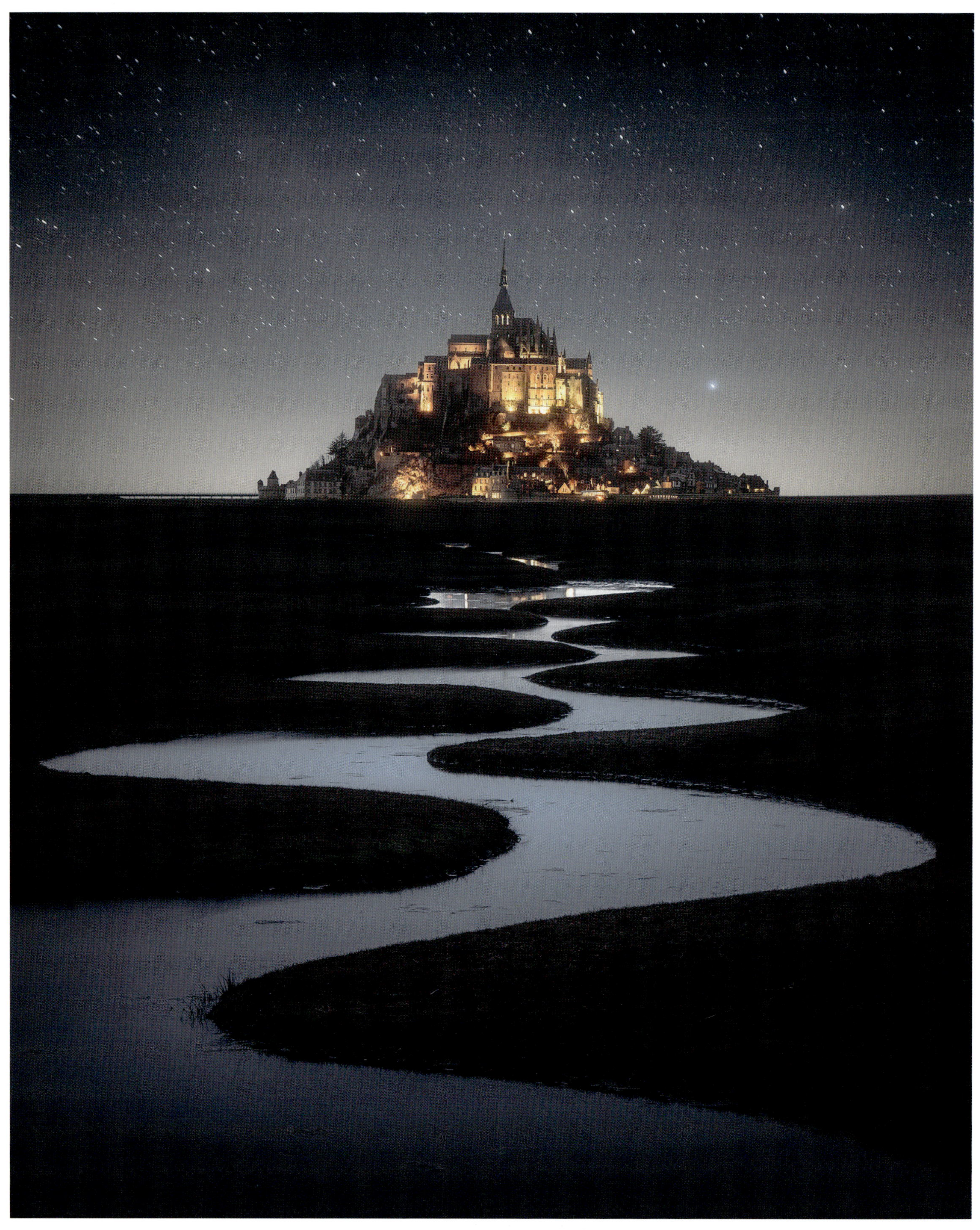

Mont Saint-Michel, France

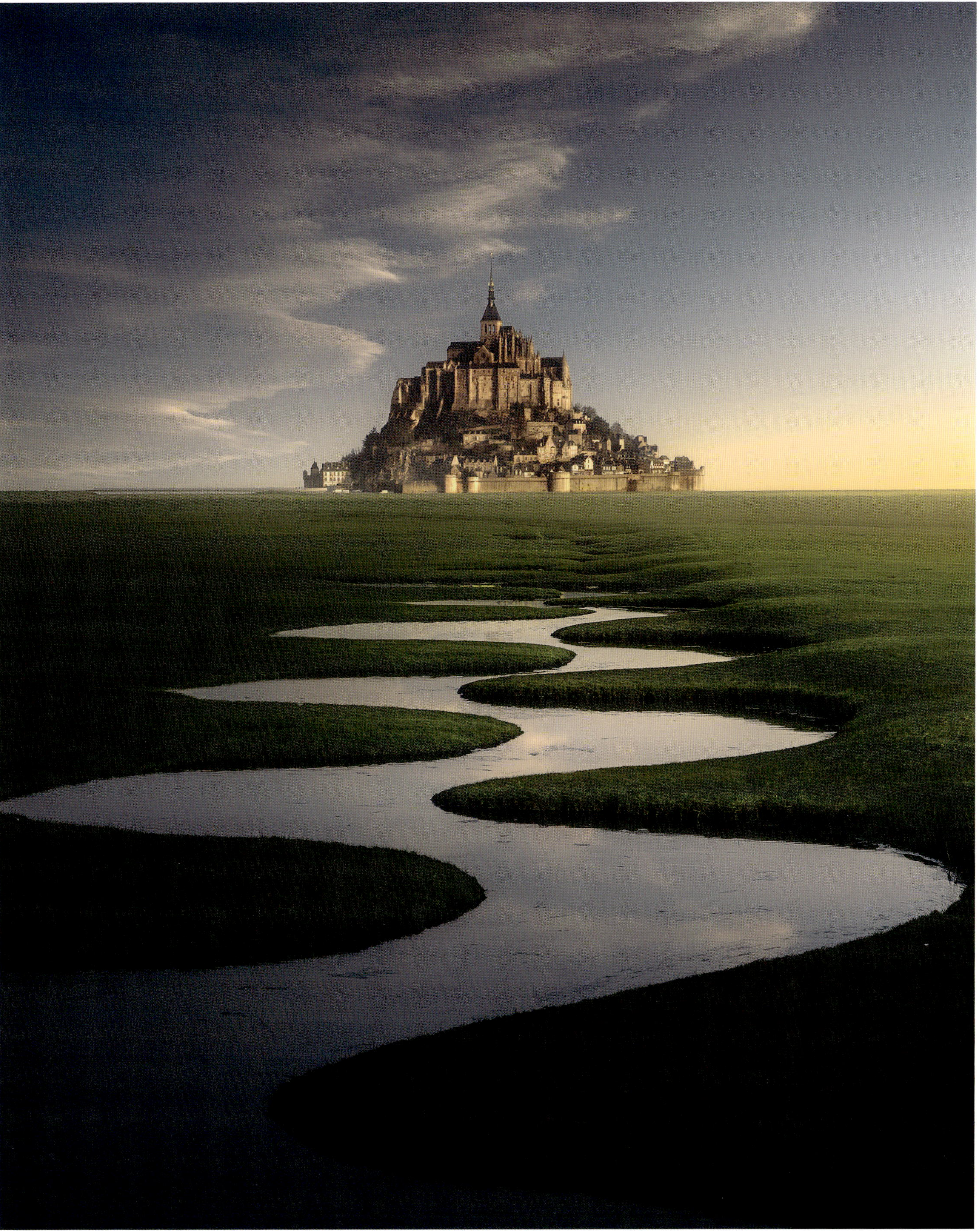

Mont Saint-Michel, France

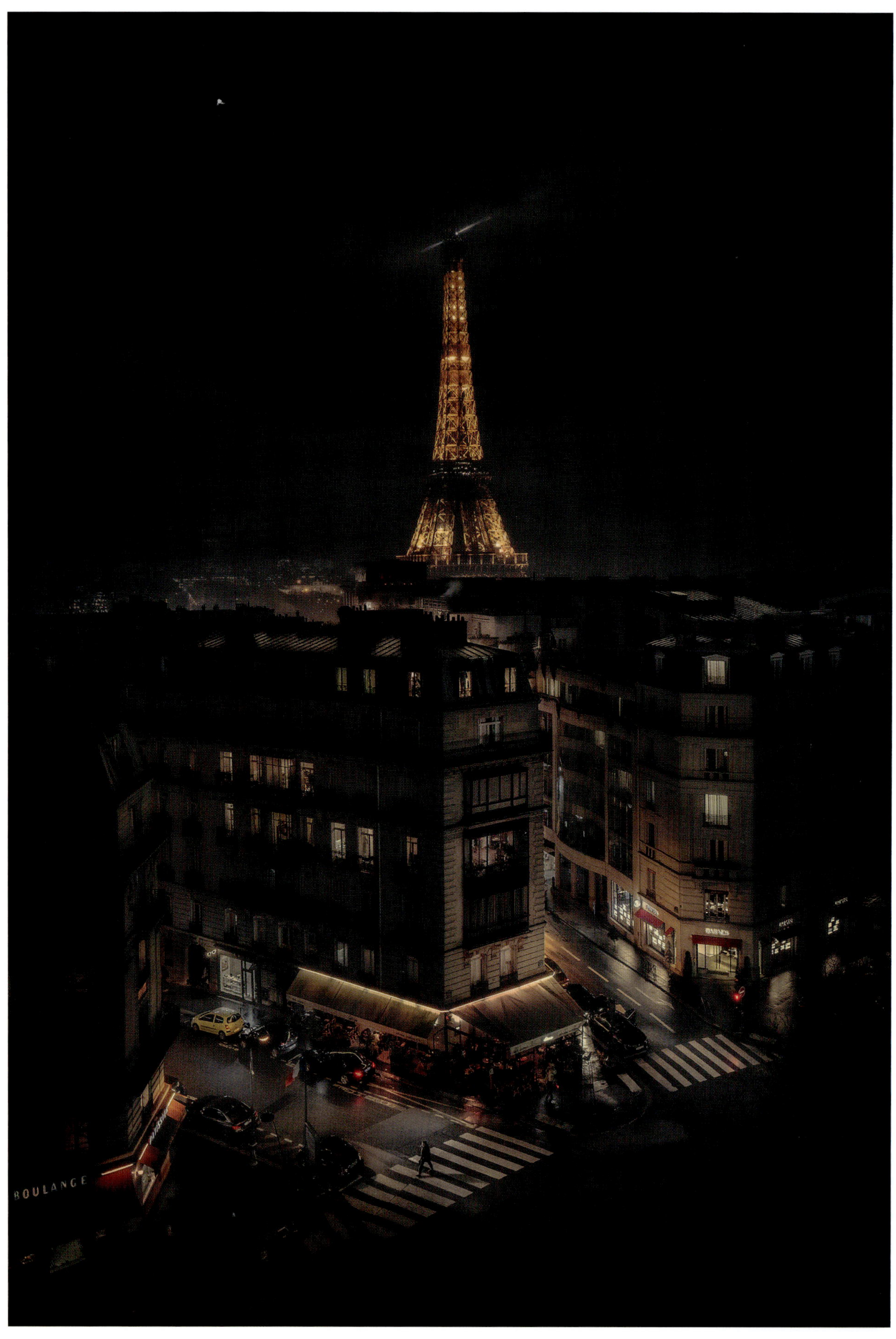

Paris, France

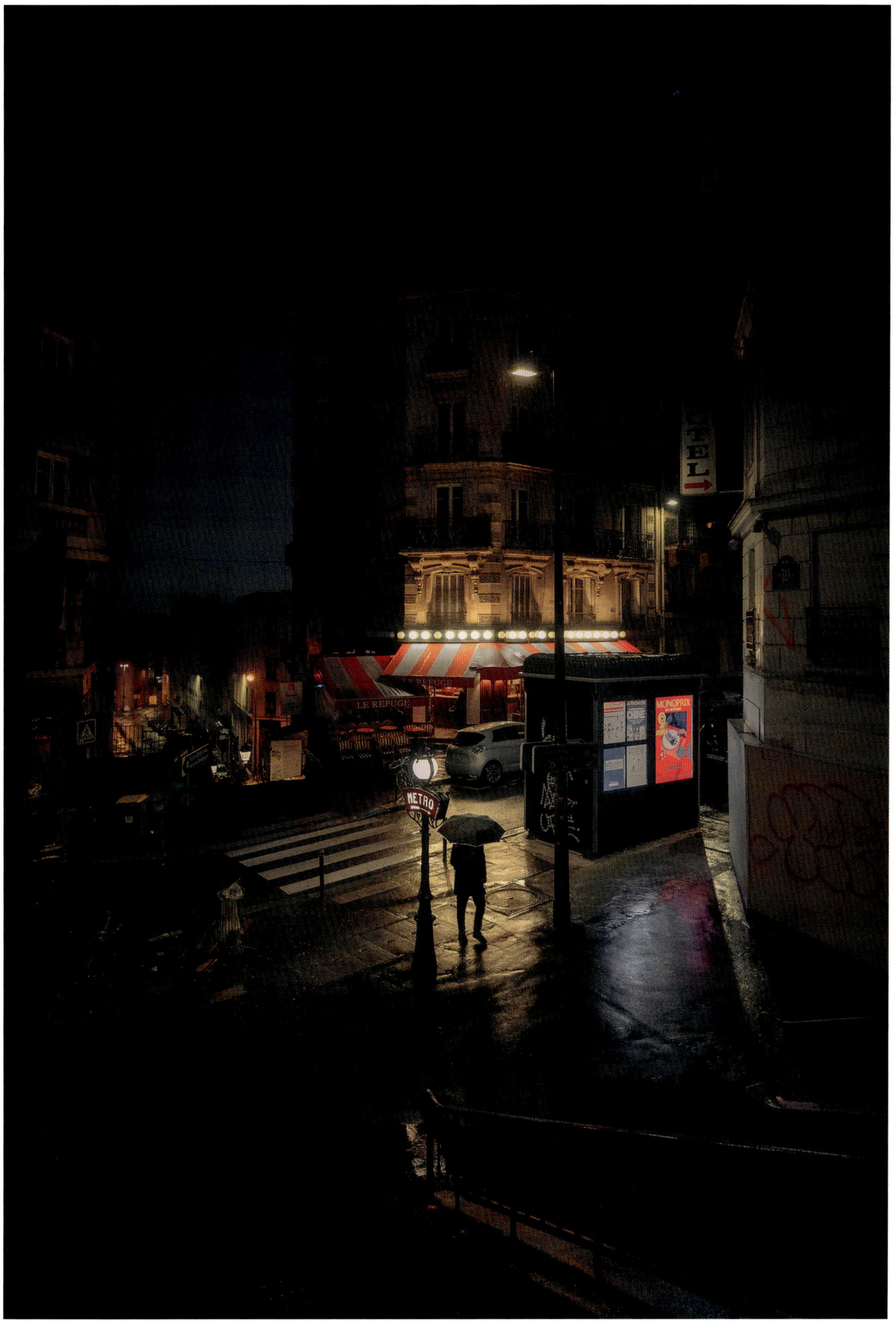

Paris, France

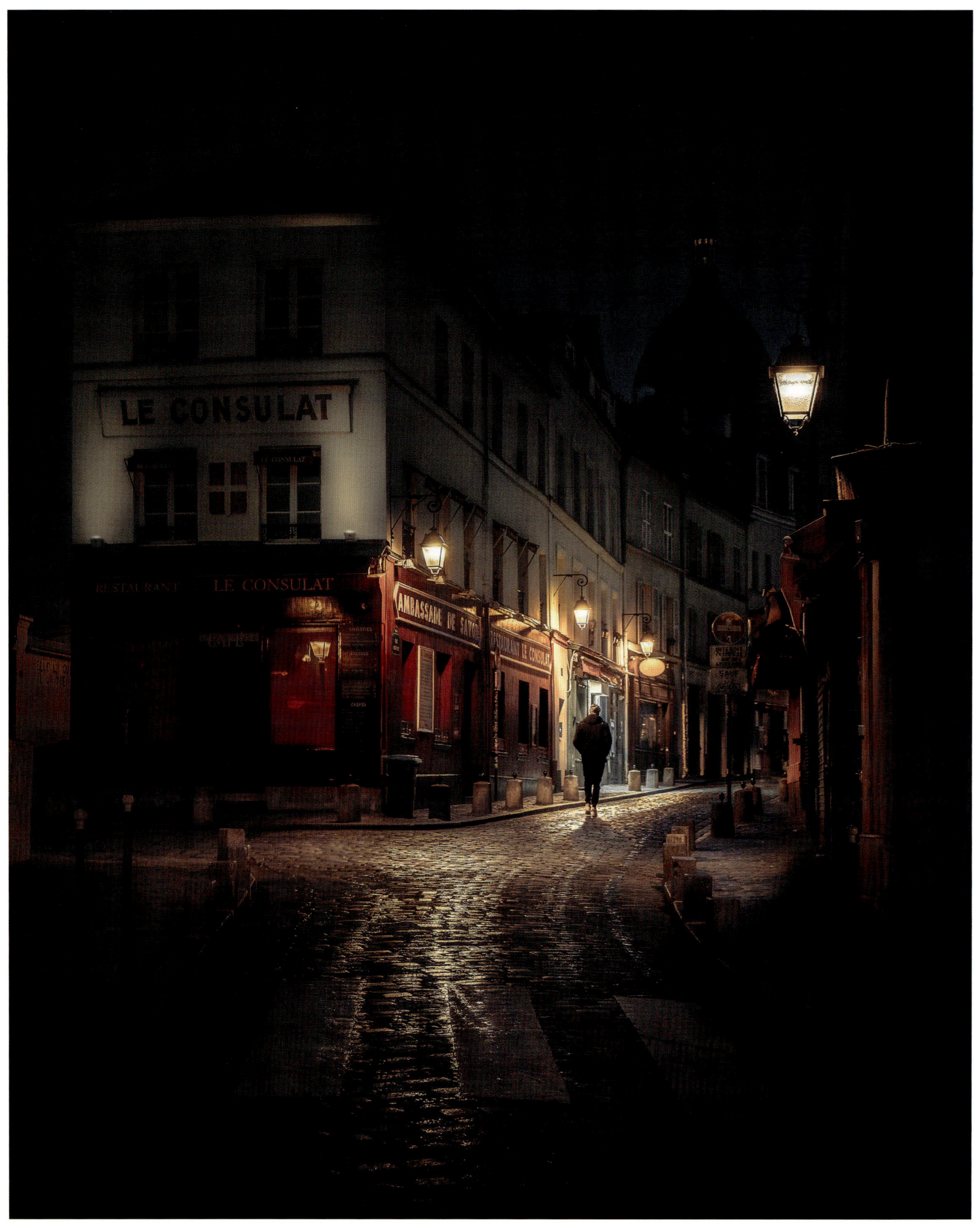

Paris, France

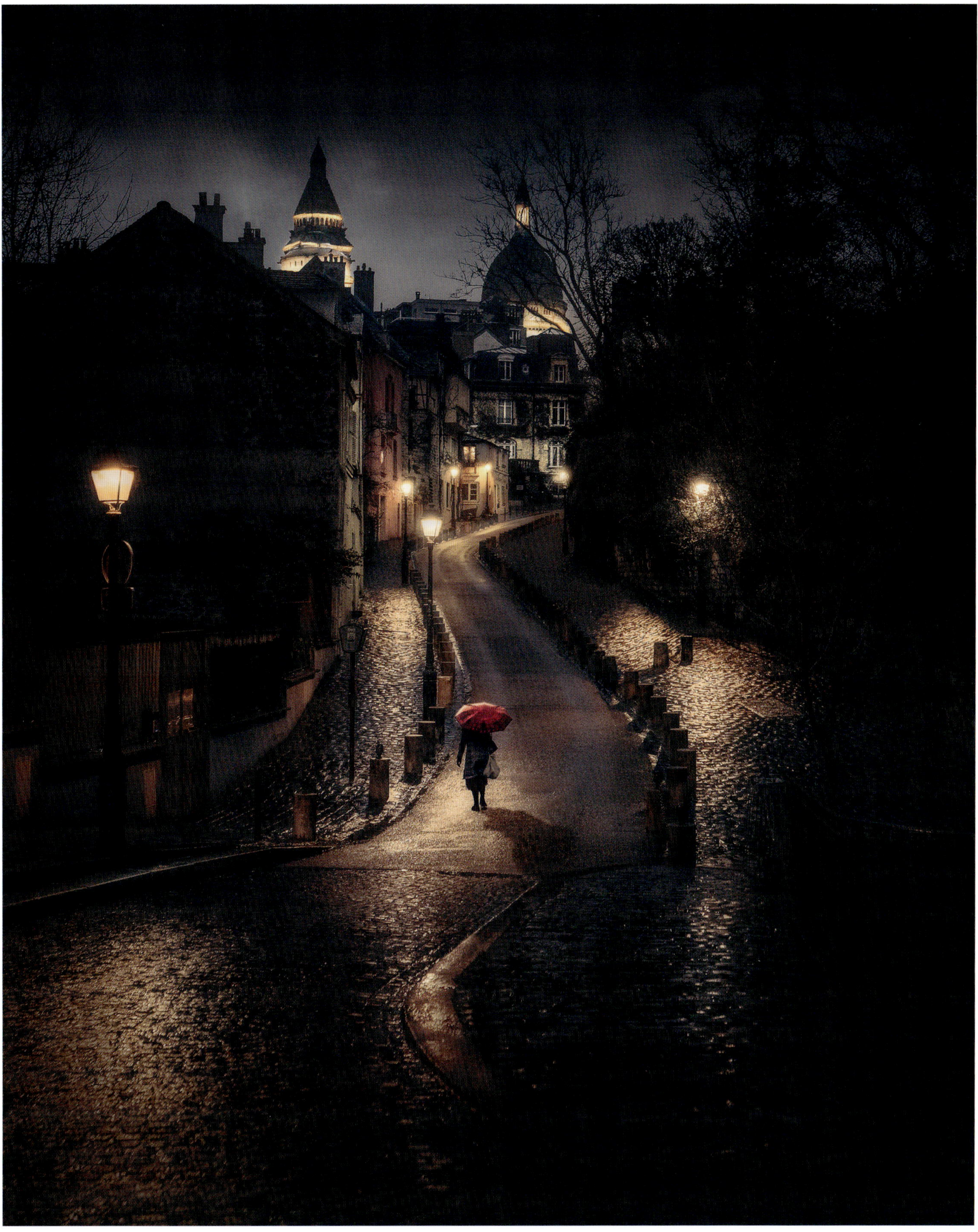

Paris, France

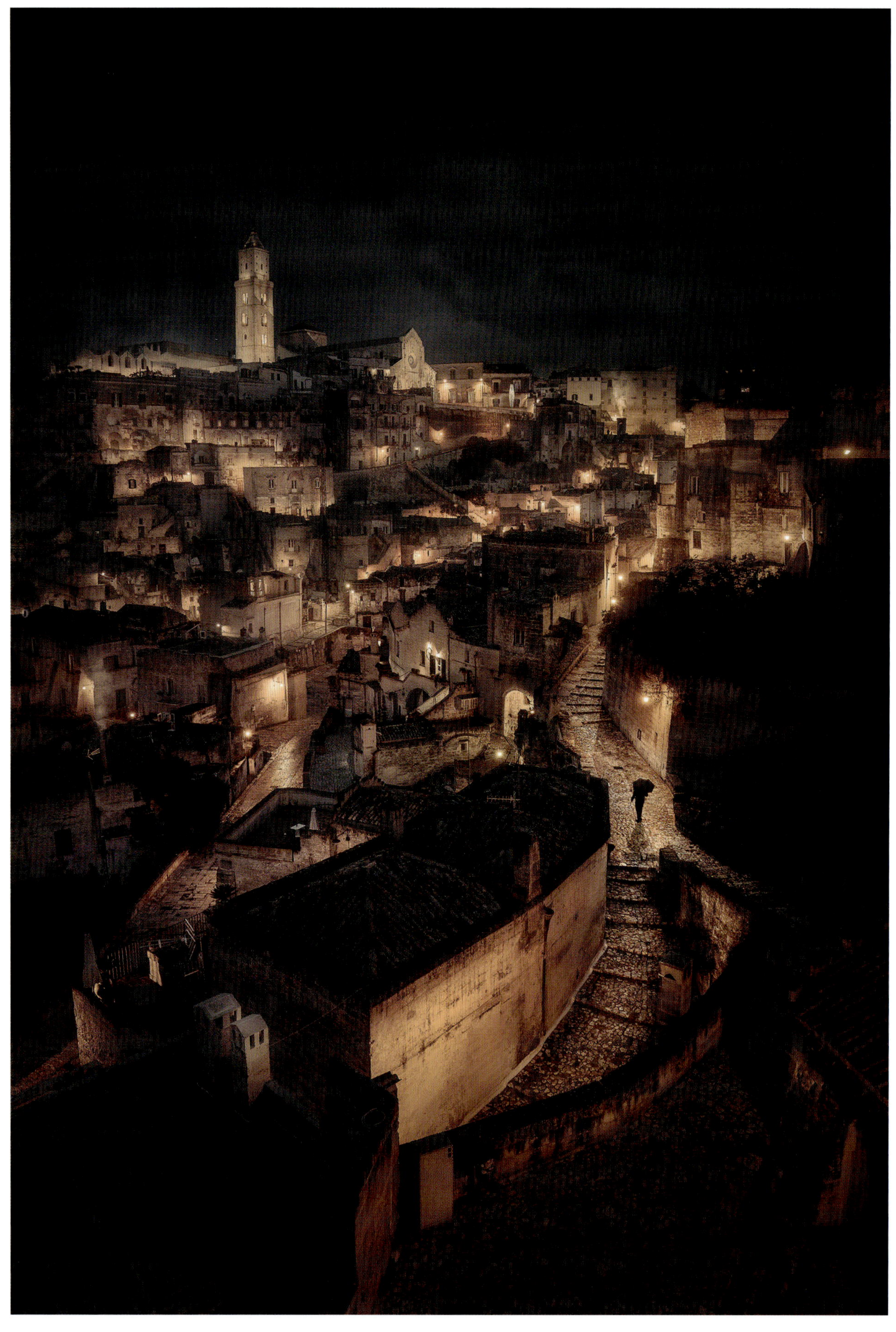

Matera, Italy

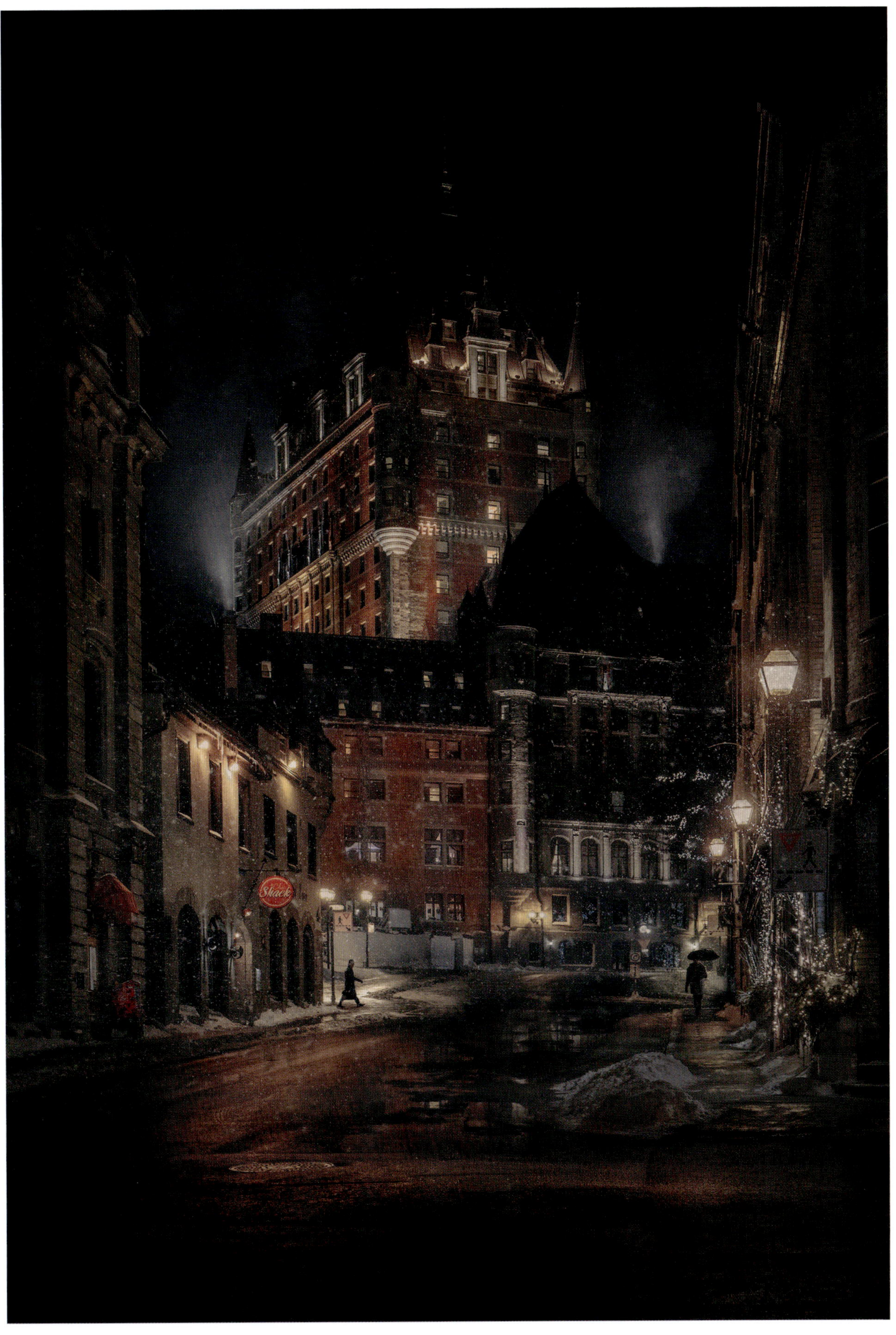

Québec City, Canada

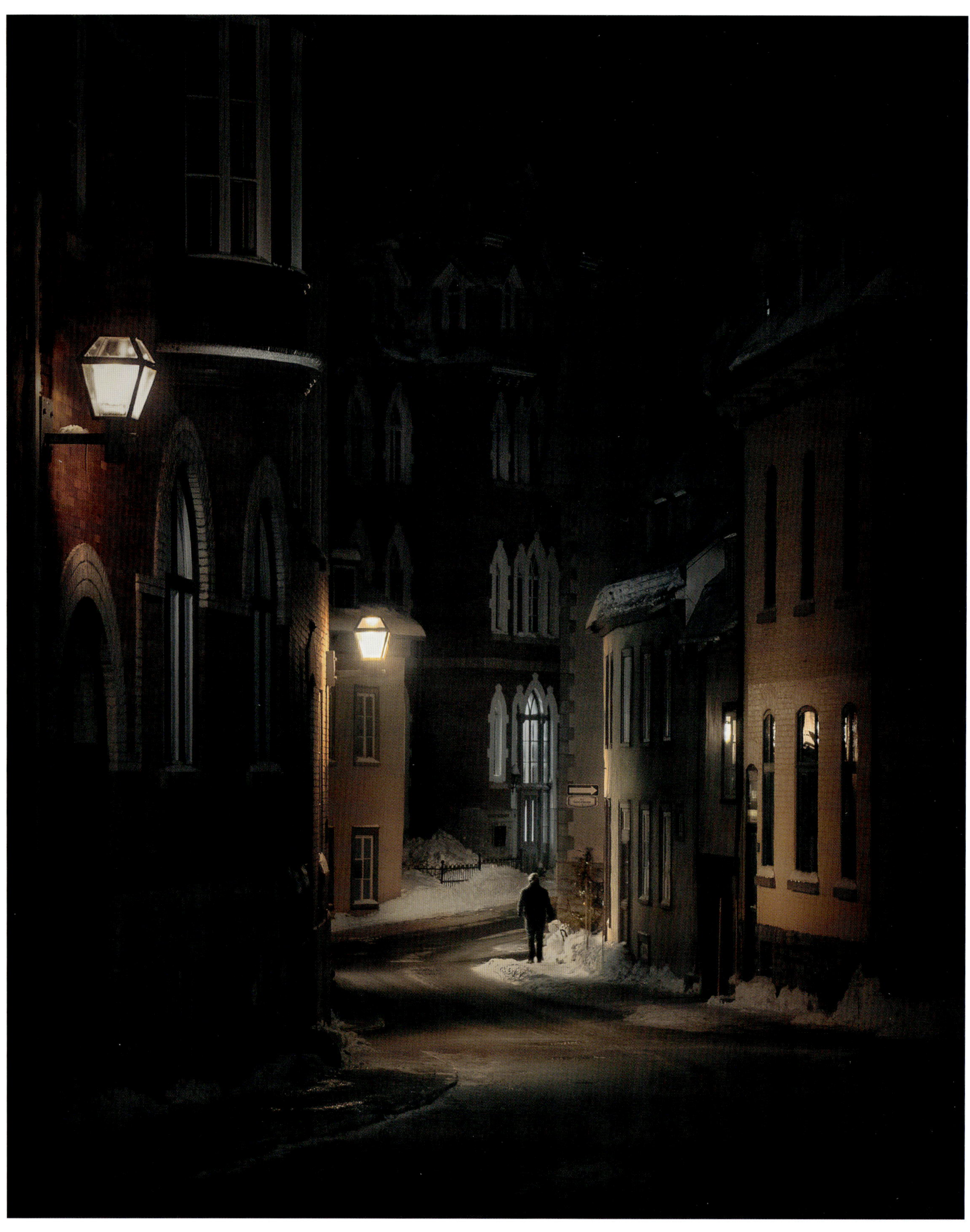

Québec City, Canada

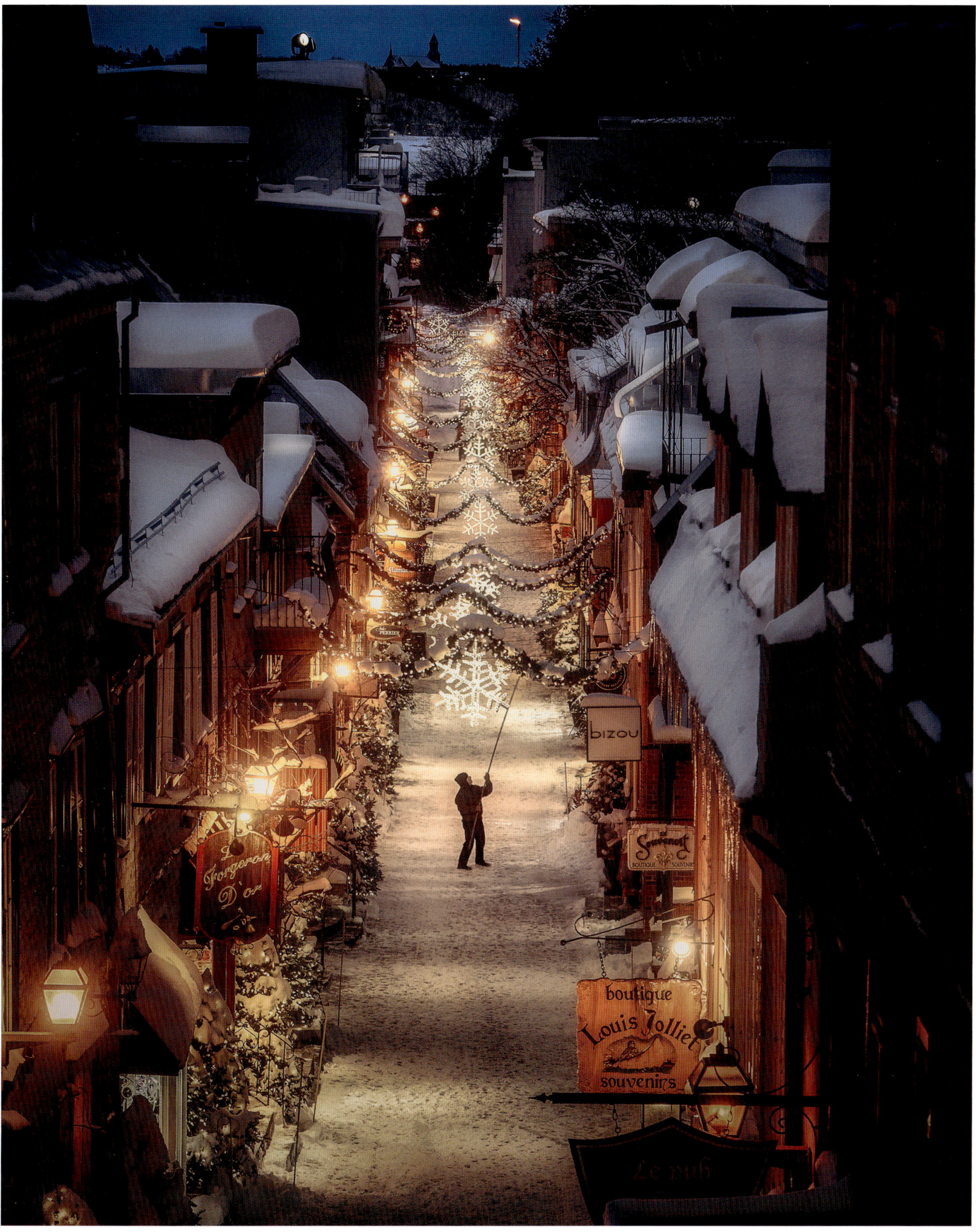

Québec City, Canada

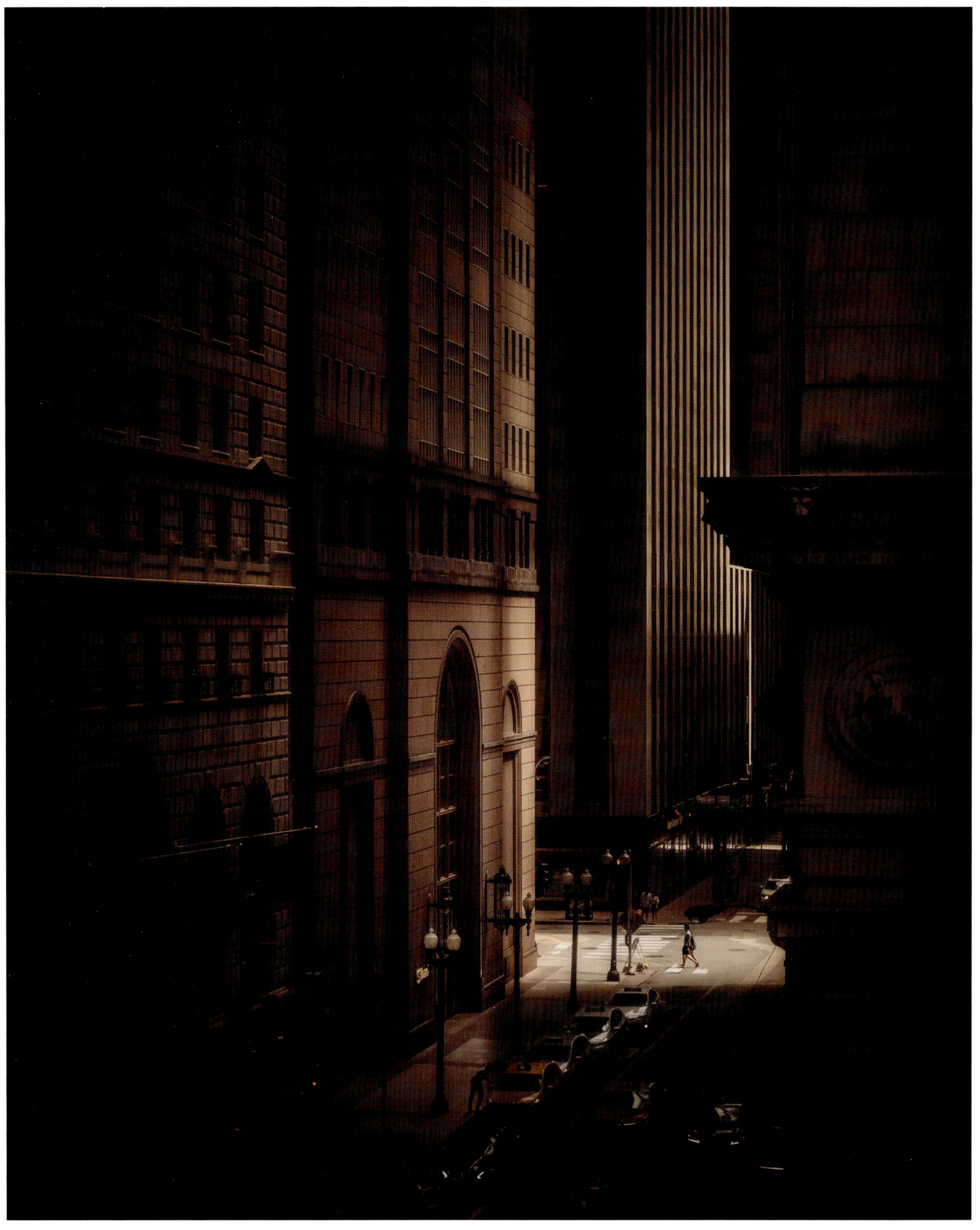

Chicago, Illinois, USA

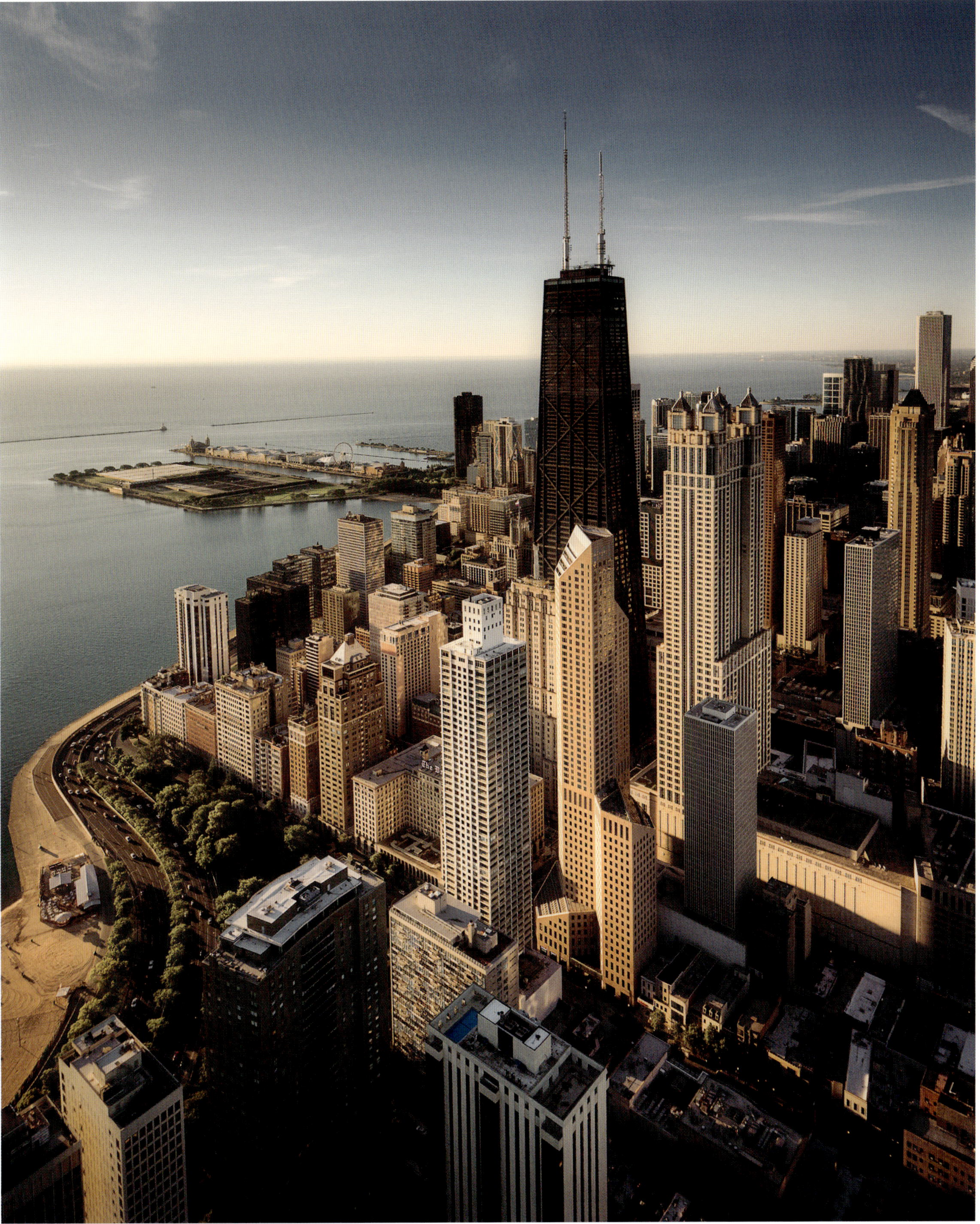

Chicago, Illinois, USA

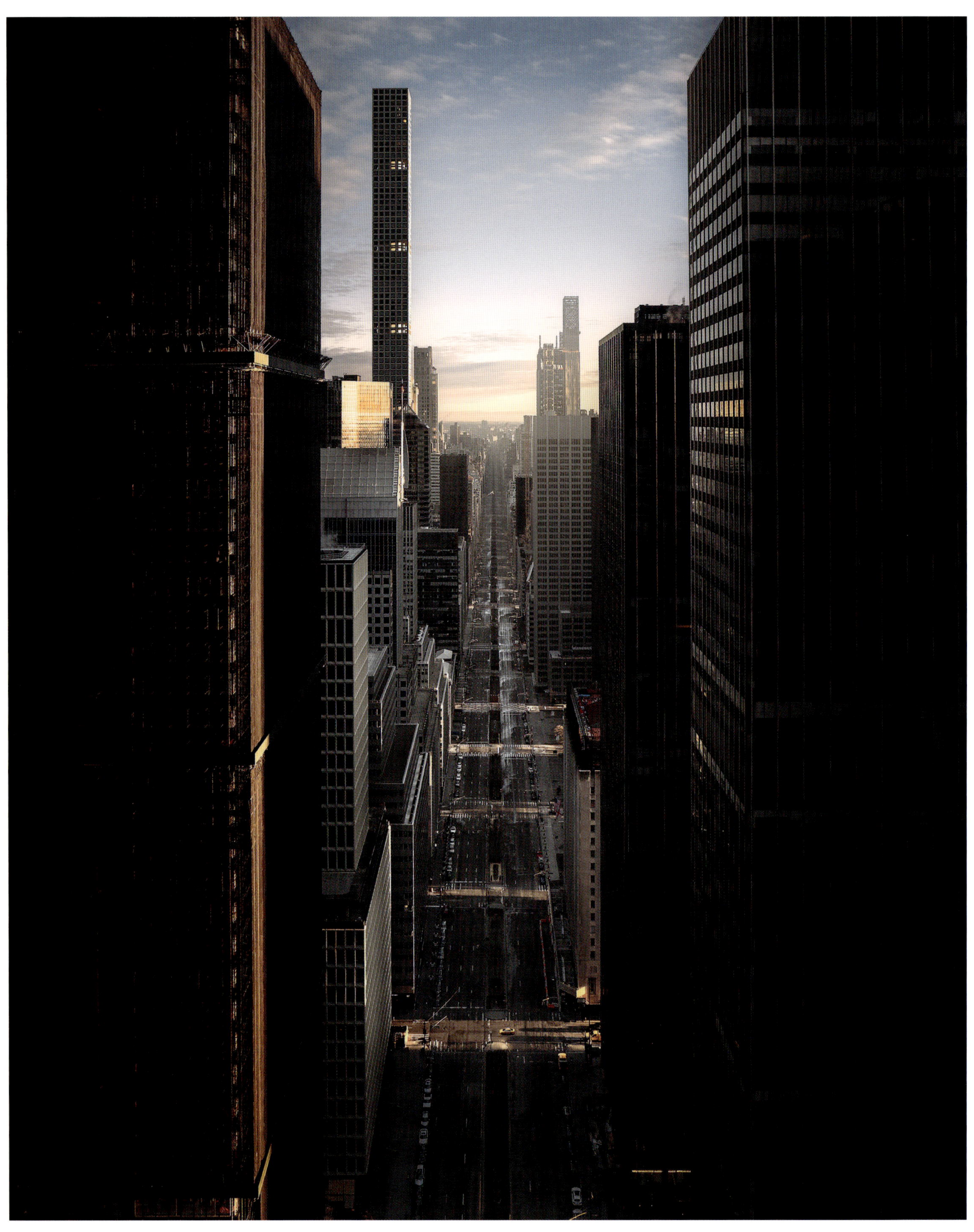

New York, New York, USA

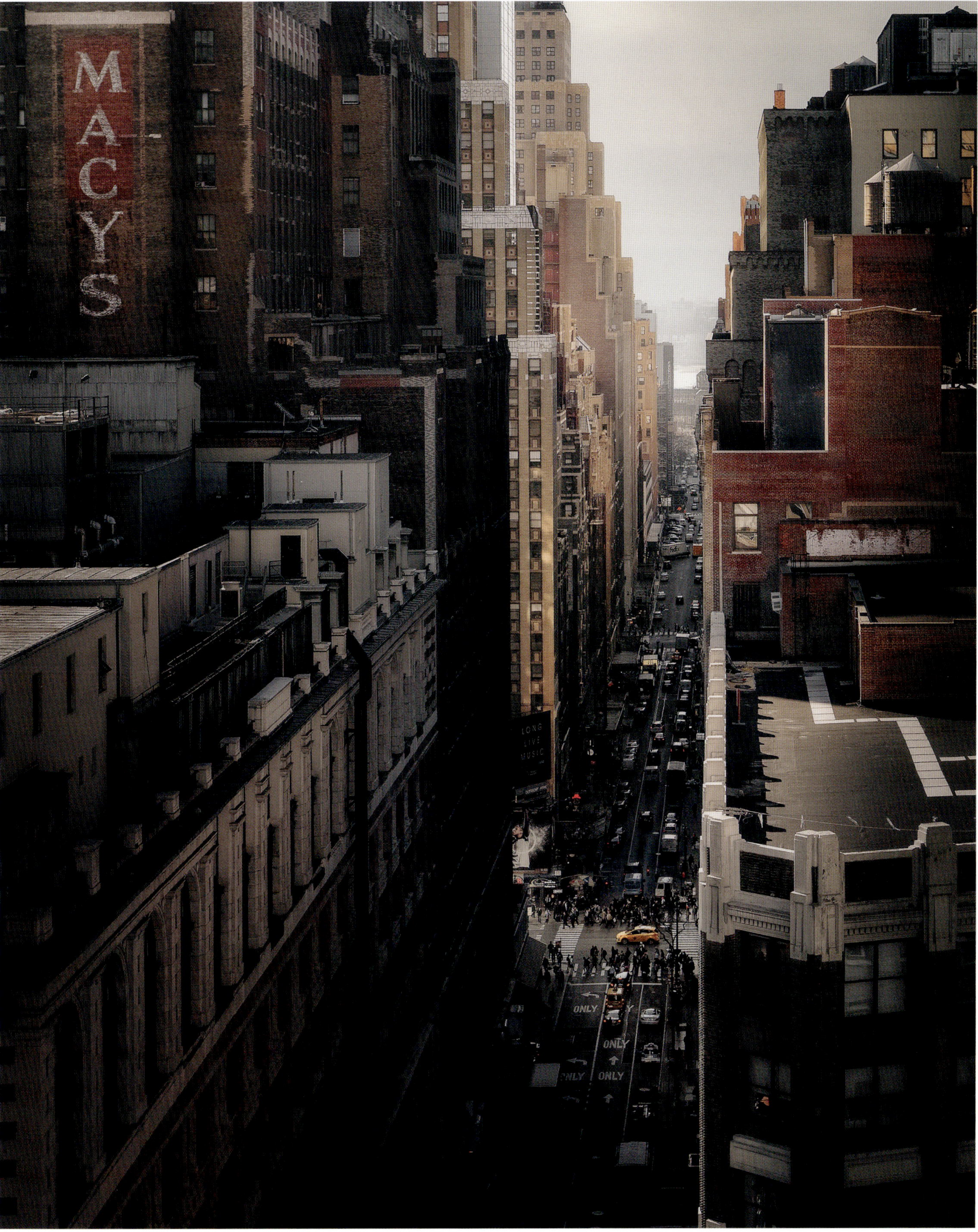

New York, New York, USA

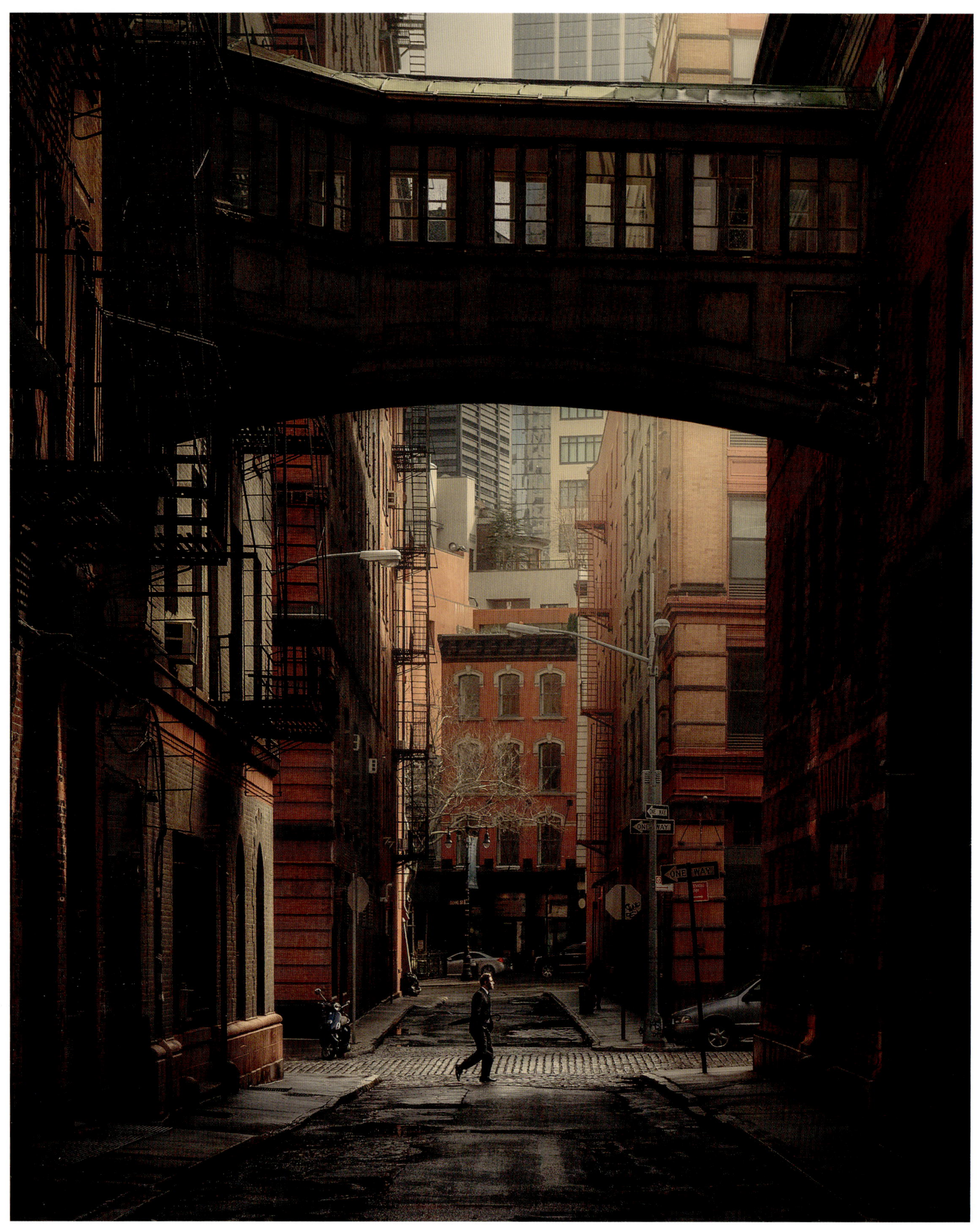

New York, New York, USA

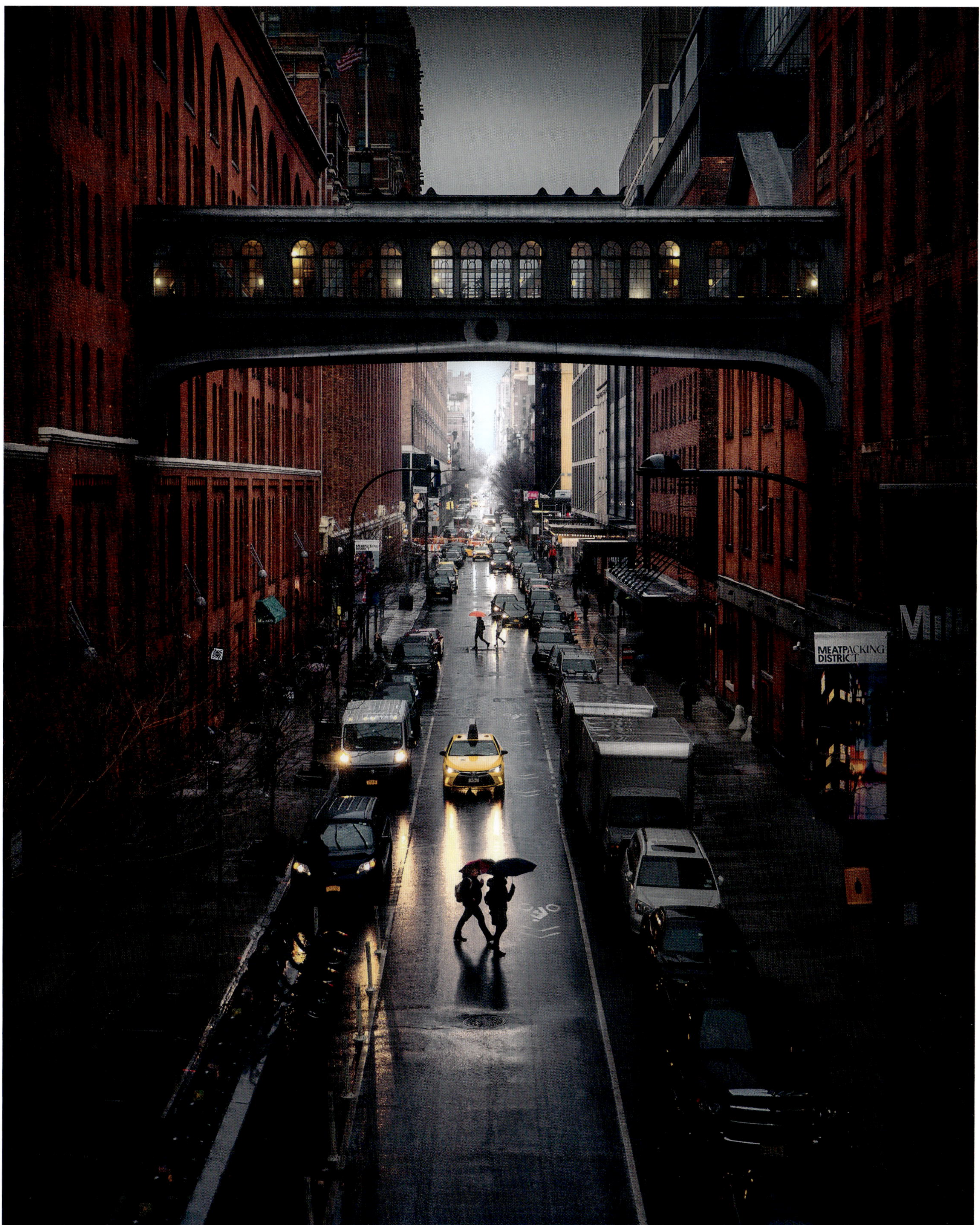

New York, New York, USA

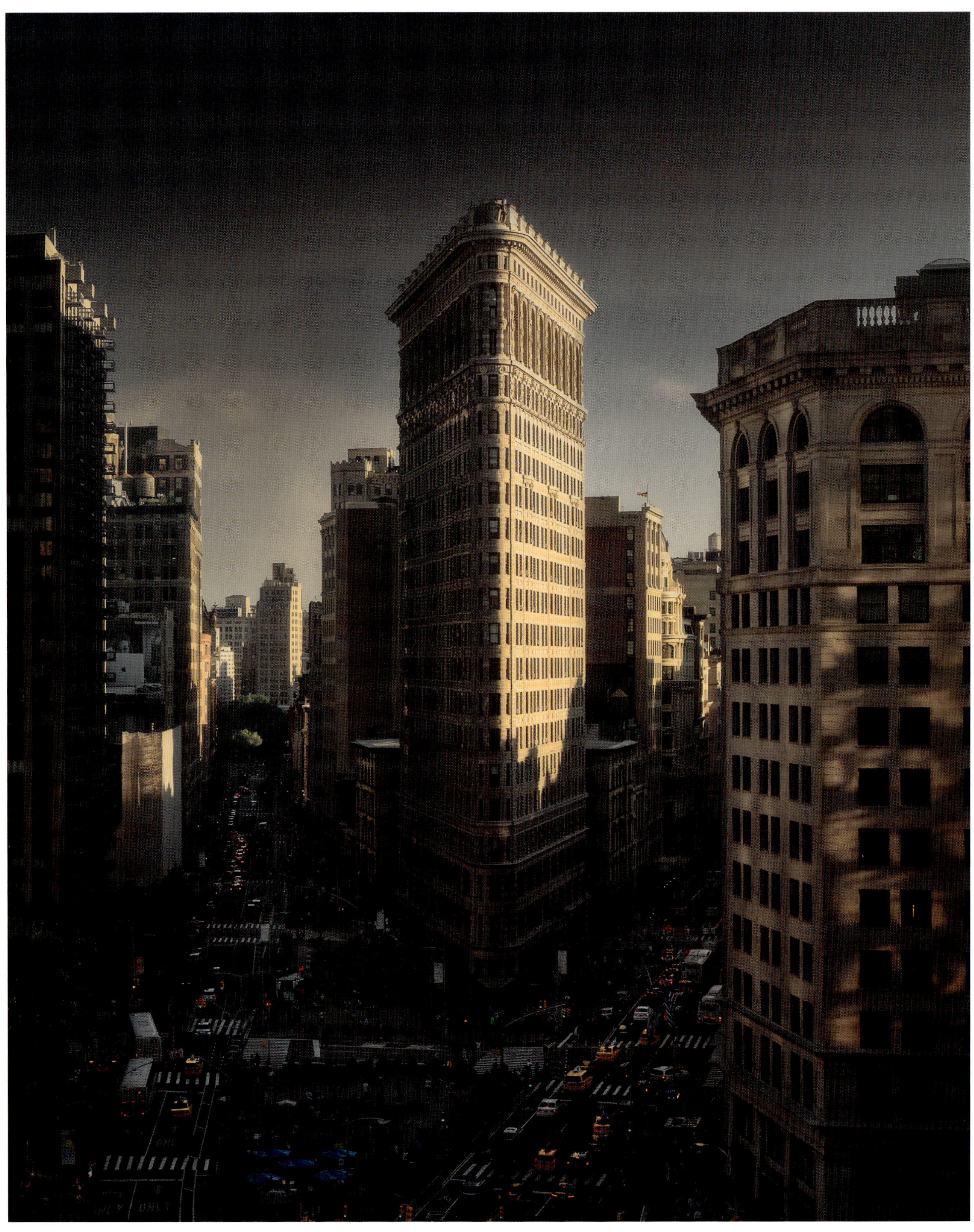

New York, New York, USA

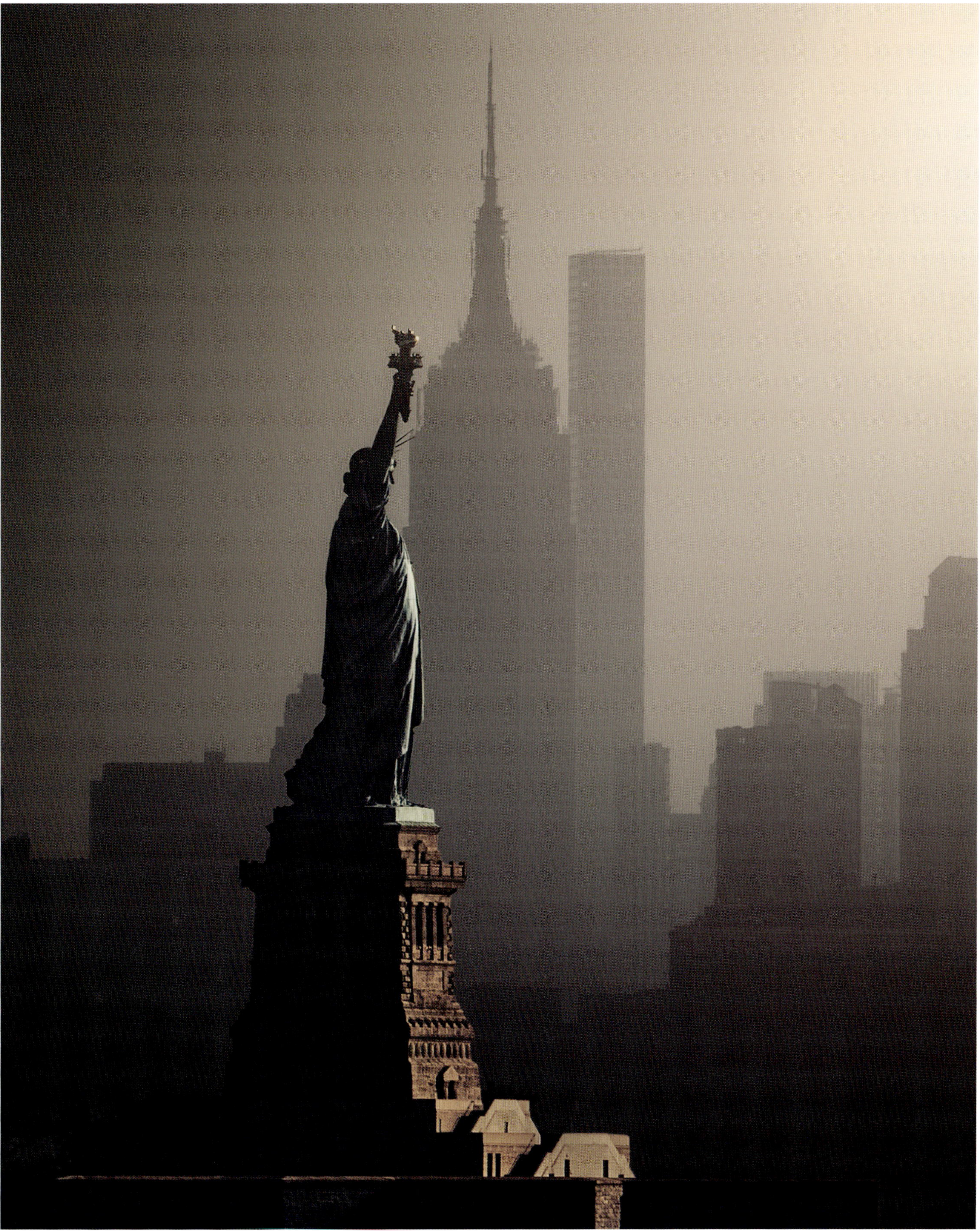

New York, New York, USA

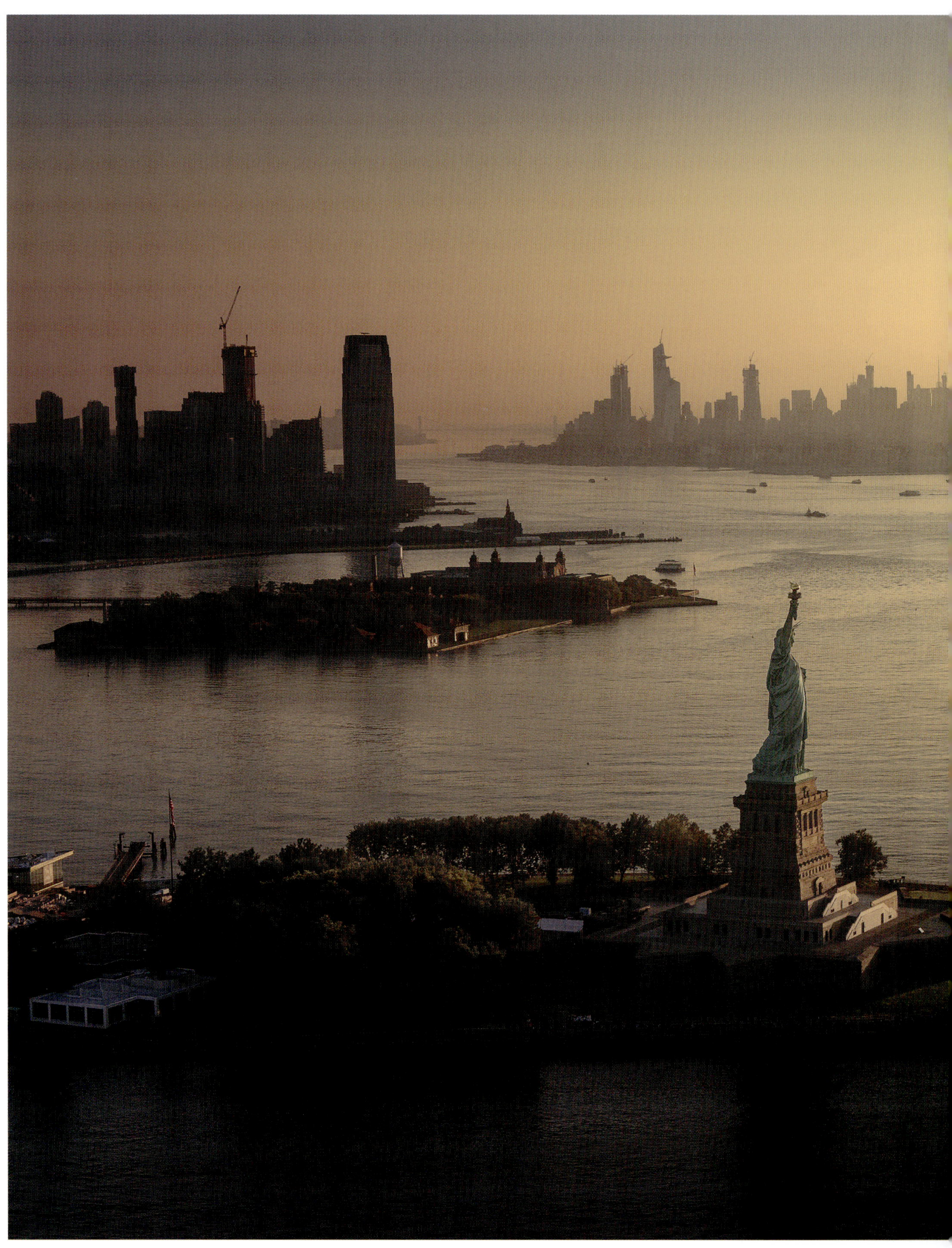

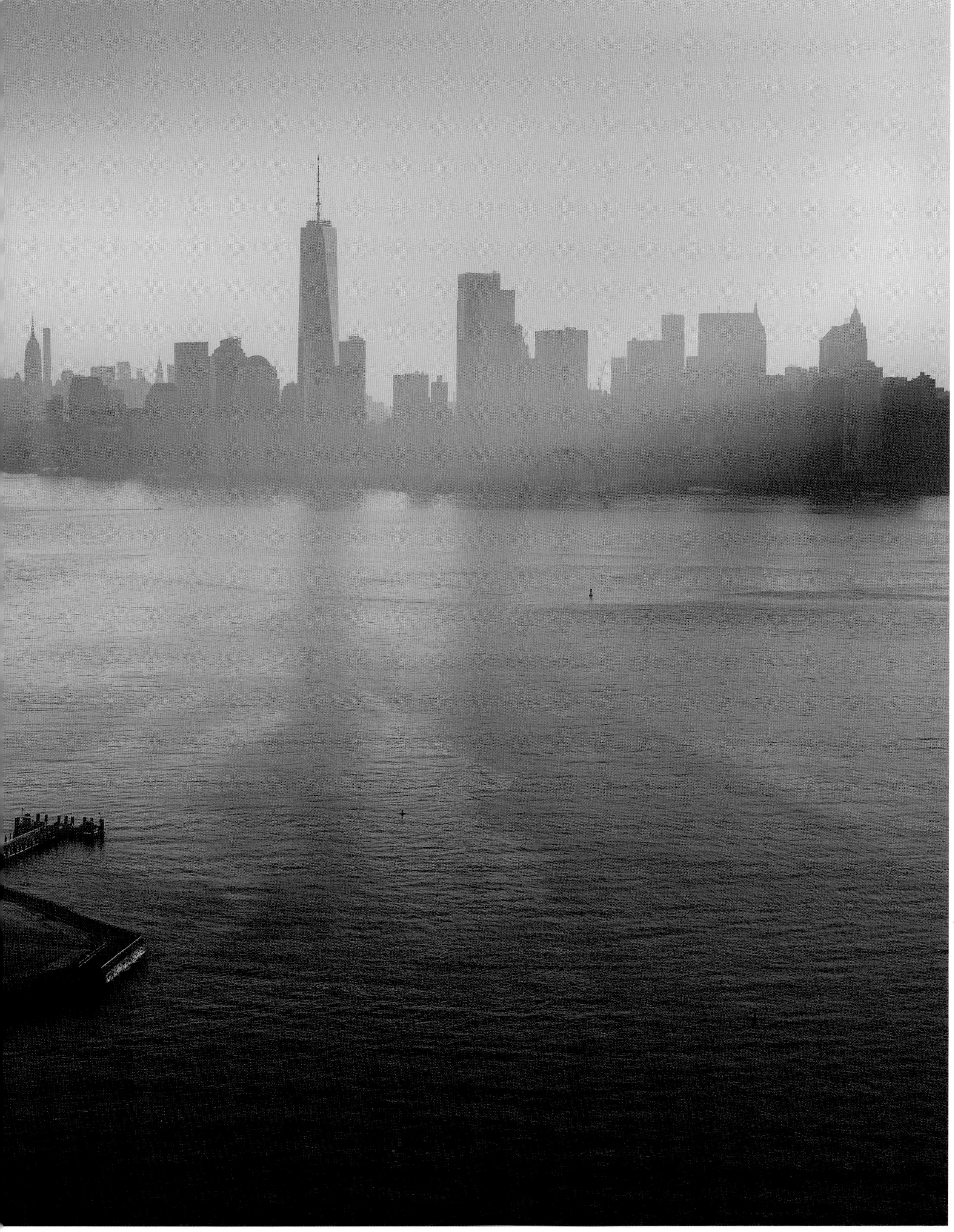

New York, New York, USA

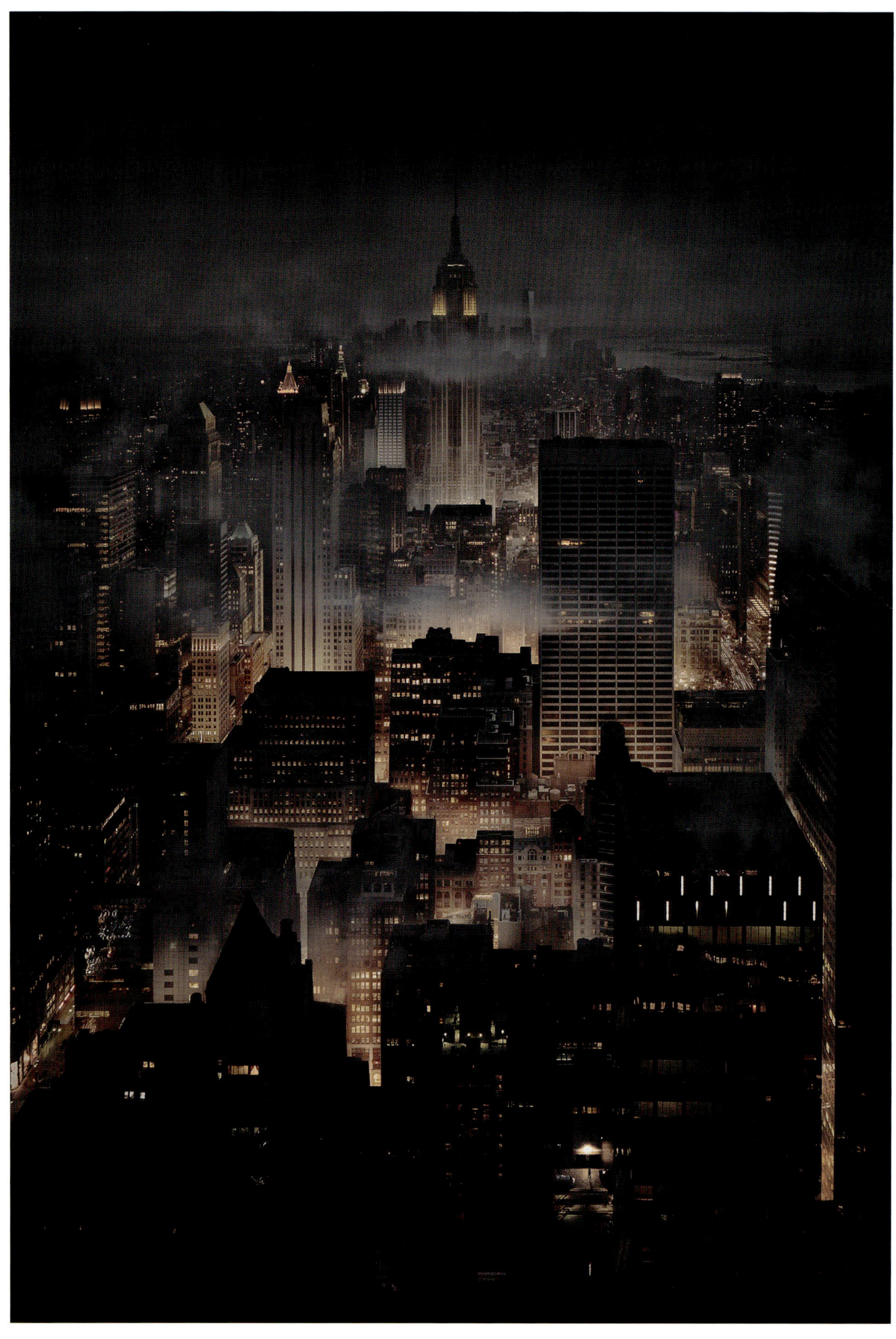

New York, New York, USA

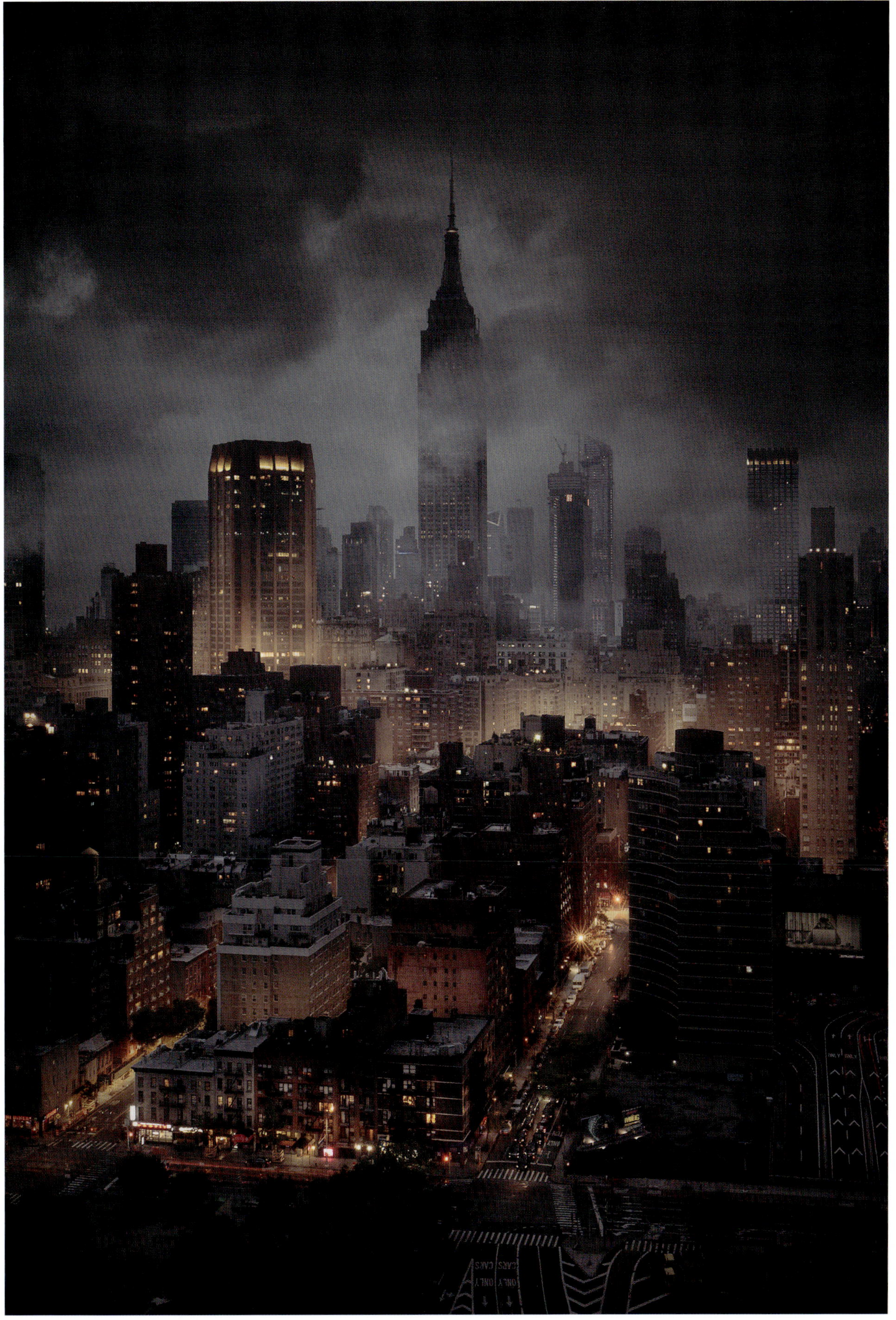

New York, New York, USA

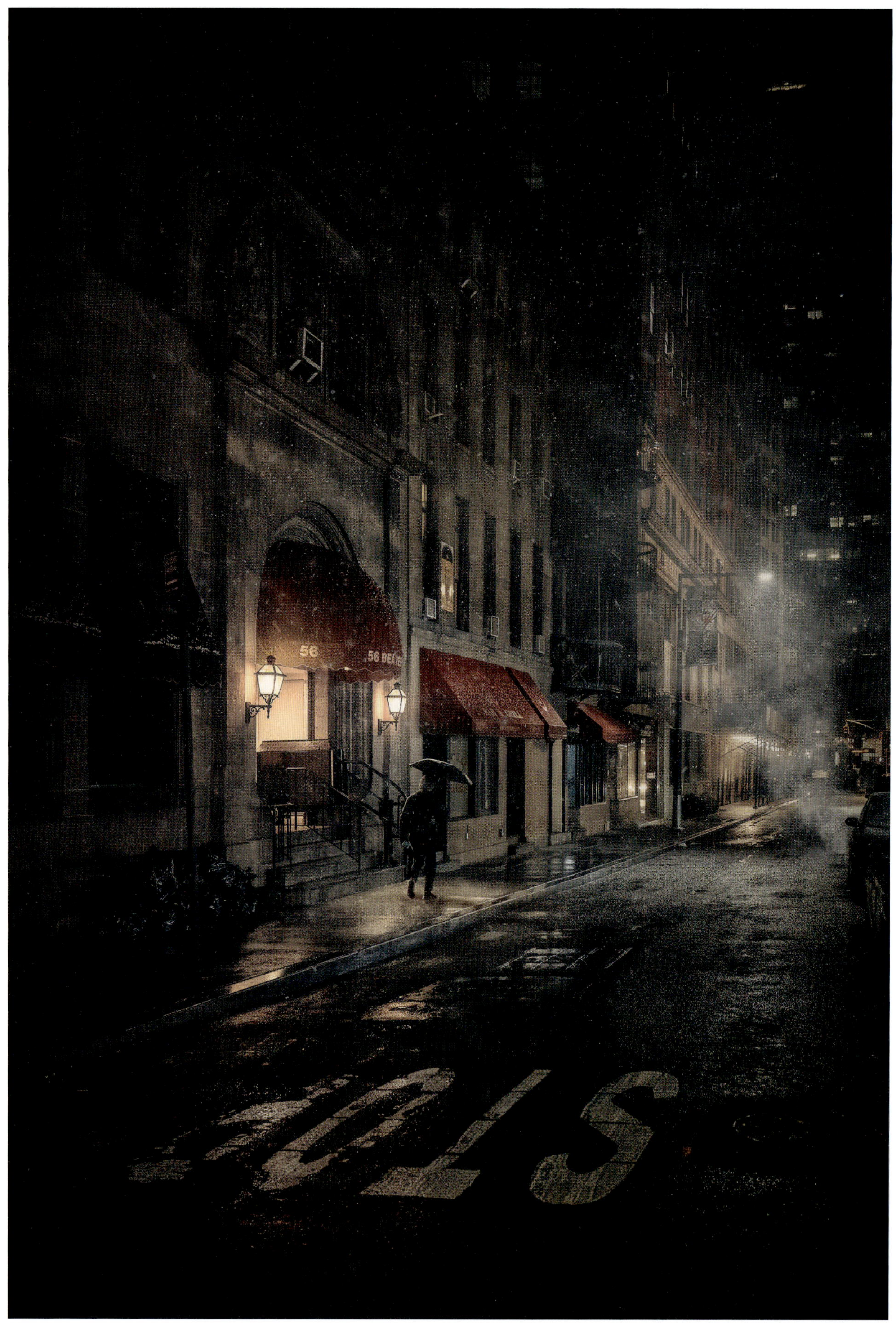

New York, New York, USA

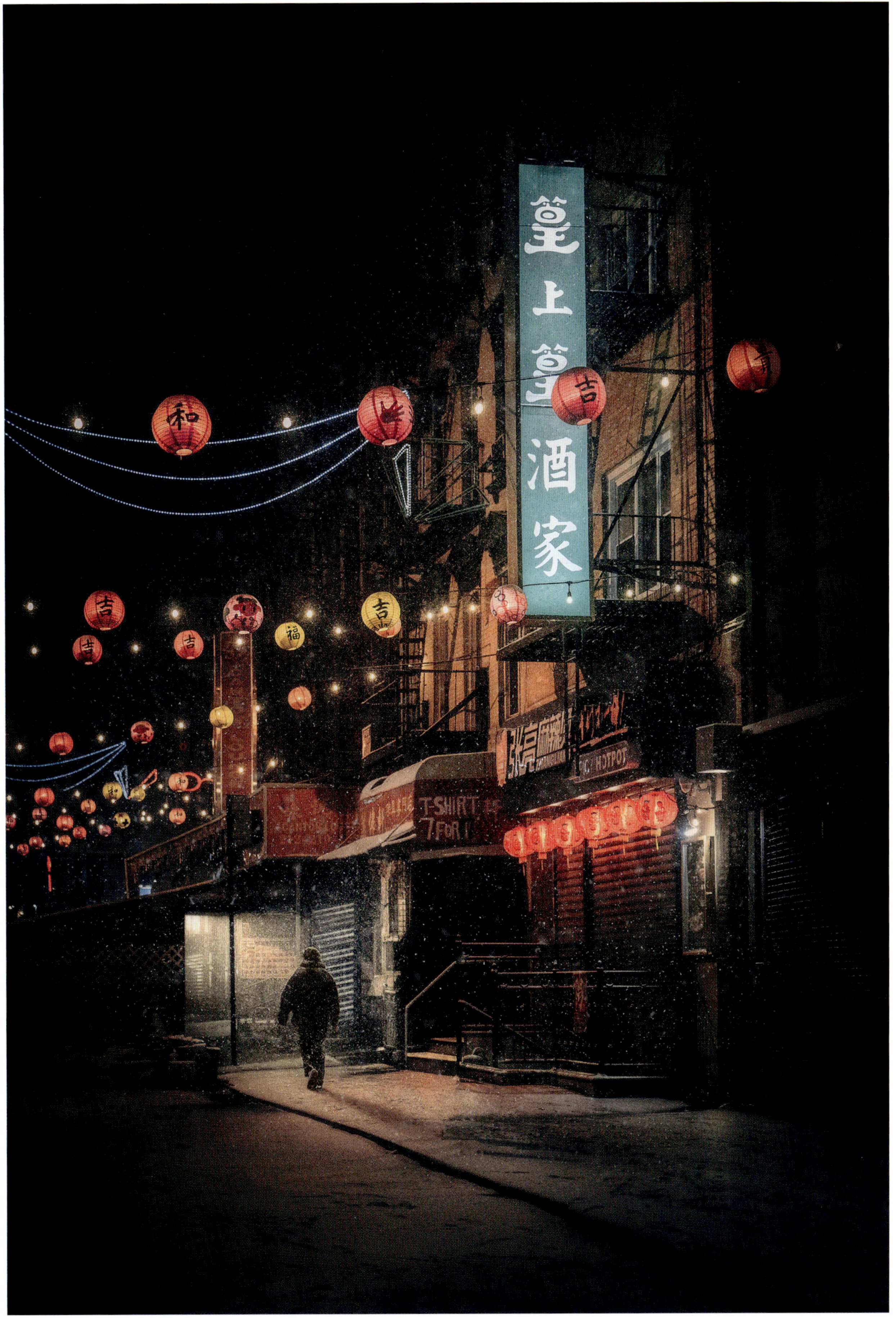

New York, New York, USA

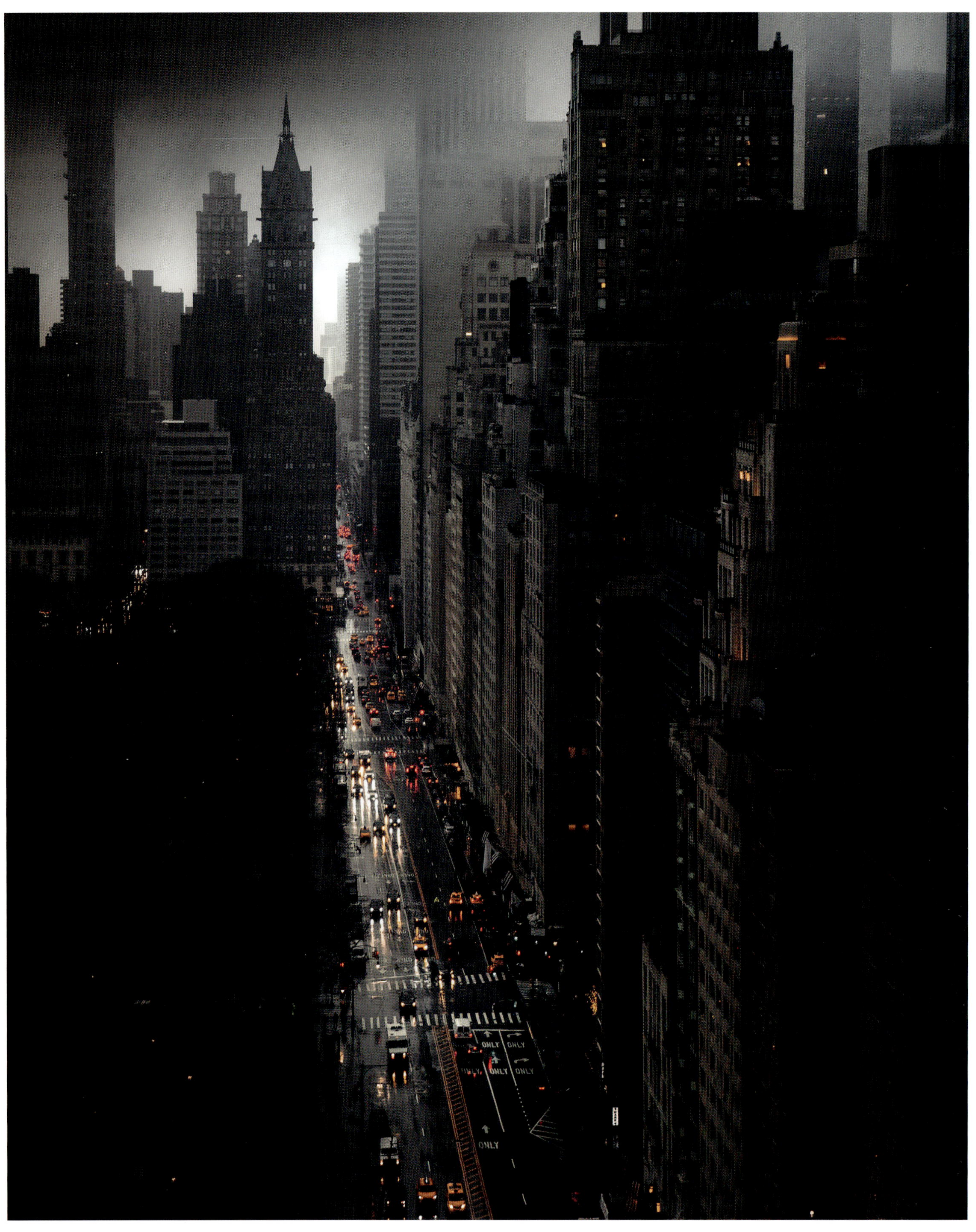

New York, New York, USA

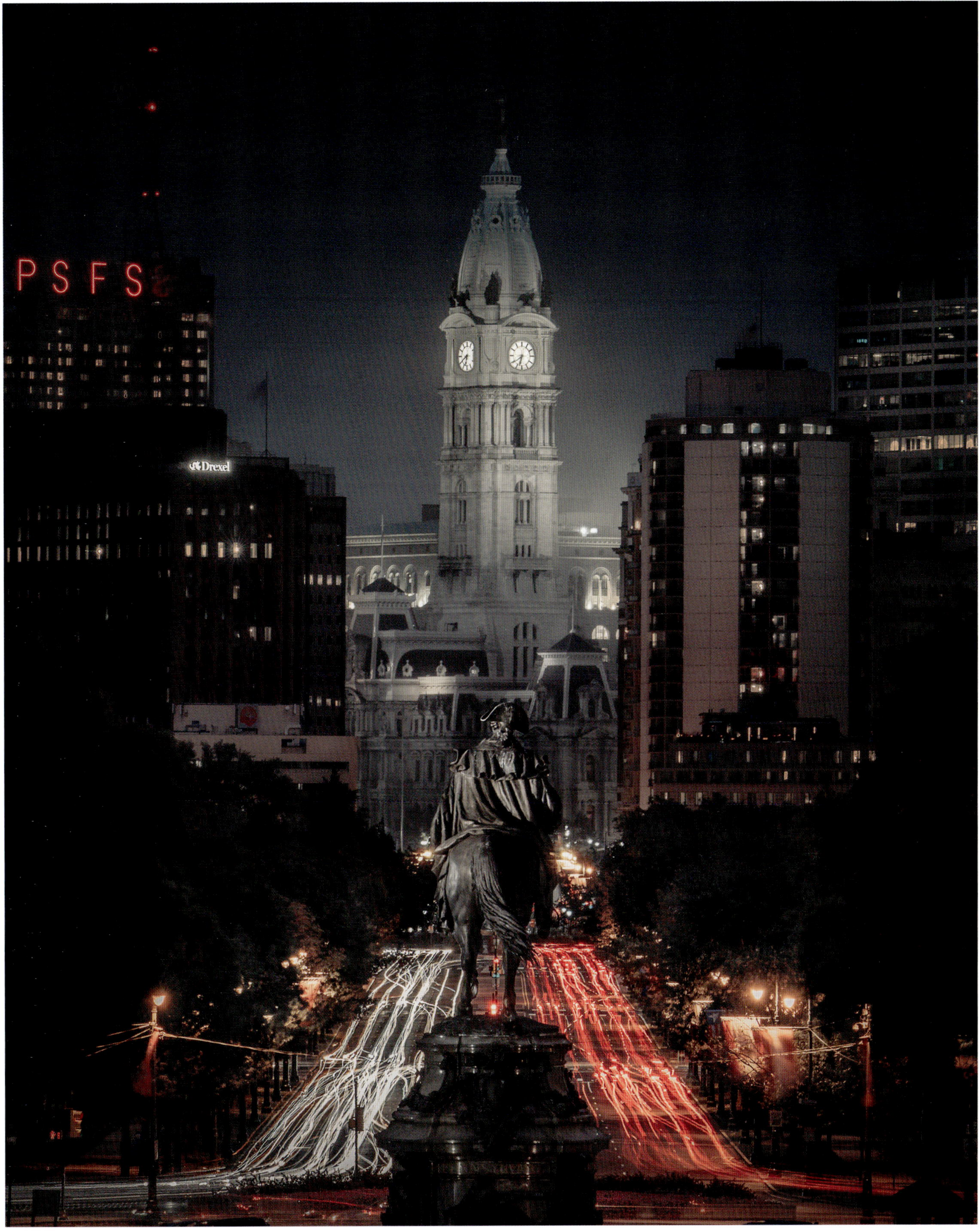

Philadelphia, Pennsylvania, USA

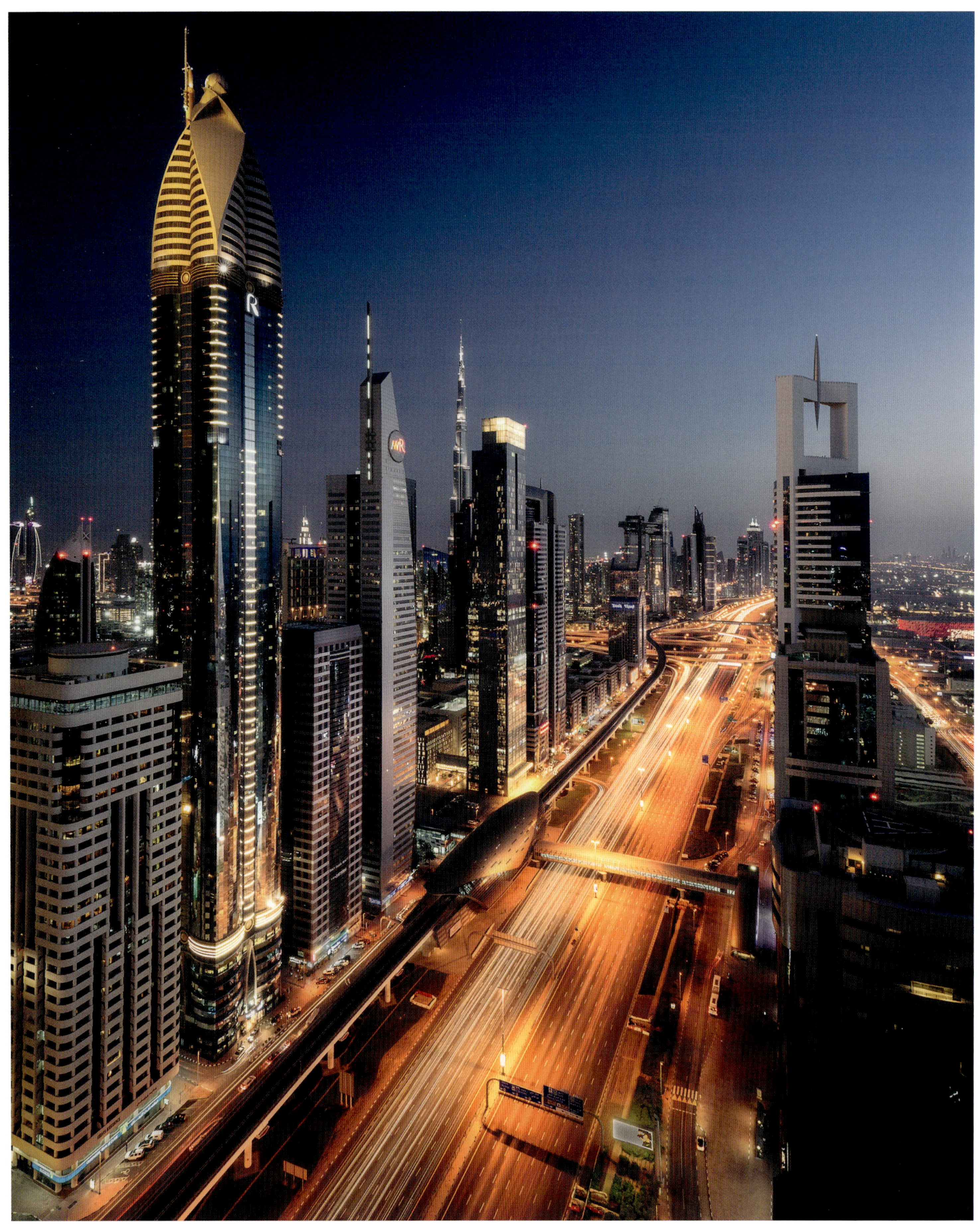

Dubai, United Arab Emirates

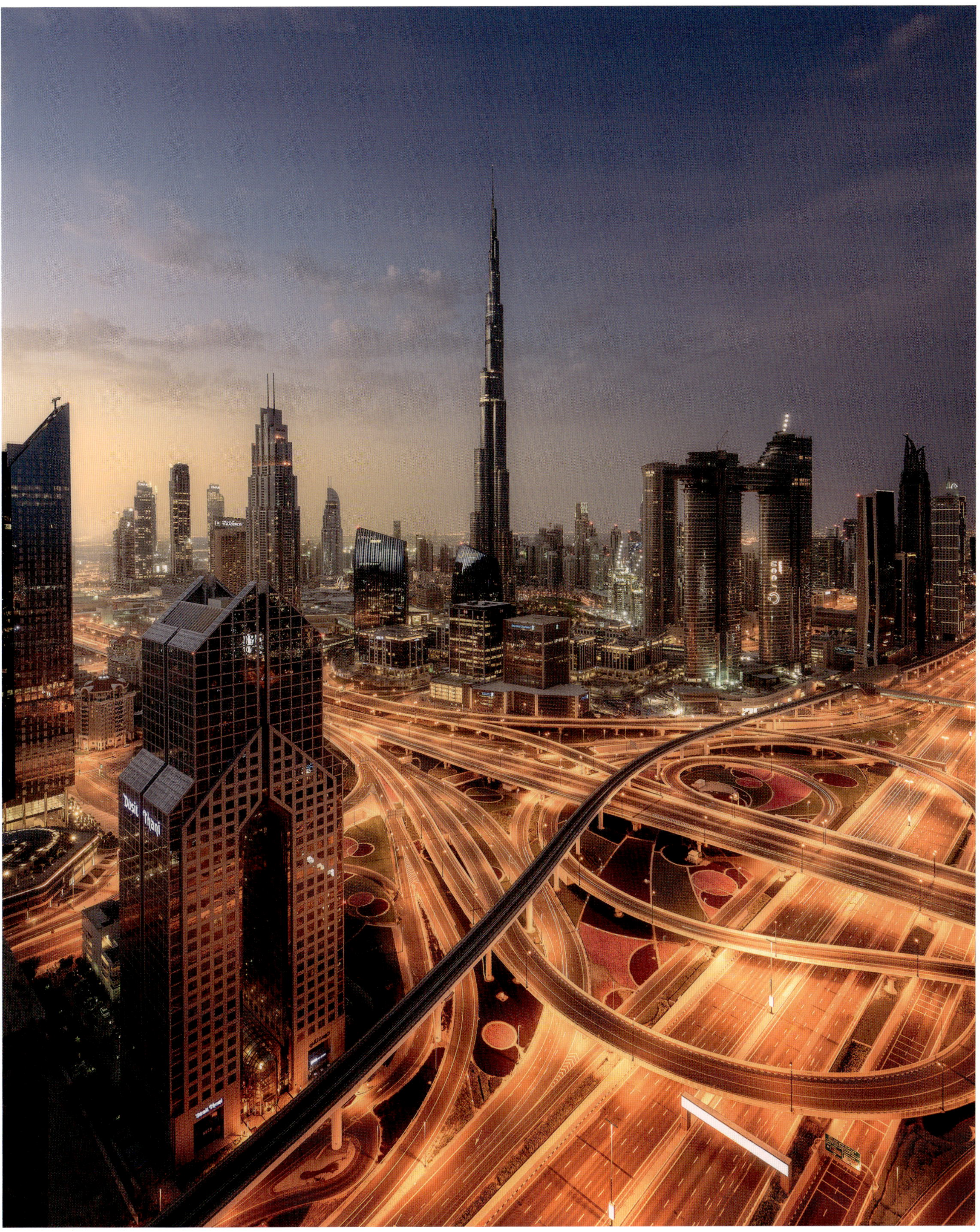

Dubai, United Arab Emirates

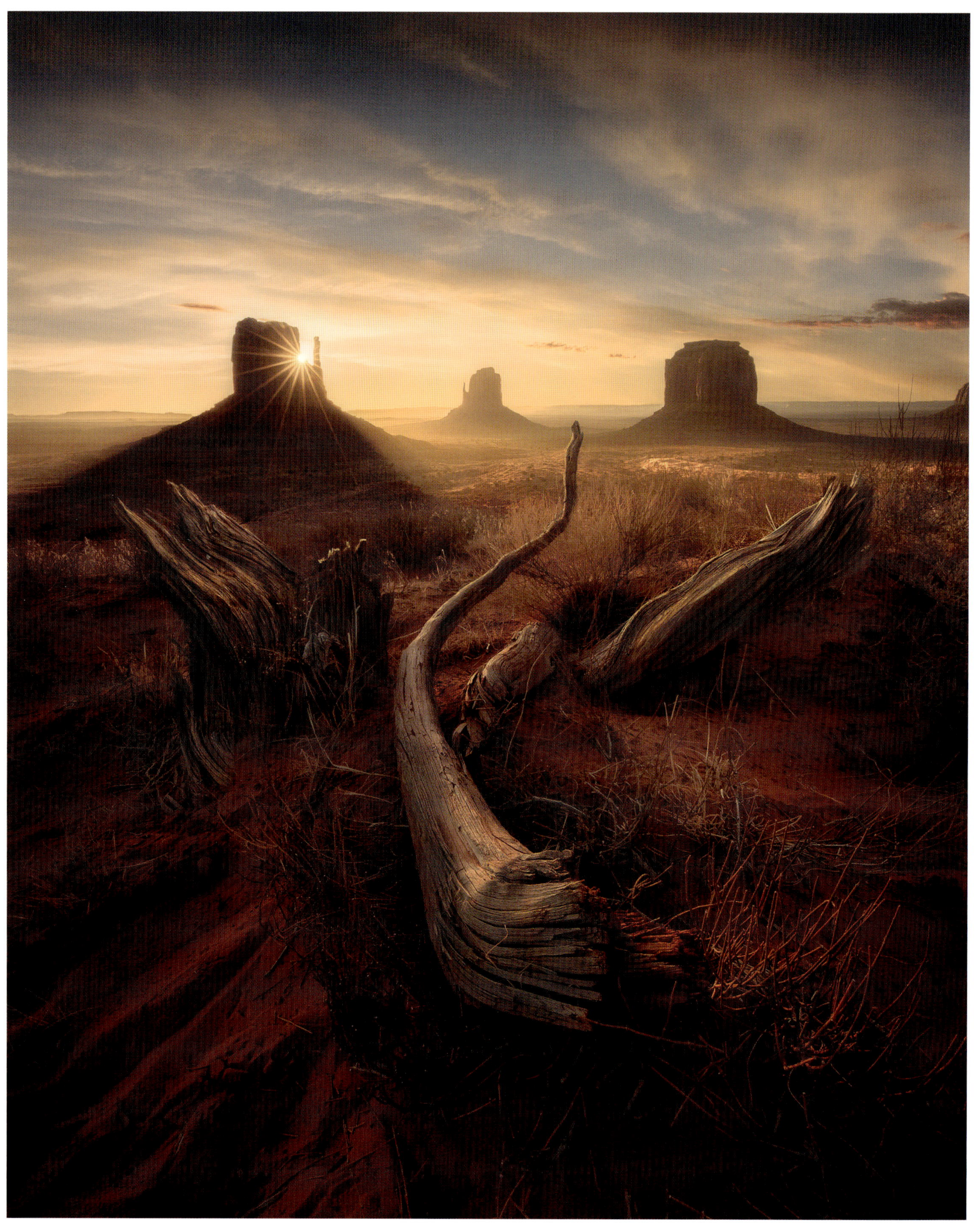

Monument Valley, Arizona, USA

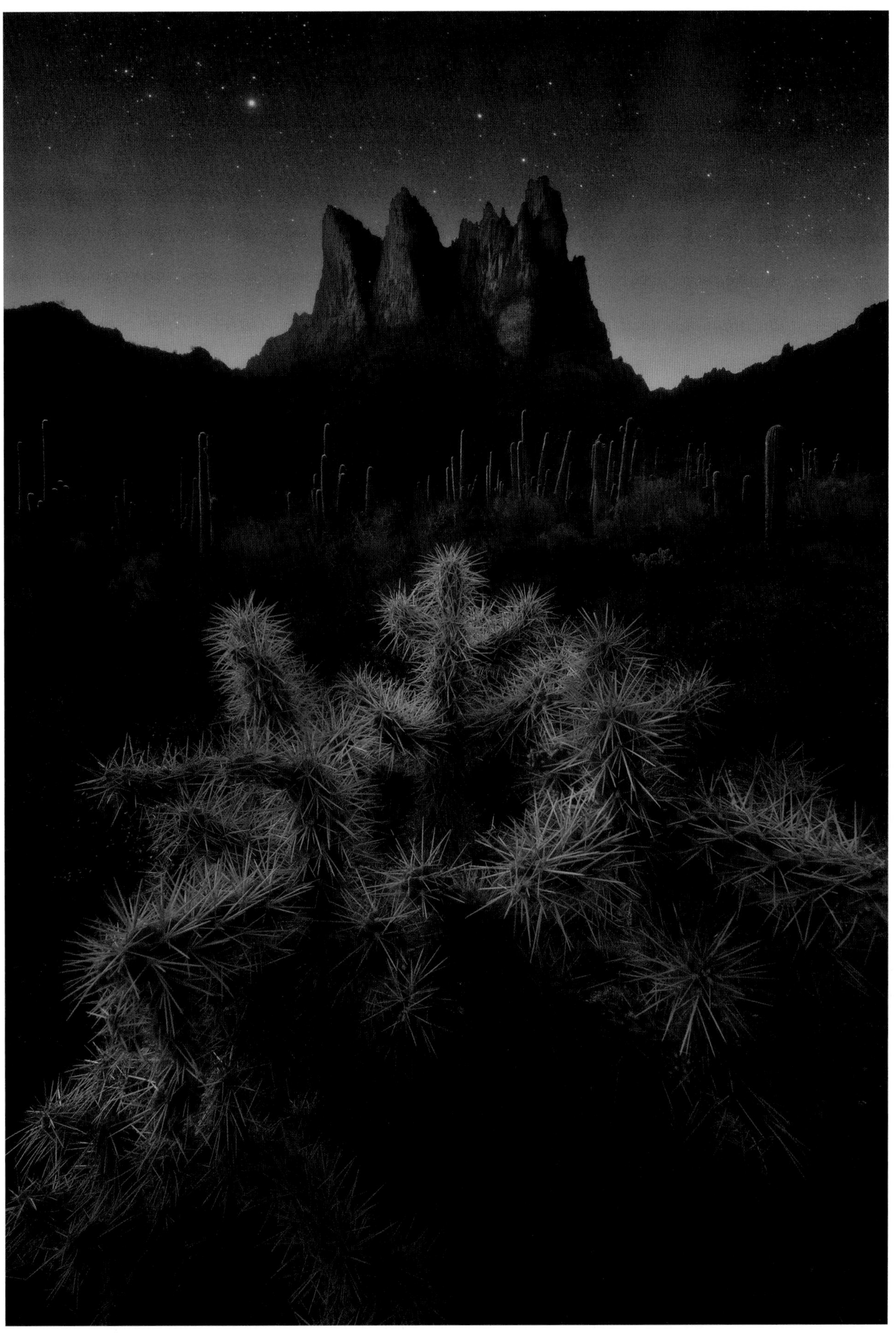

Superstition Mountains, Arizona, USA

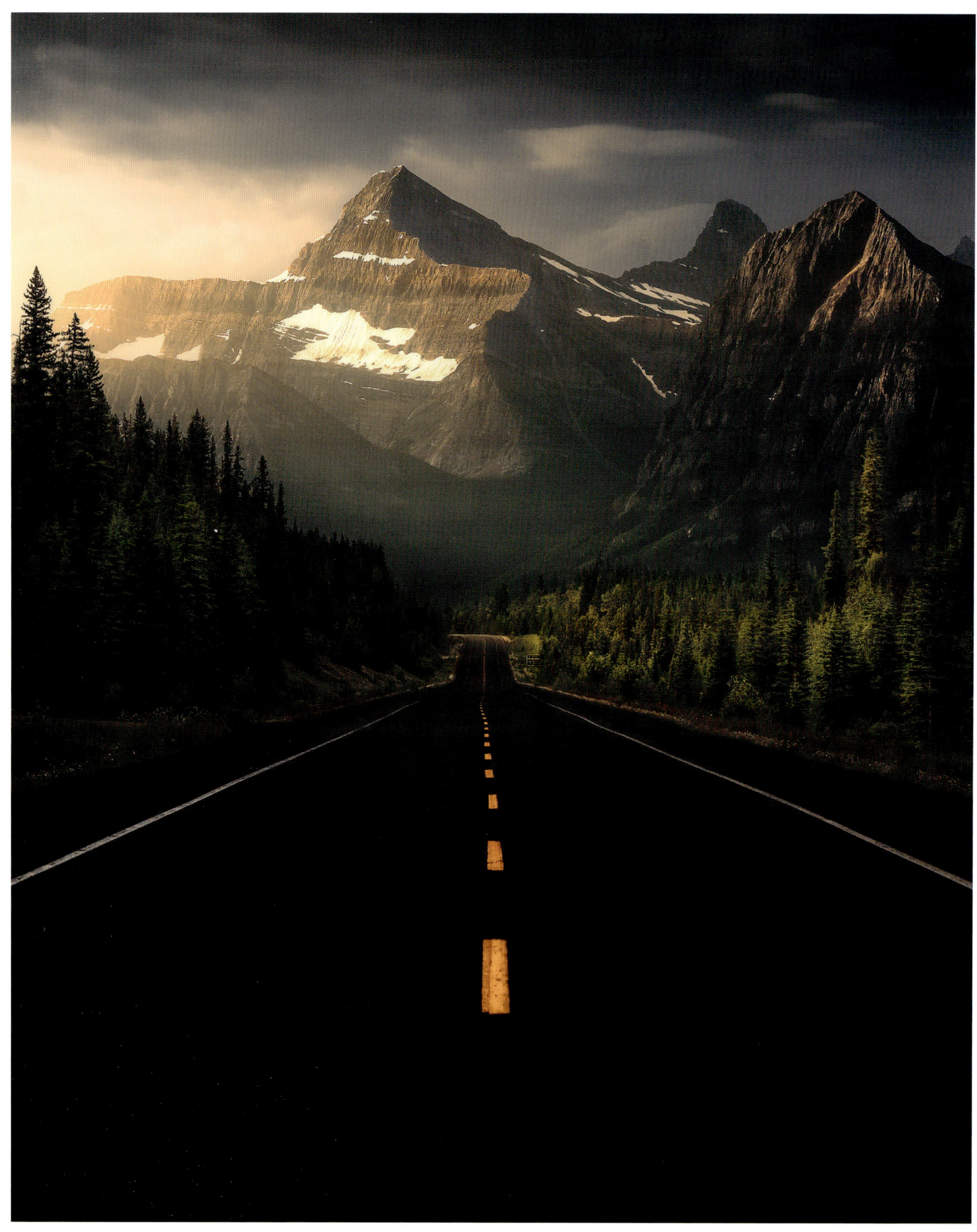

Icefields Parkway, Canada

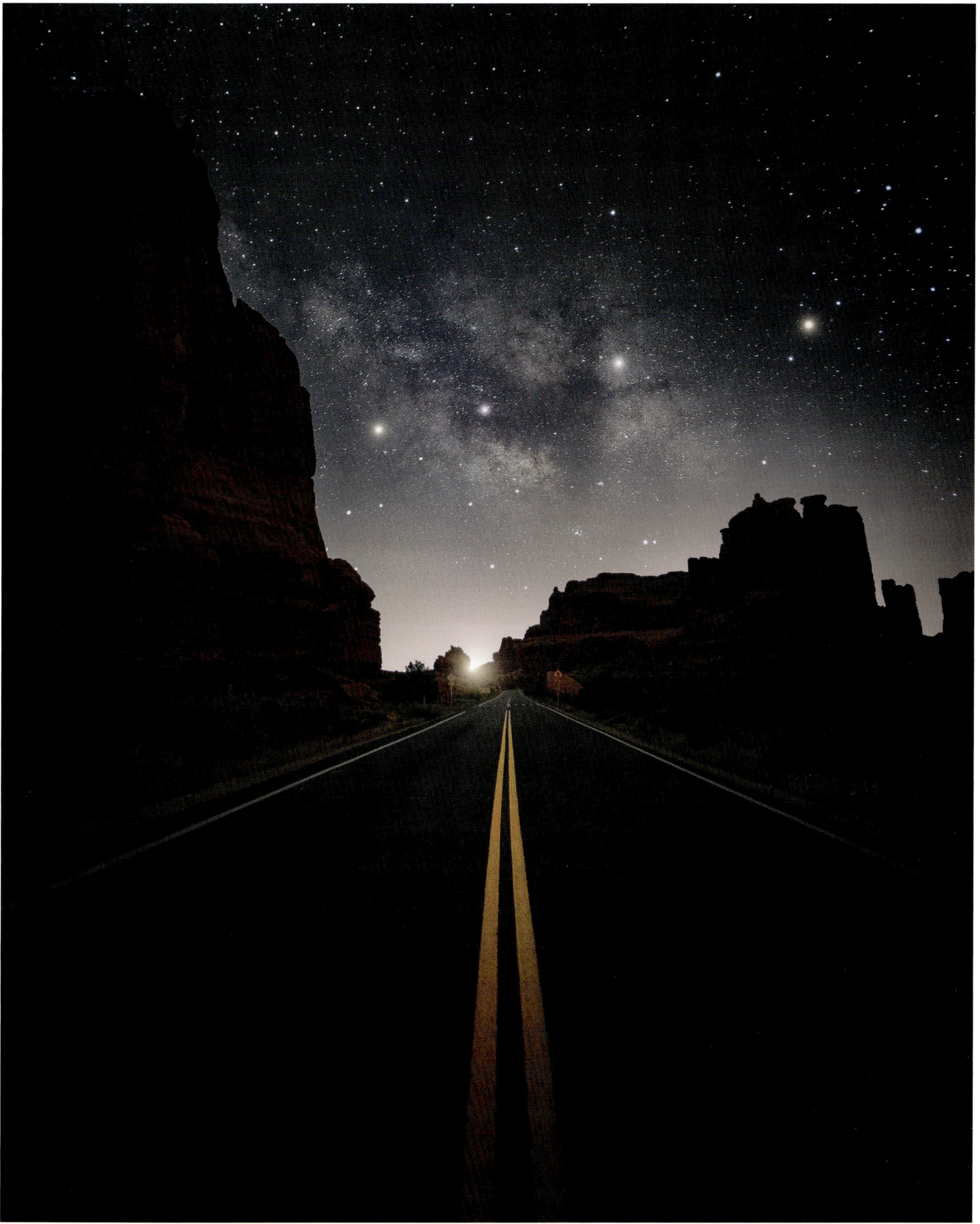

Arches National Park, Utah, USA

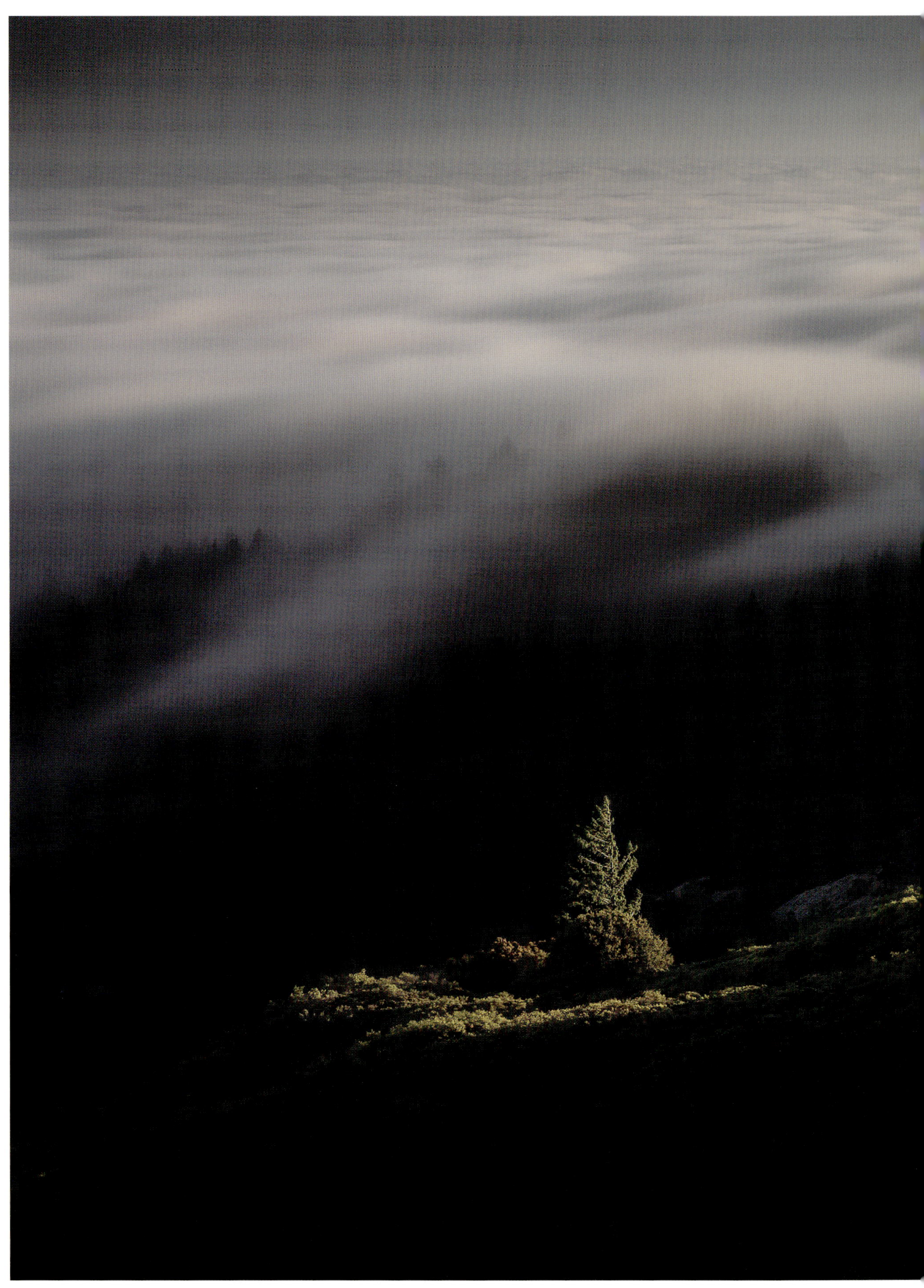

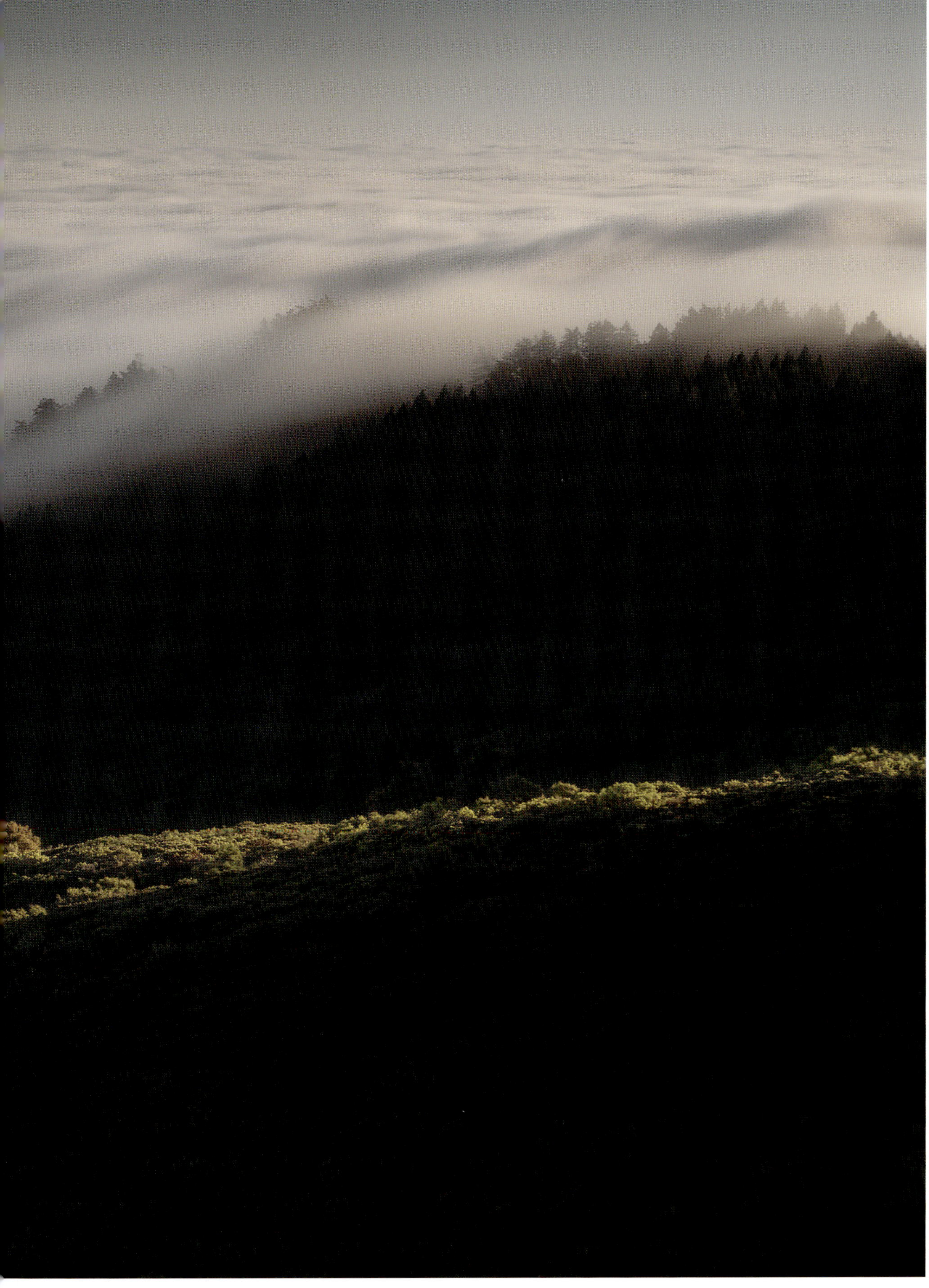

Mount Tamalpais, California, USA

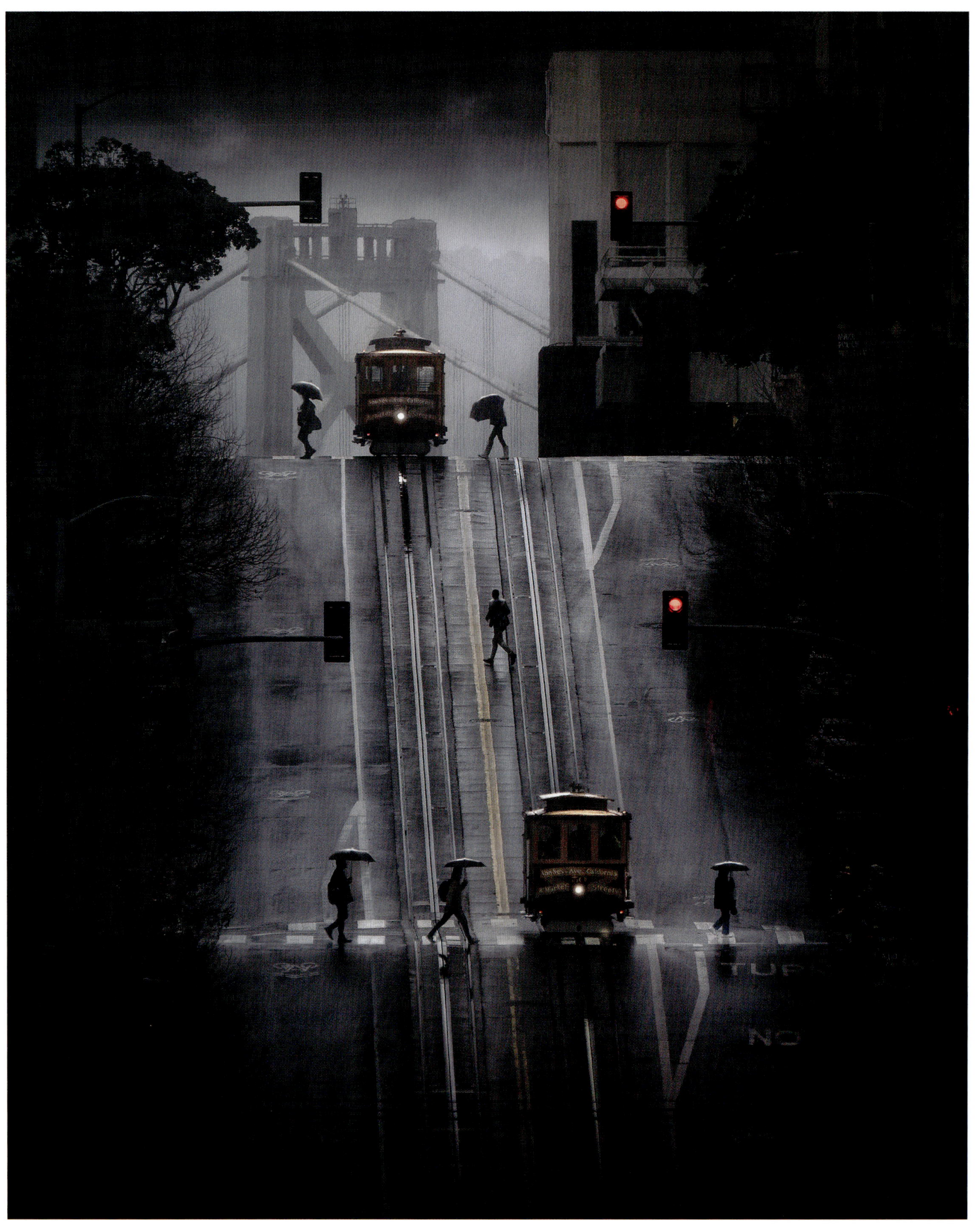

San Francisco, California, USA

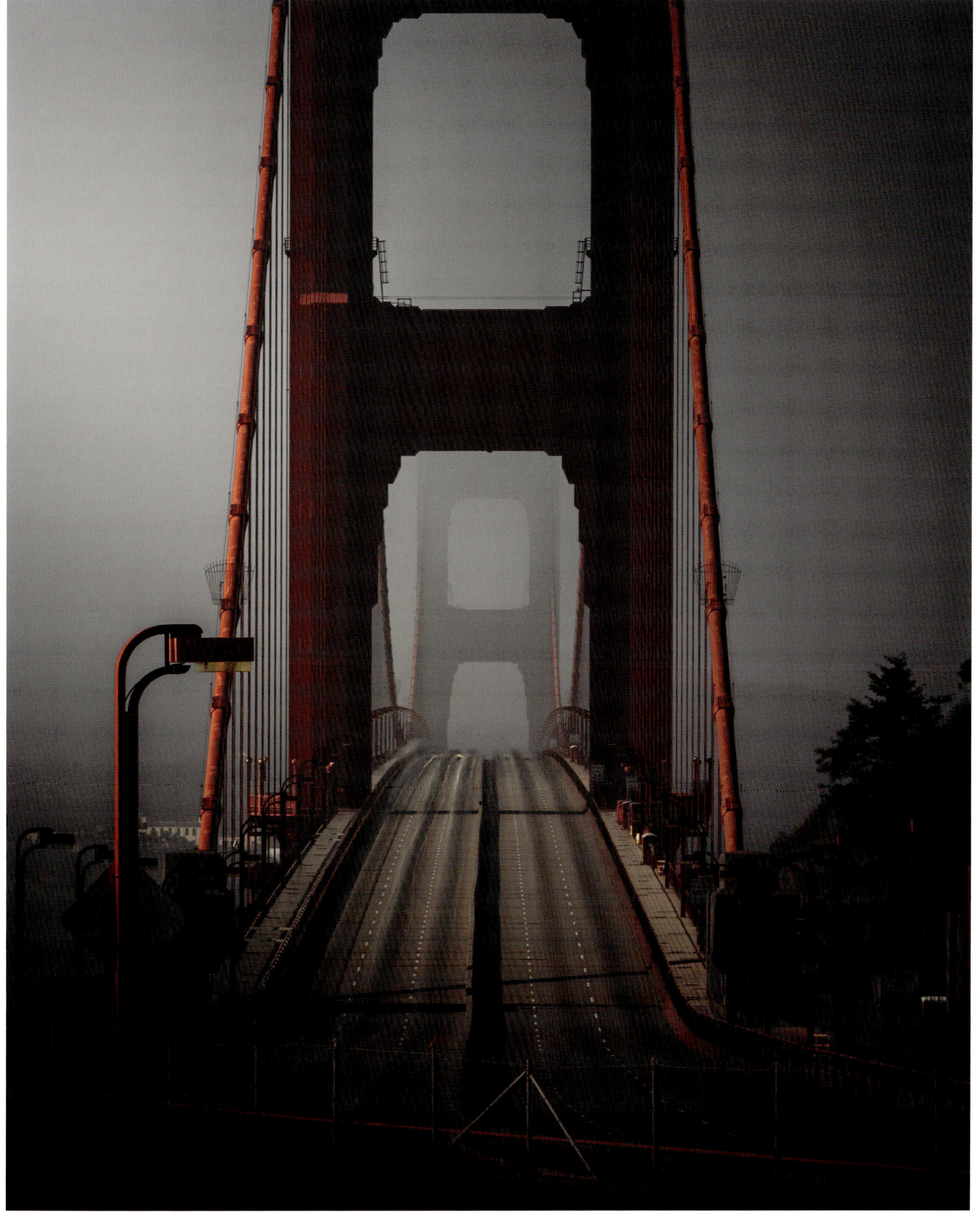

San Francisco, California, USA

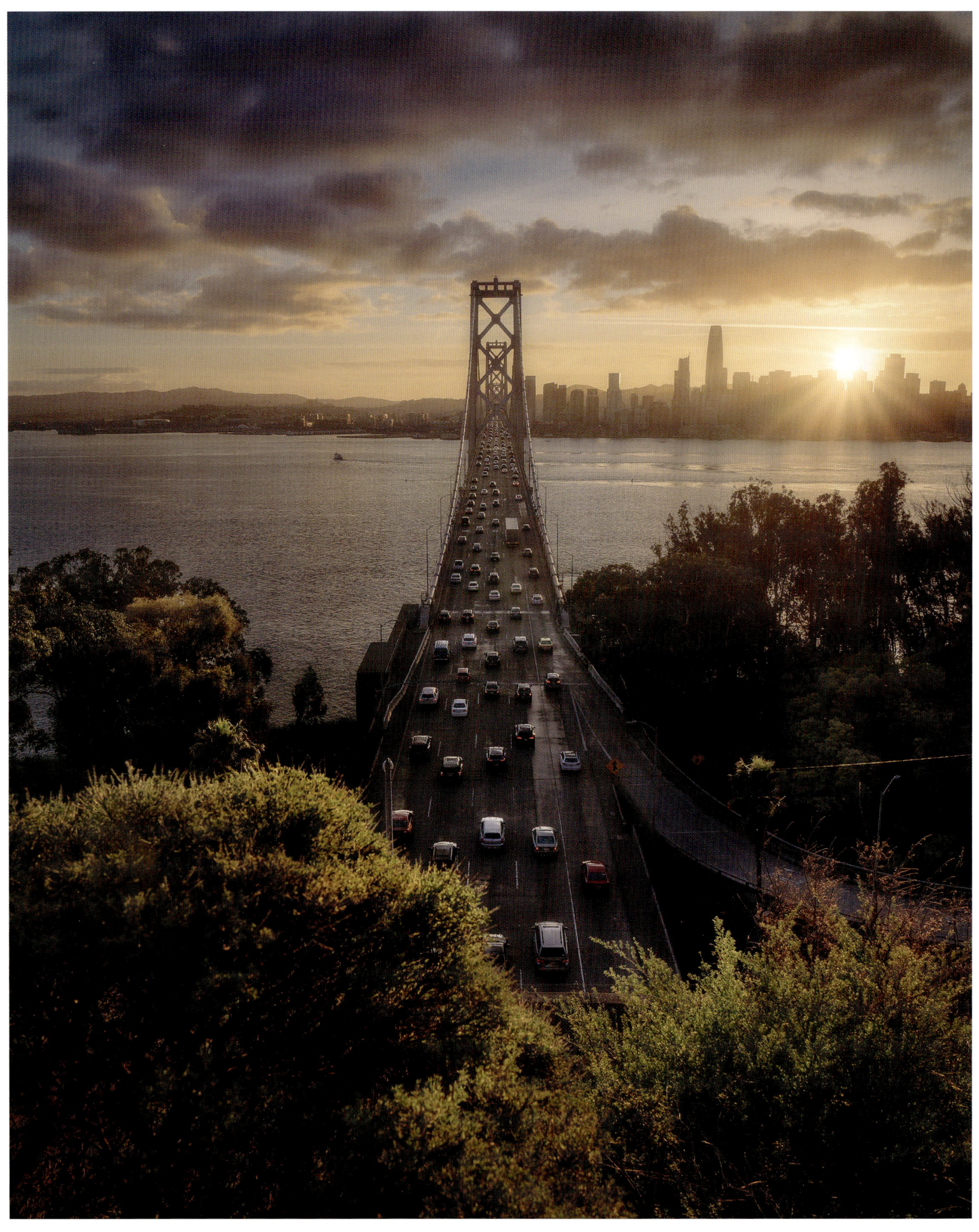

San Francisco, California, USA

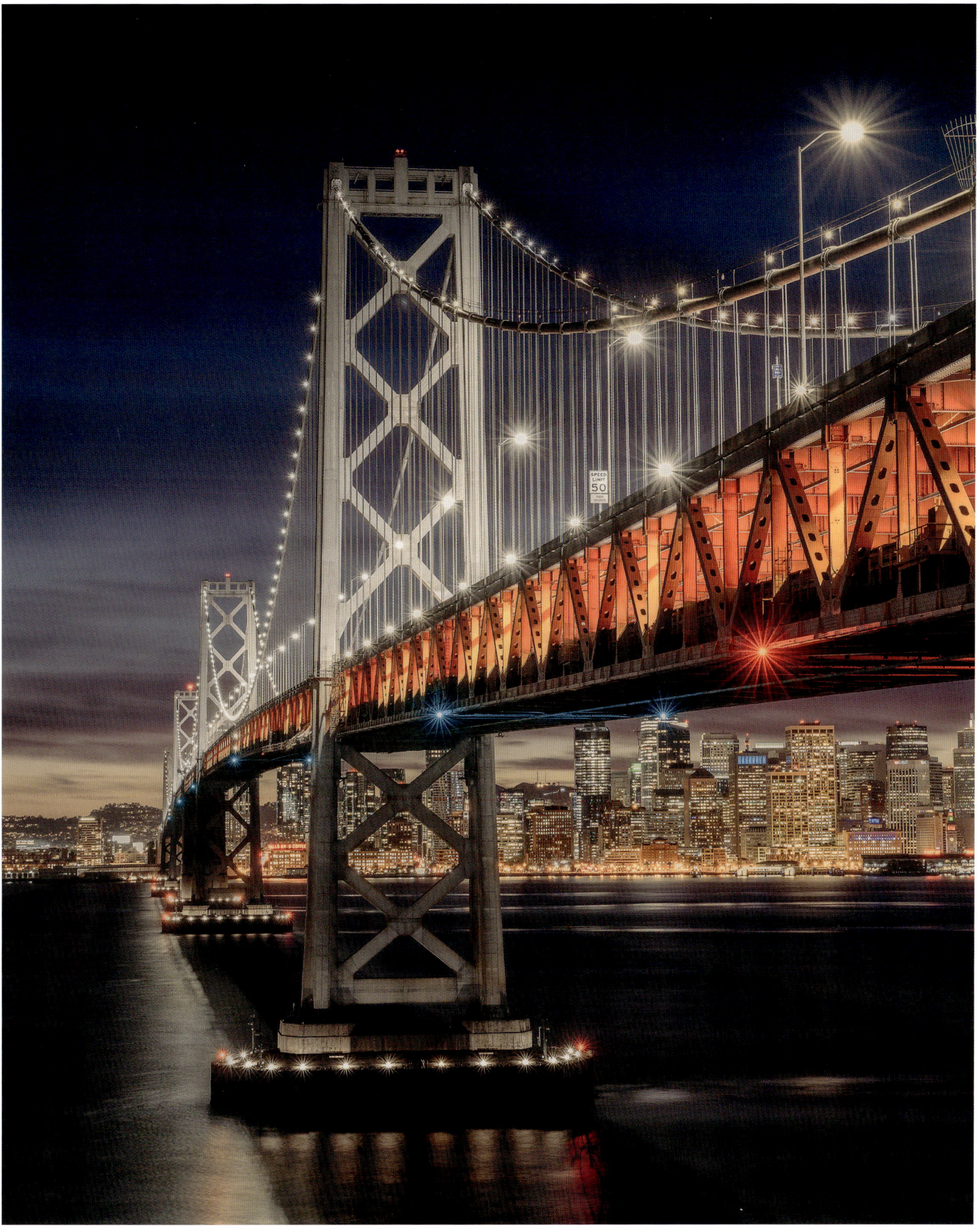

San Francisco, California, USA

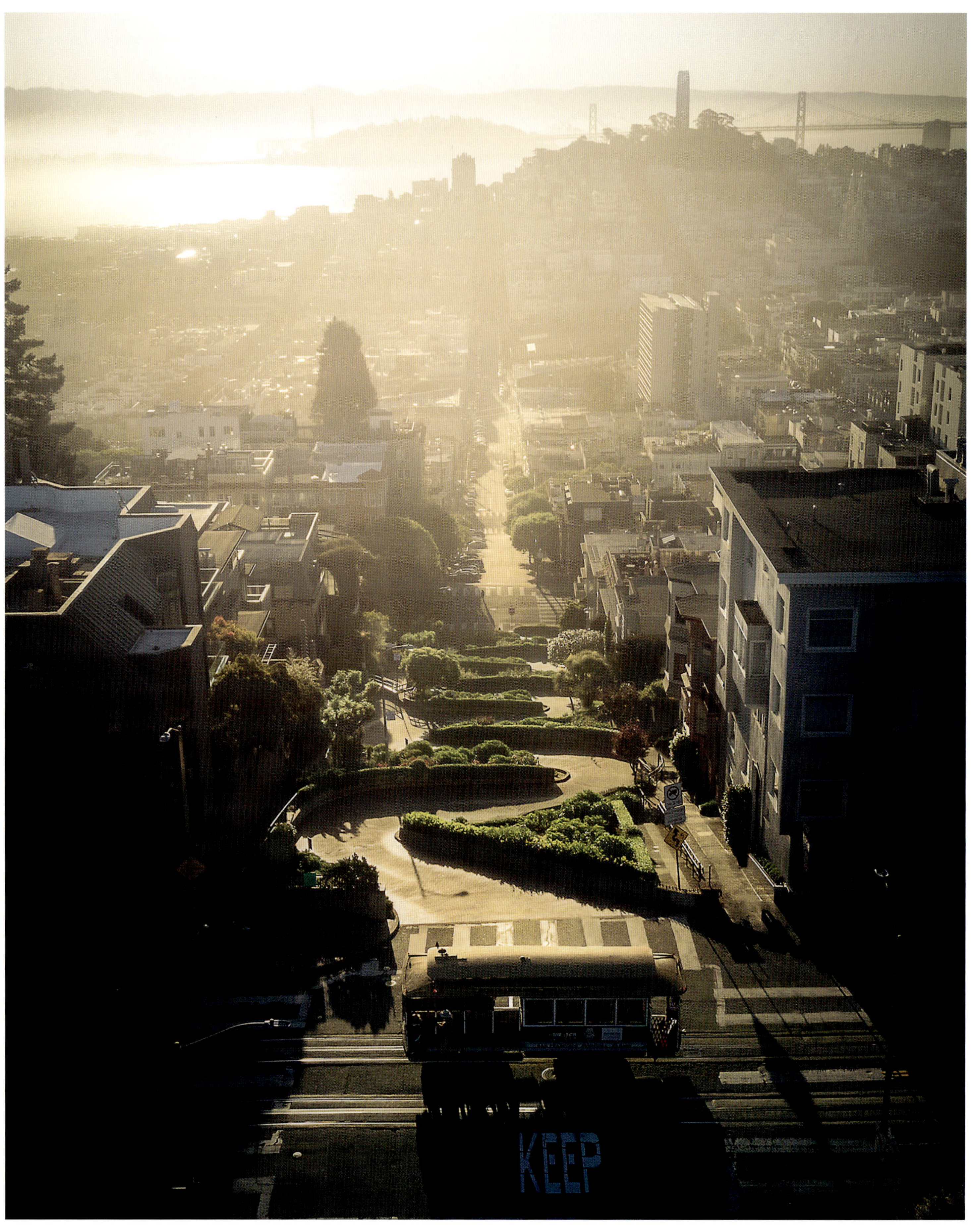

San Francisco, California, USA

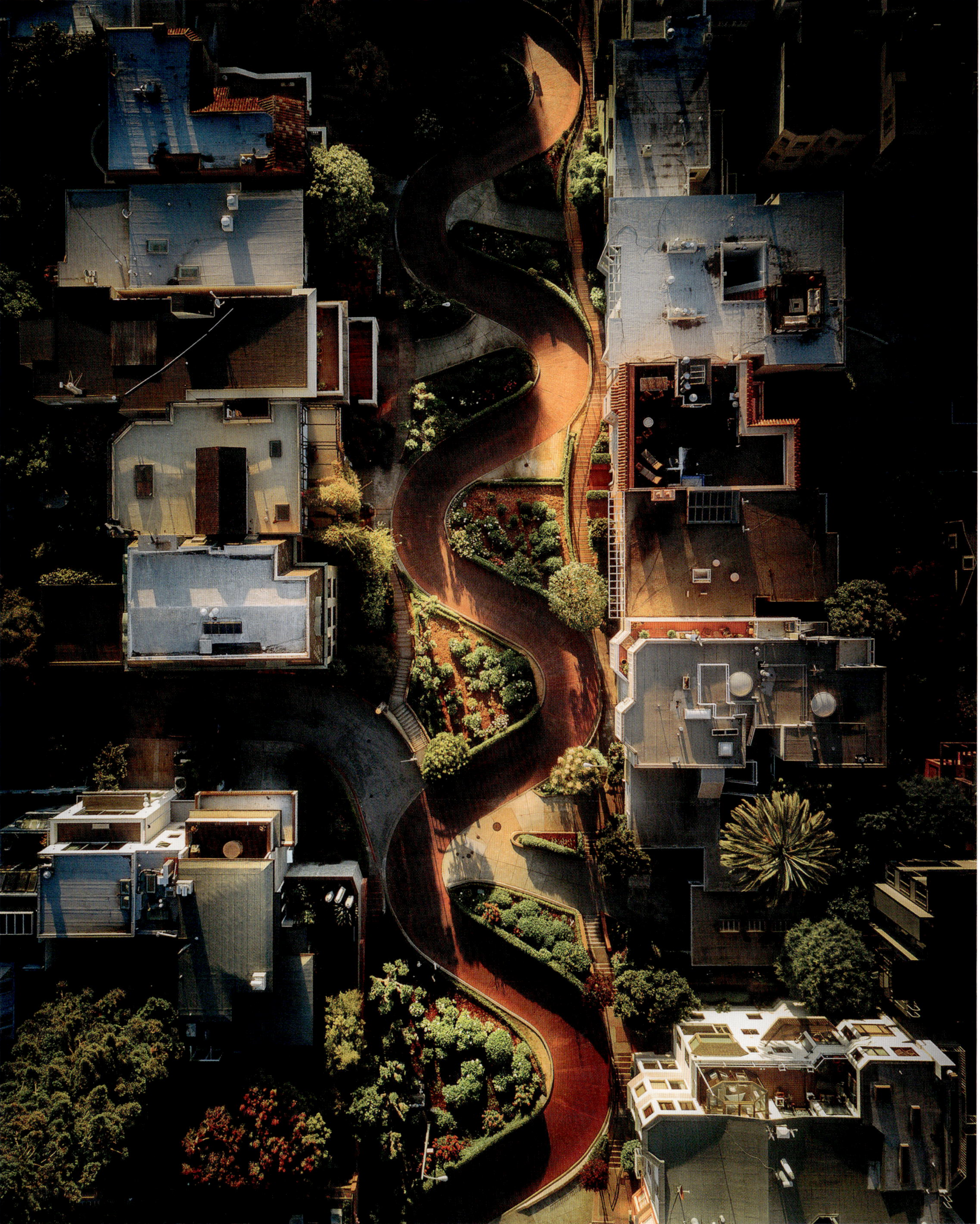

San Francisco, California, USA

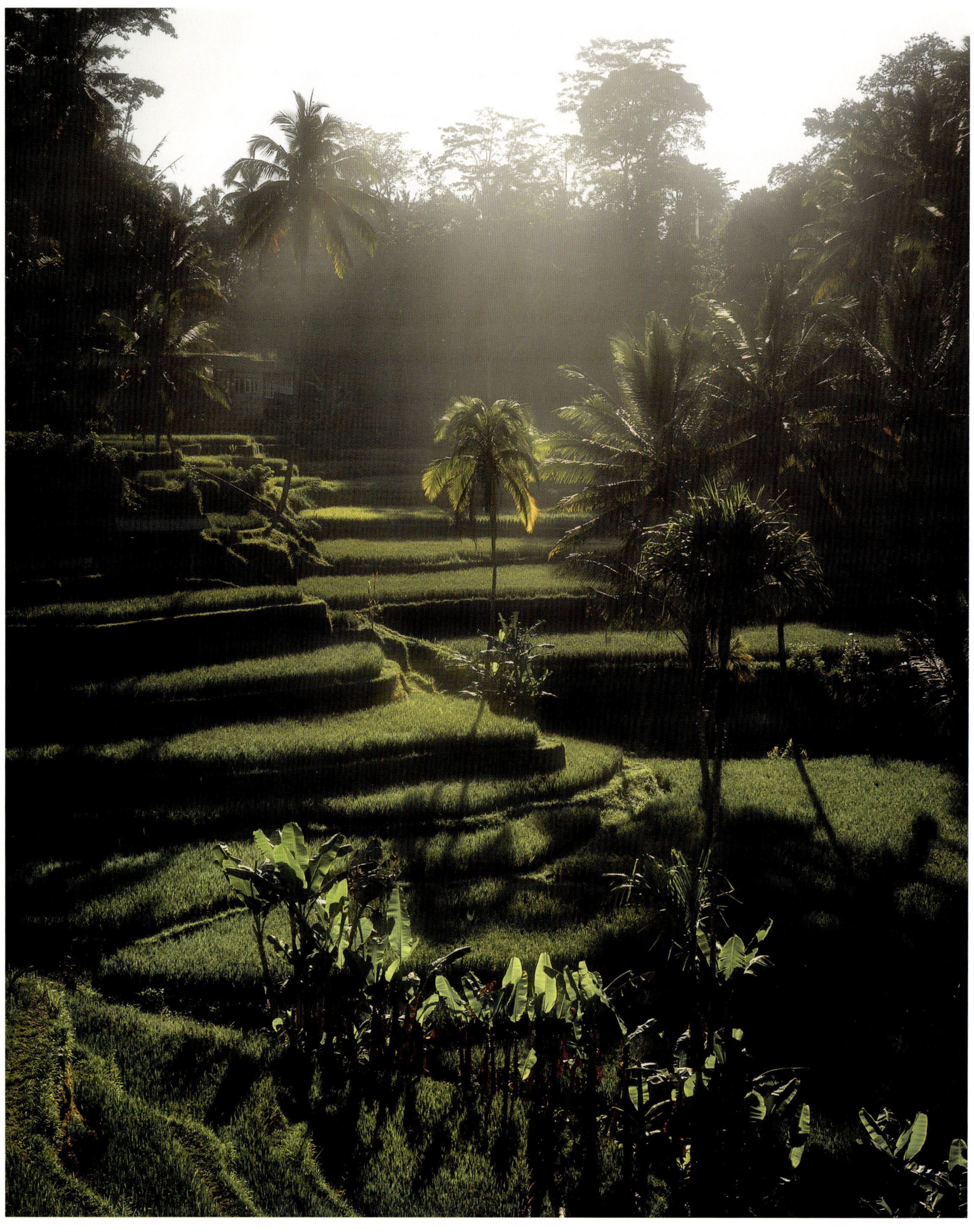

Bali, Indonesia

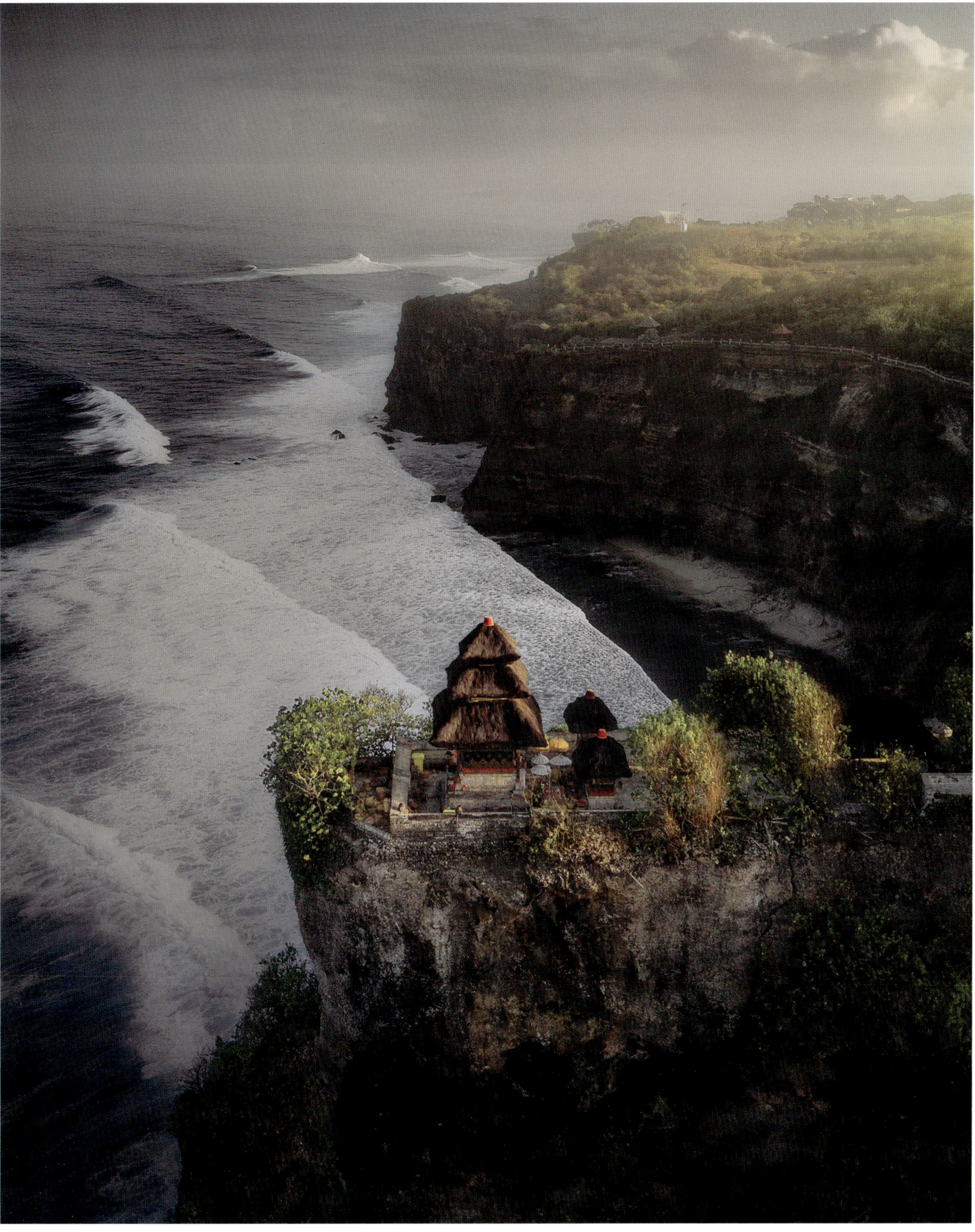

Bali, Indonesia

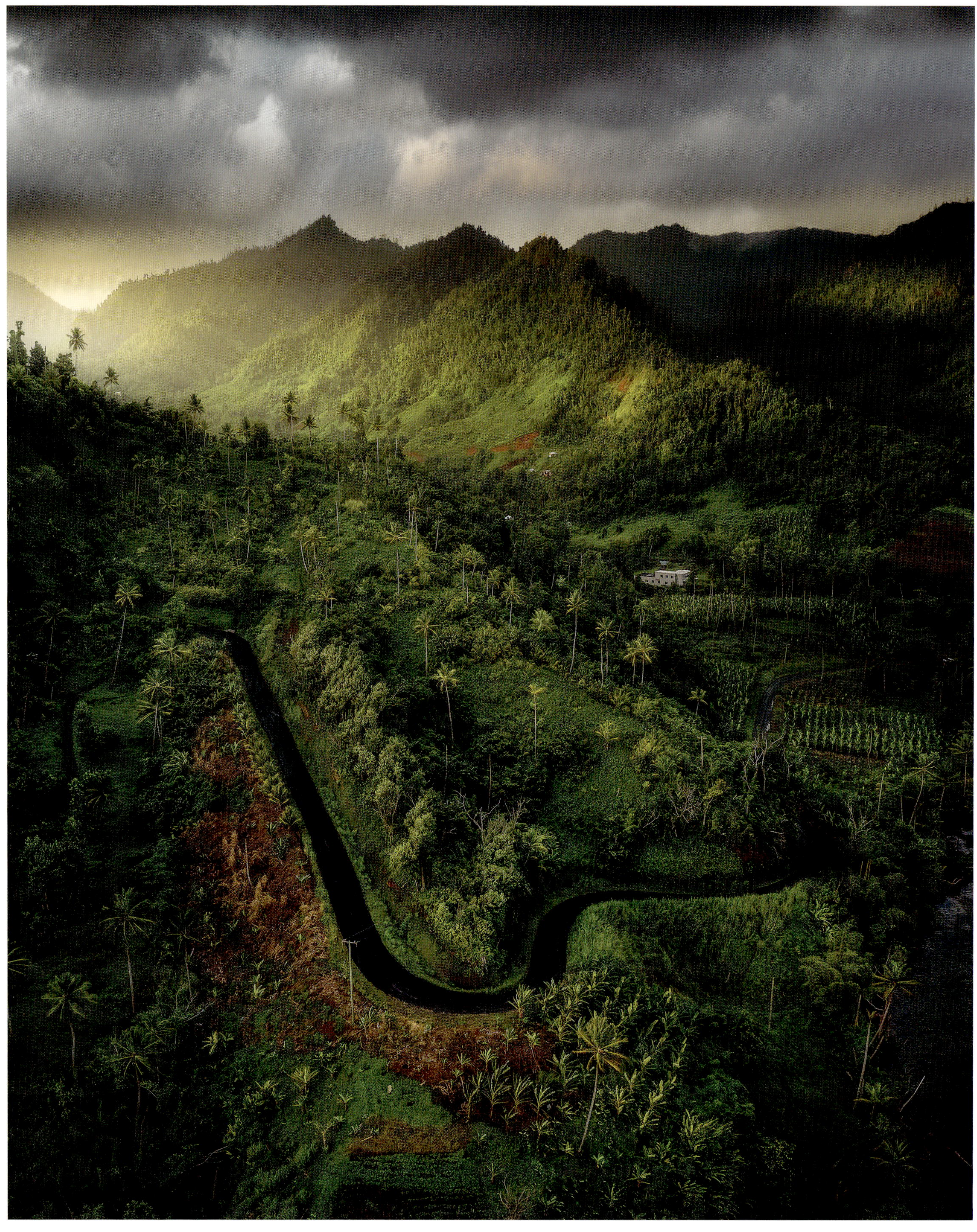

Dominica

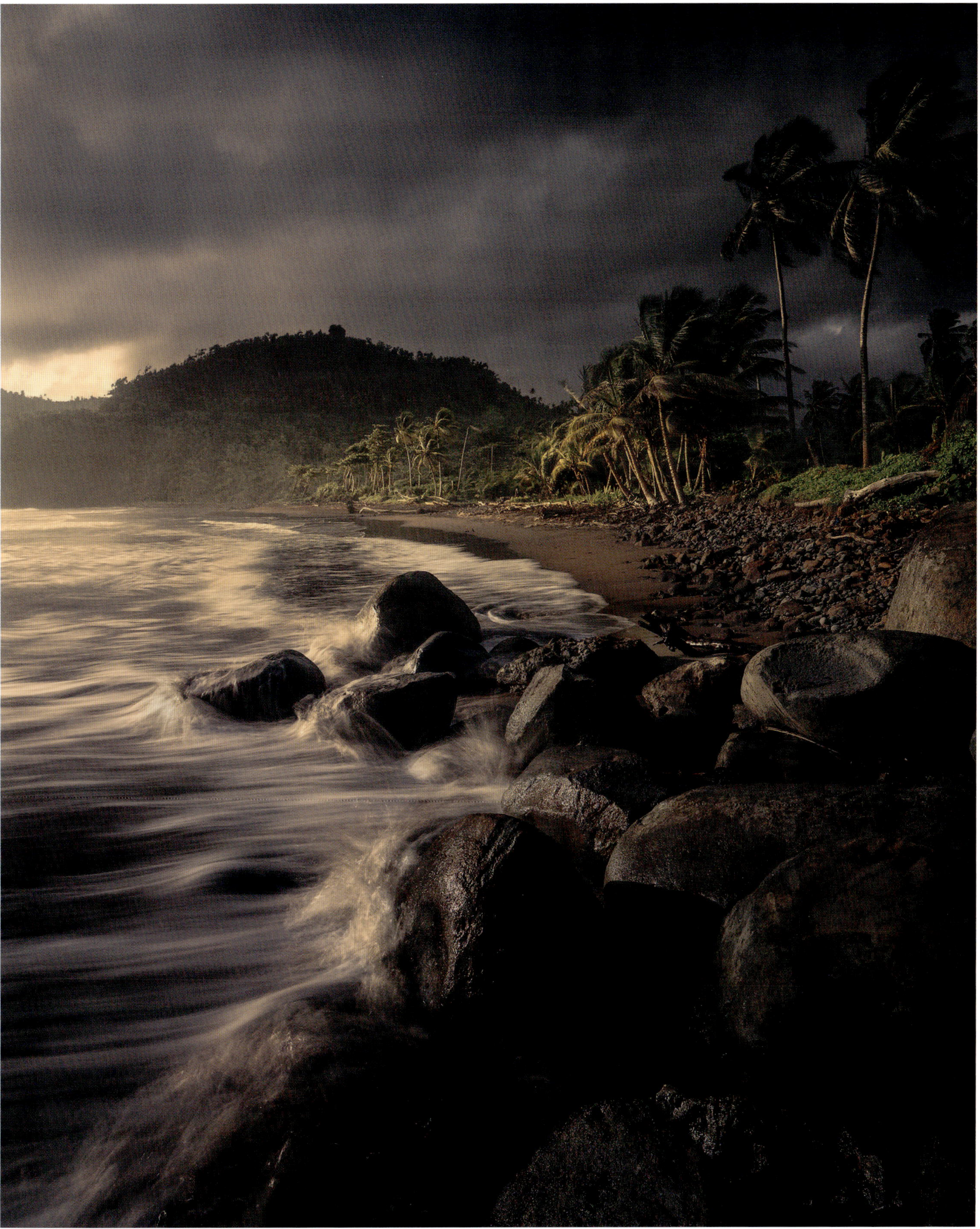

Dominica

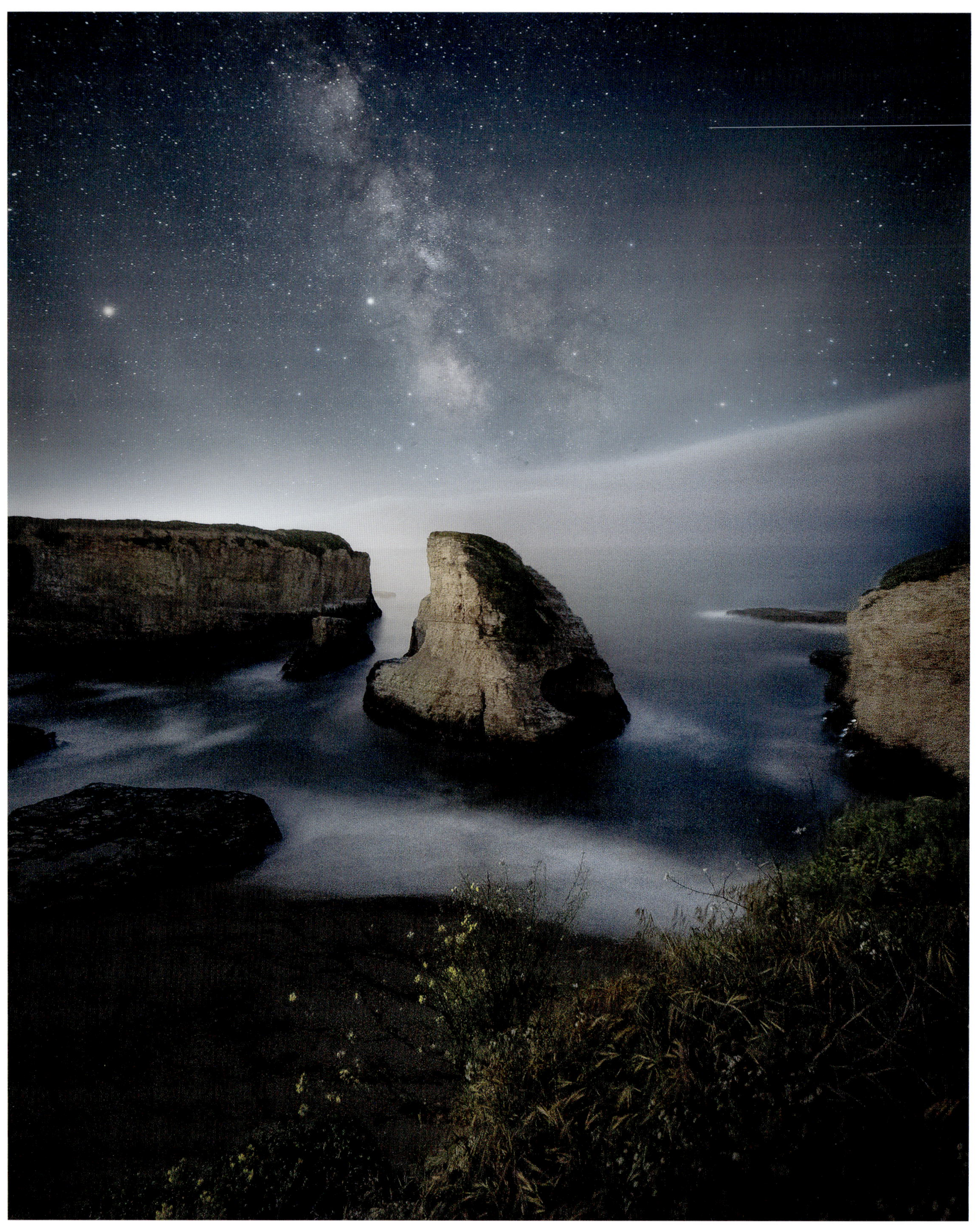

Davenport, California, USA

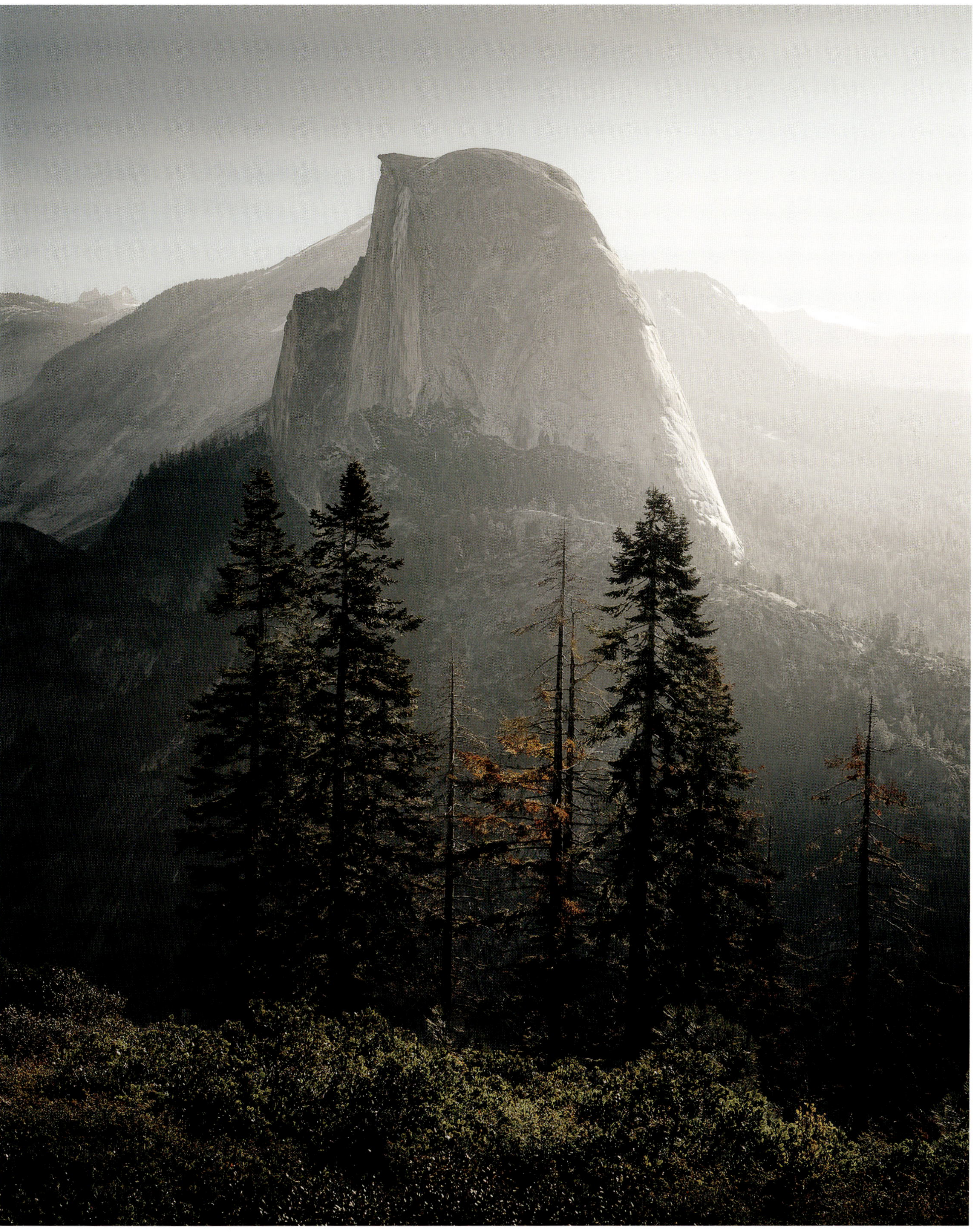

Yosemite National Park, California, USA

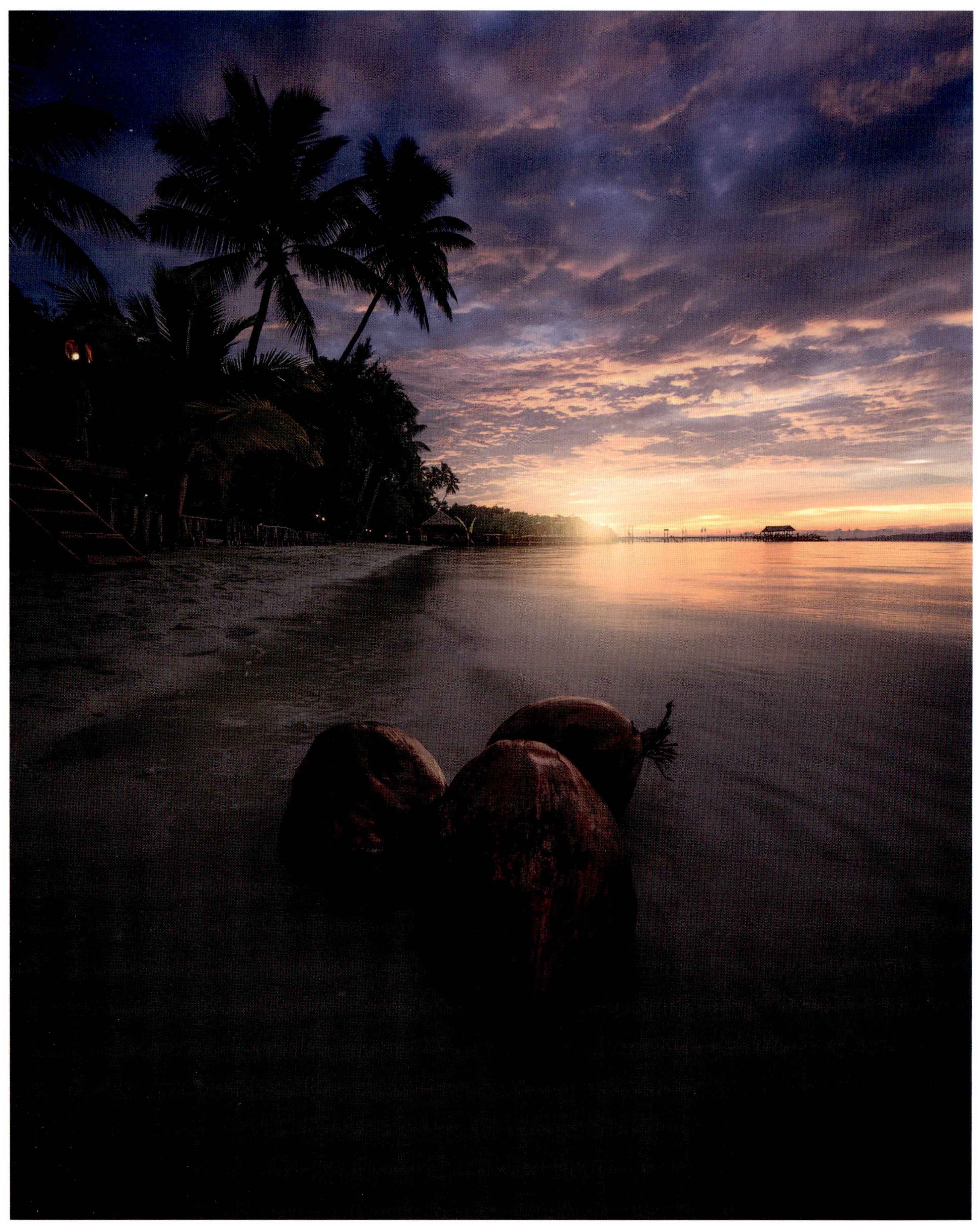

Raja Ampat, Indonesia

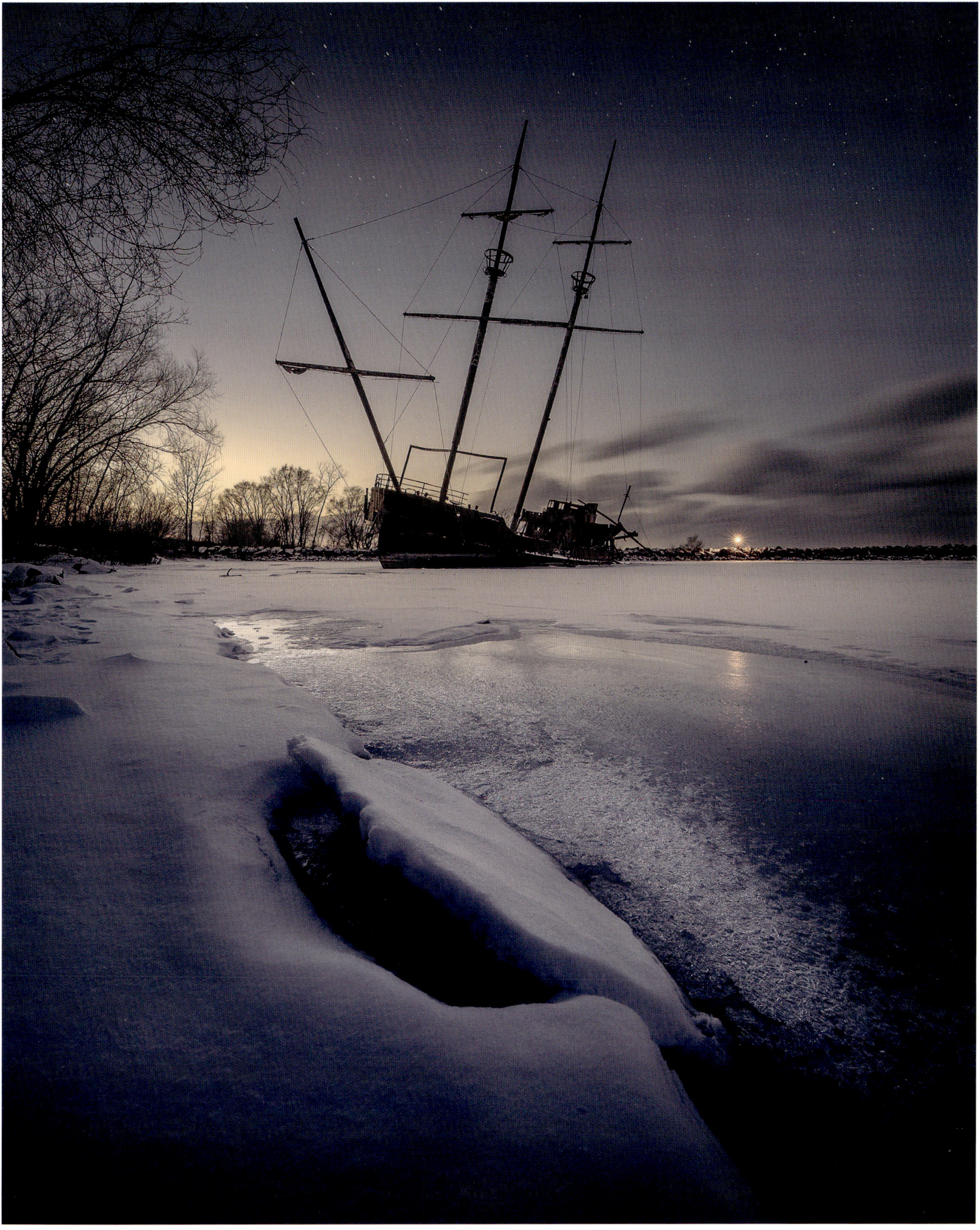

Jordan Harbour, Canada

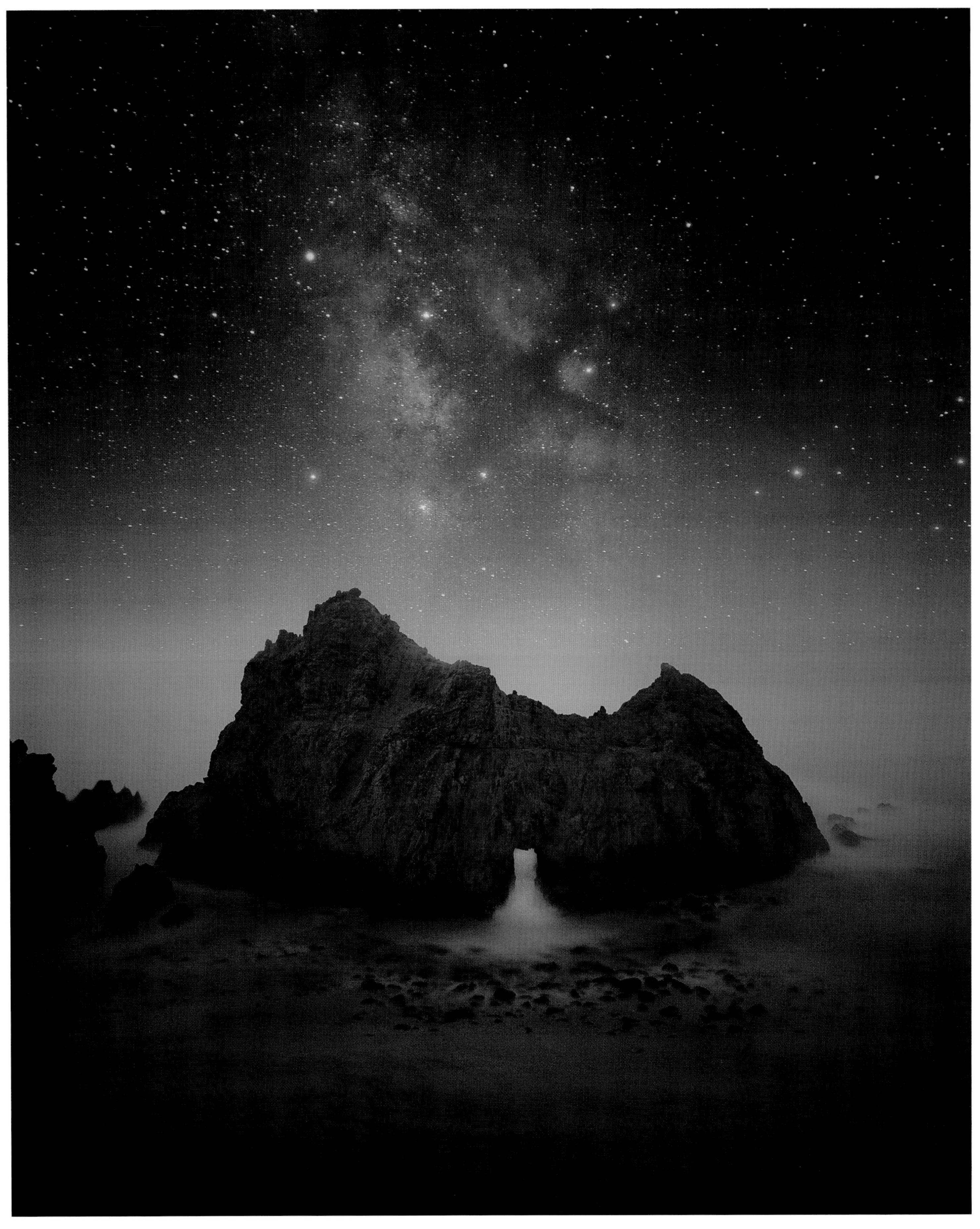

Big Sur, California, USA

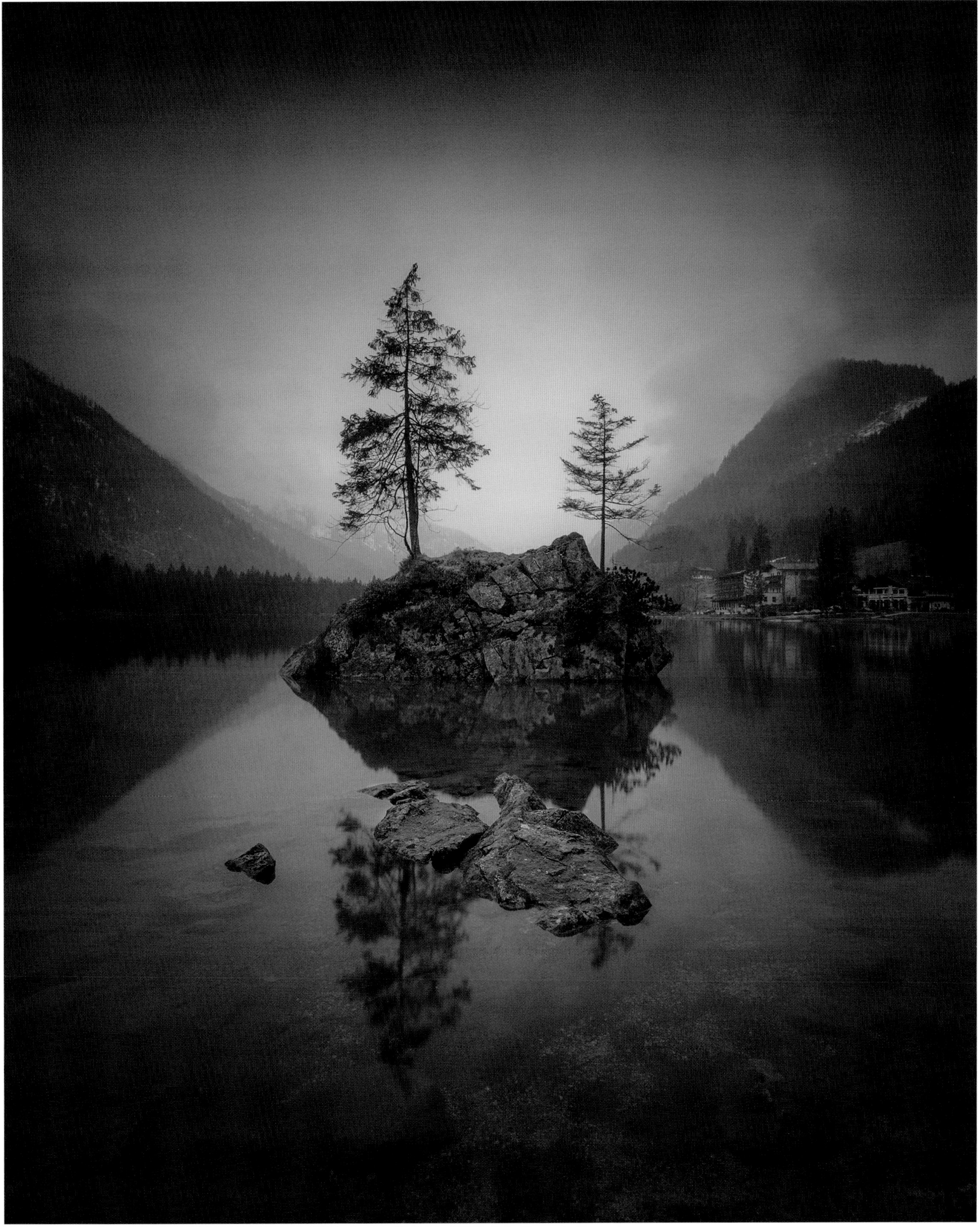

Hintersee, Germany

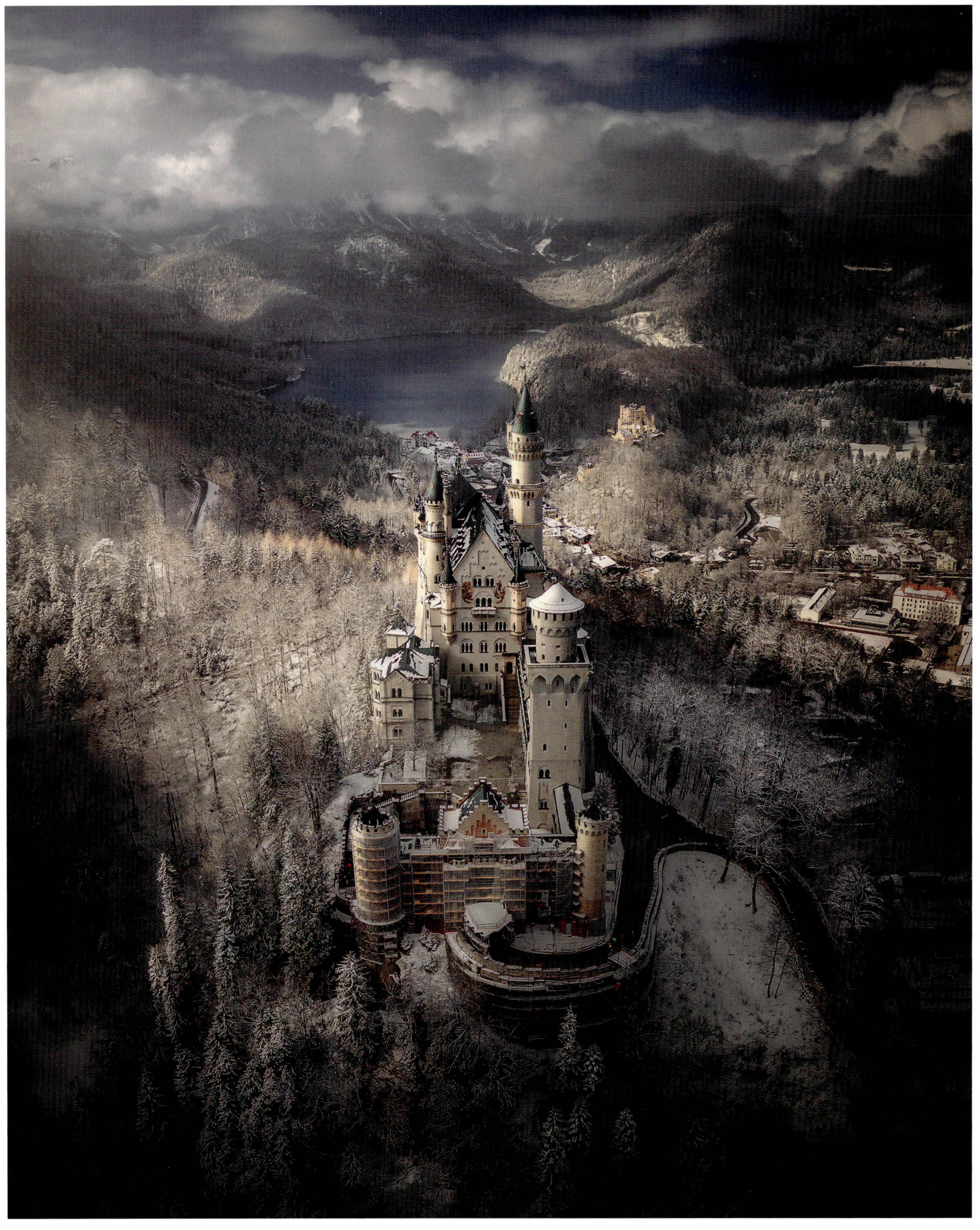

Bavaria, Germany

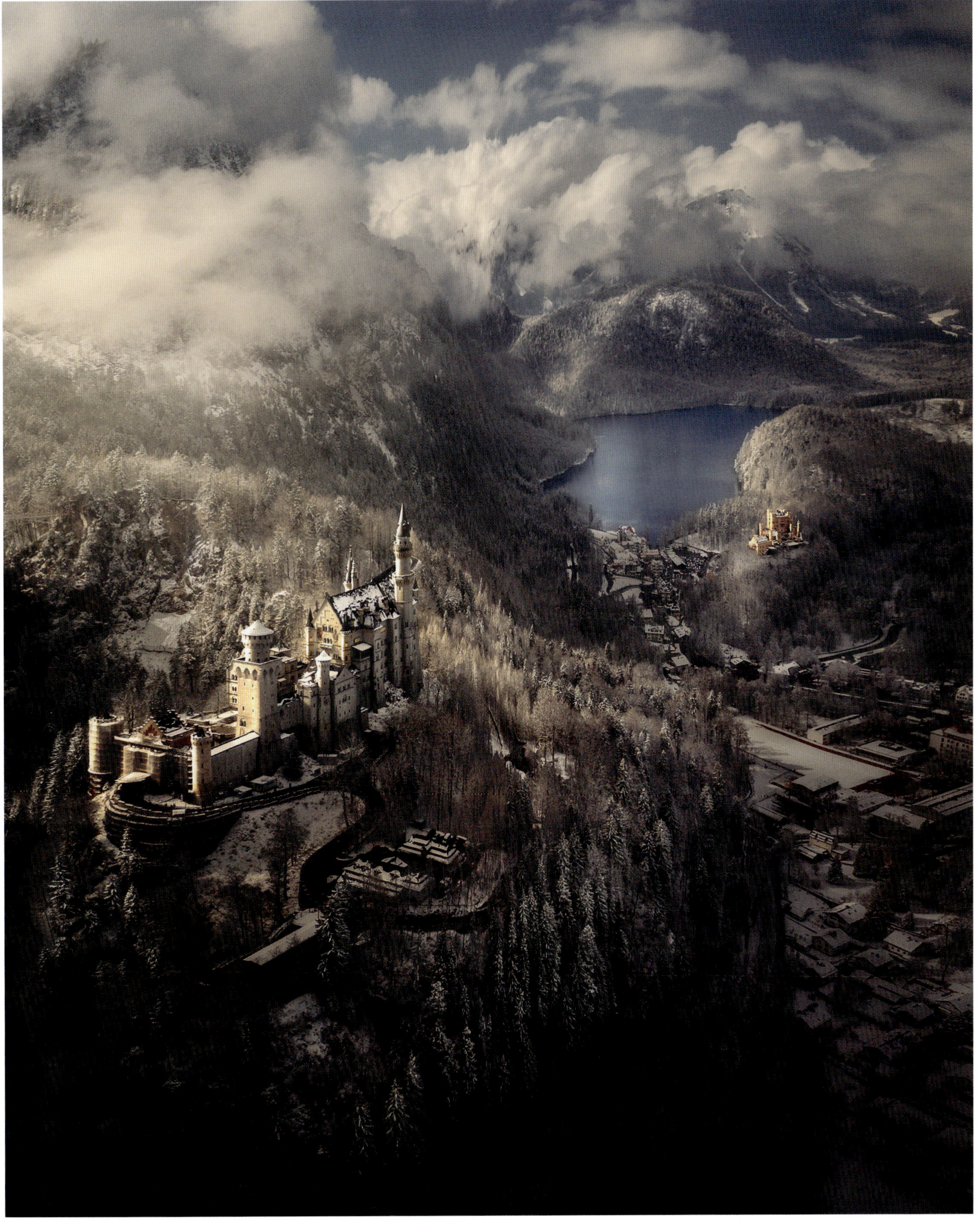

Bavaria, Germany

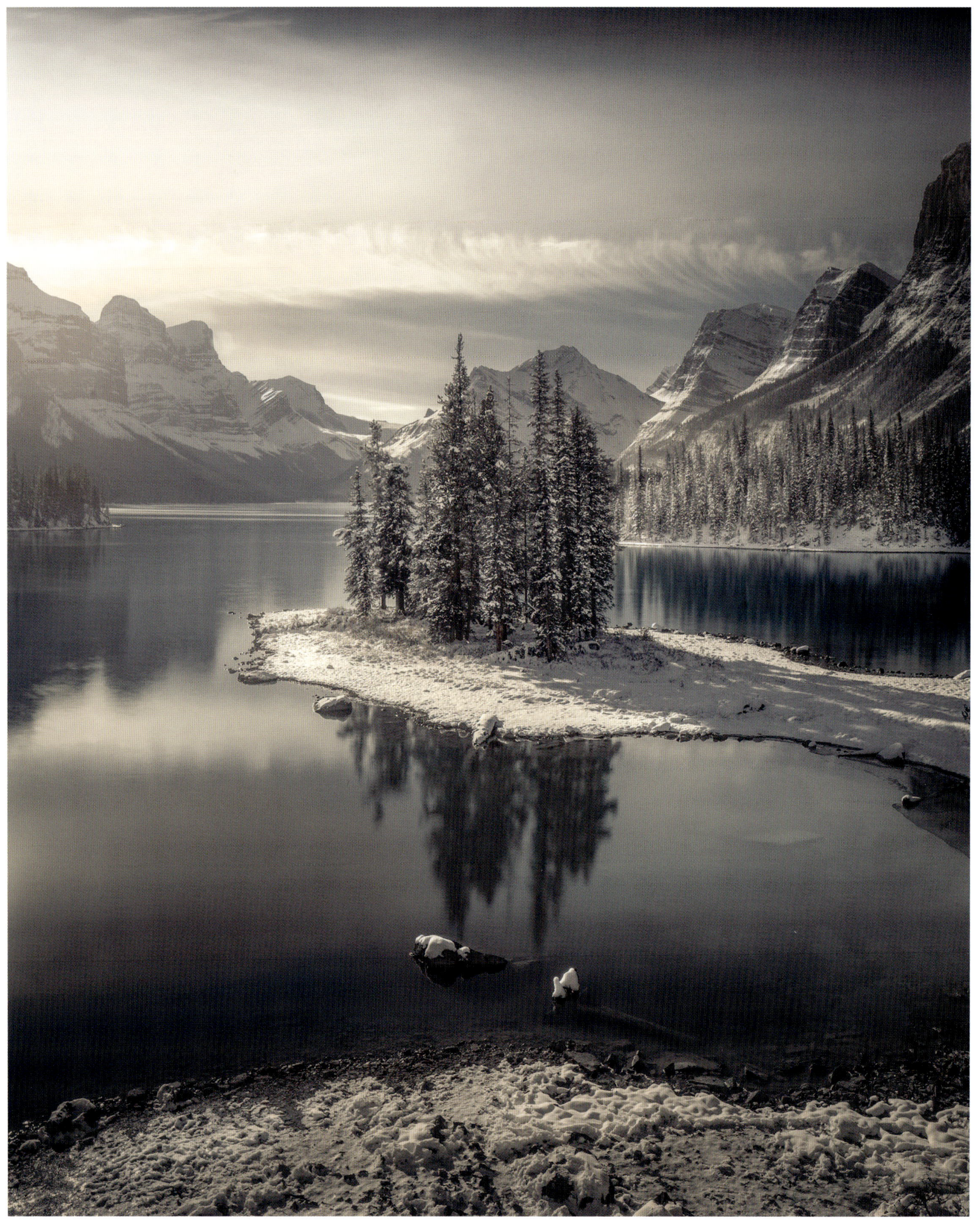

Bavaria, Germany

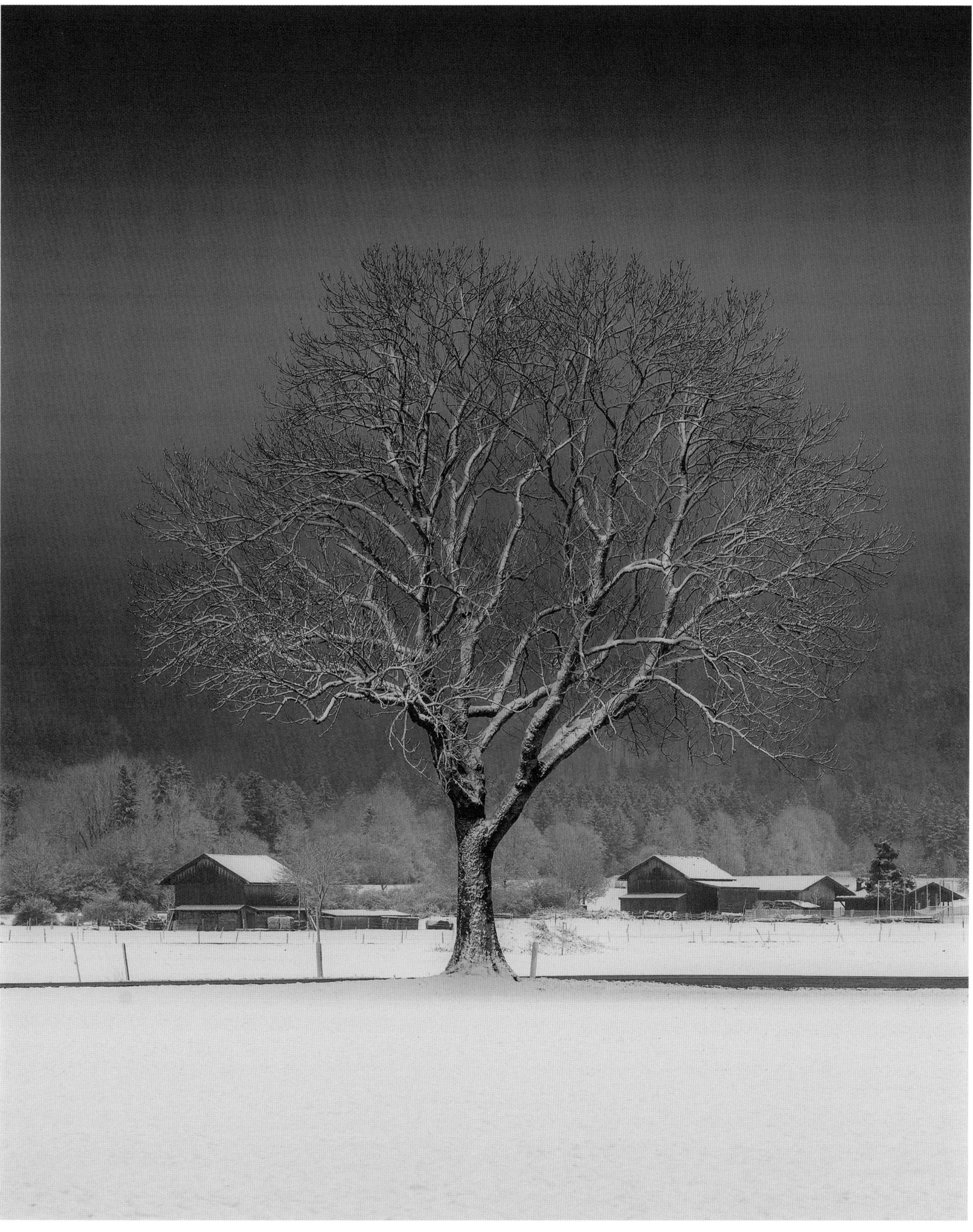

Bavaria, Germany

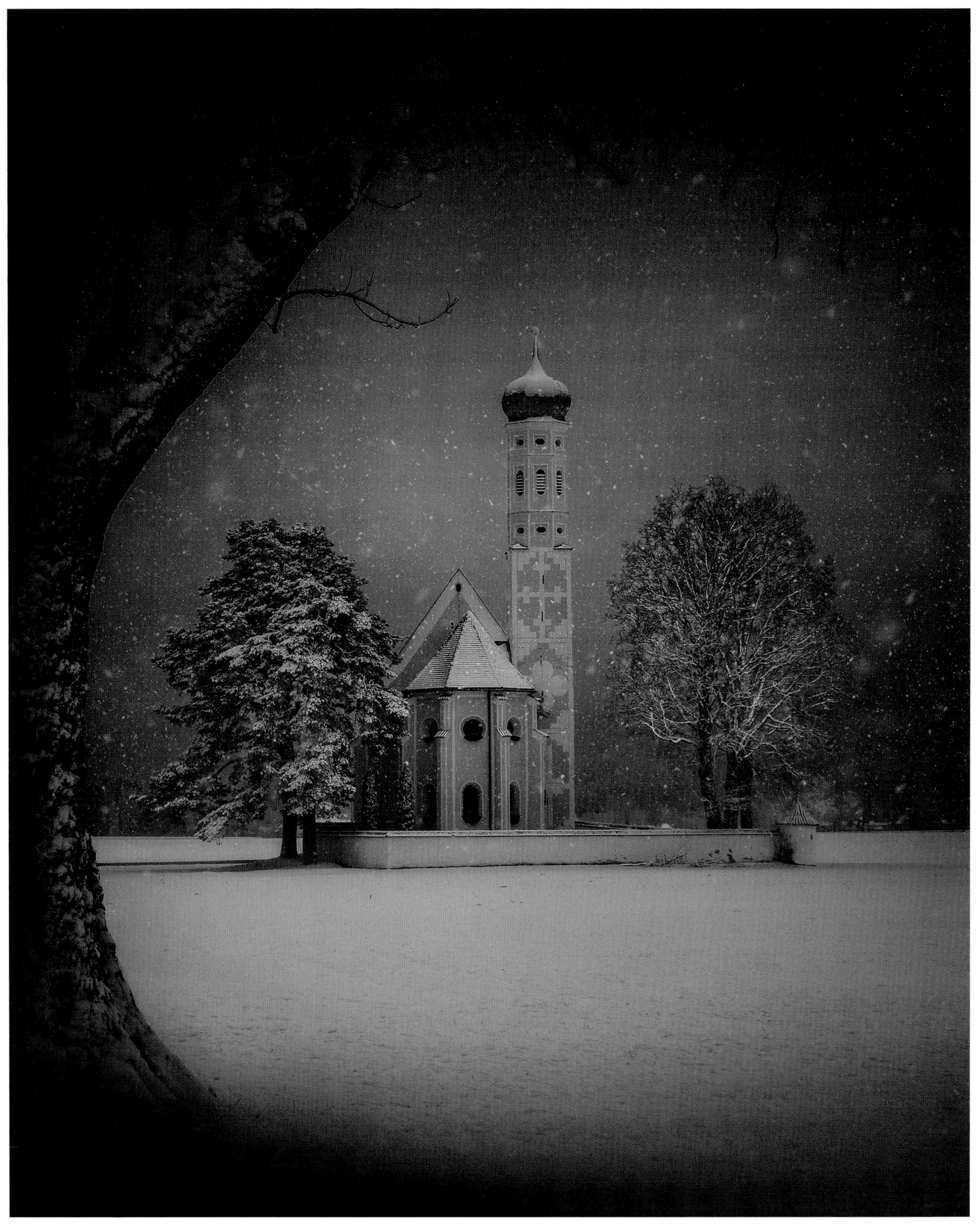

Bavaria, Germany

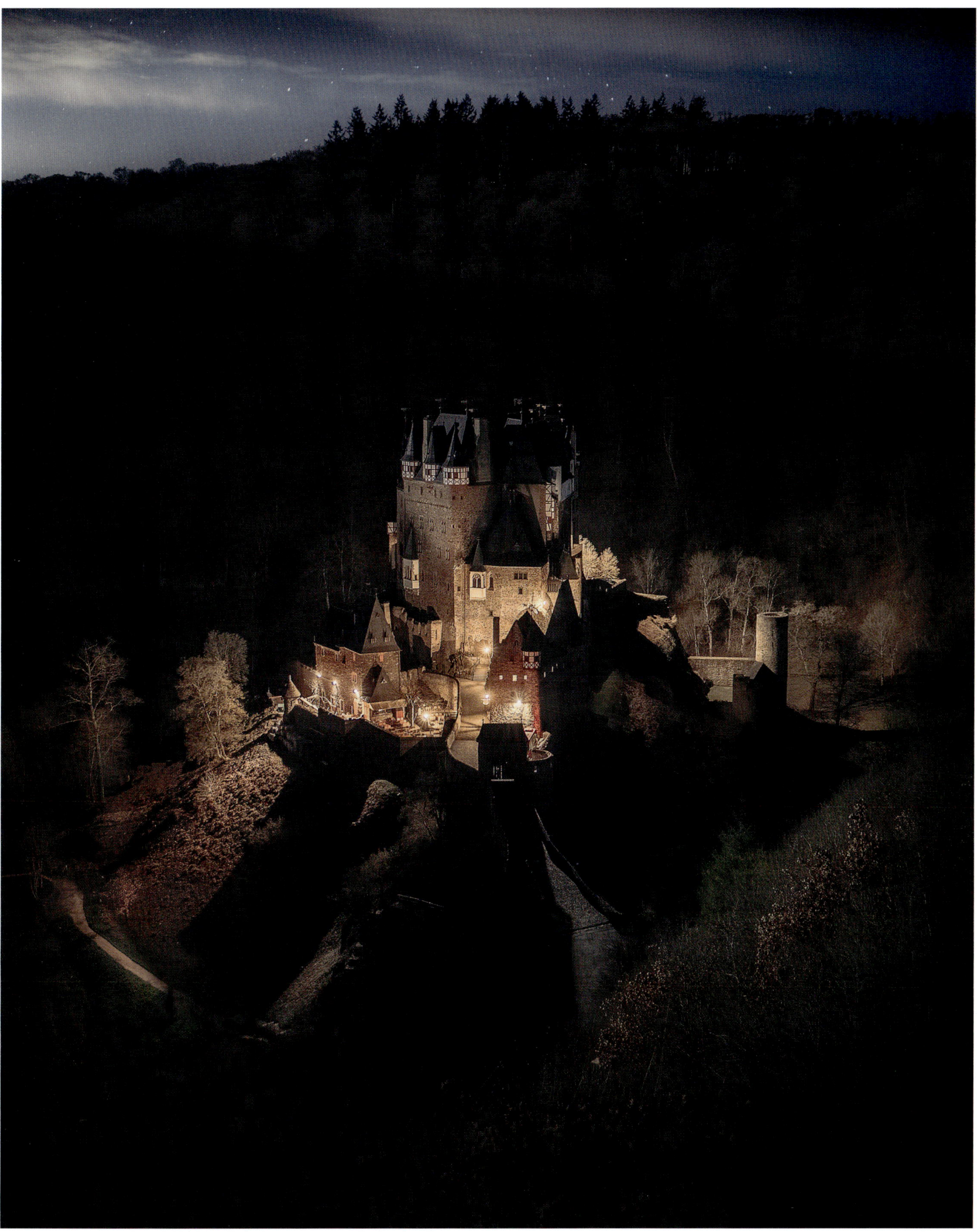

Burg Eltz, Germany

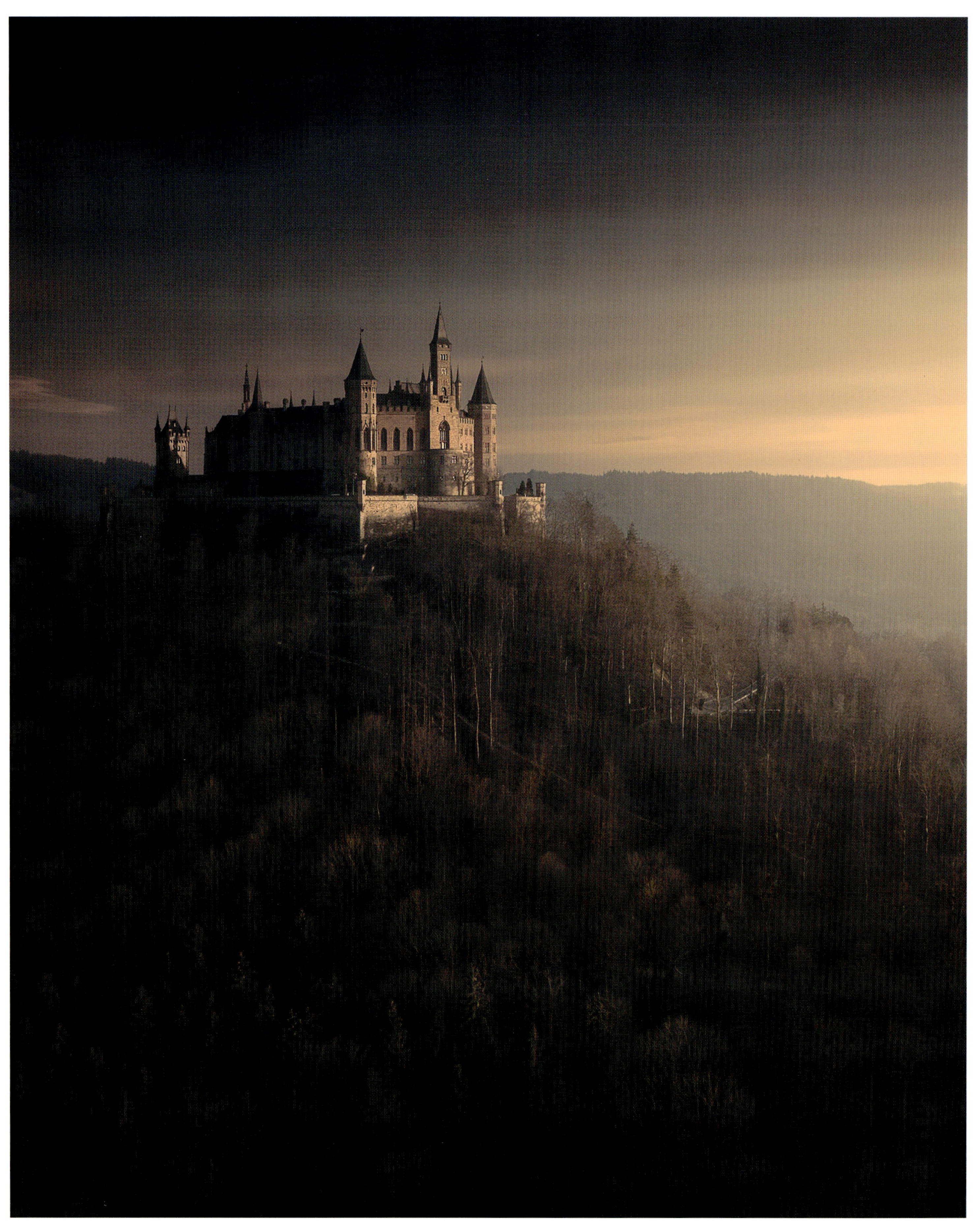

House of Hohenzollern, Germany

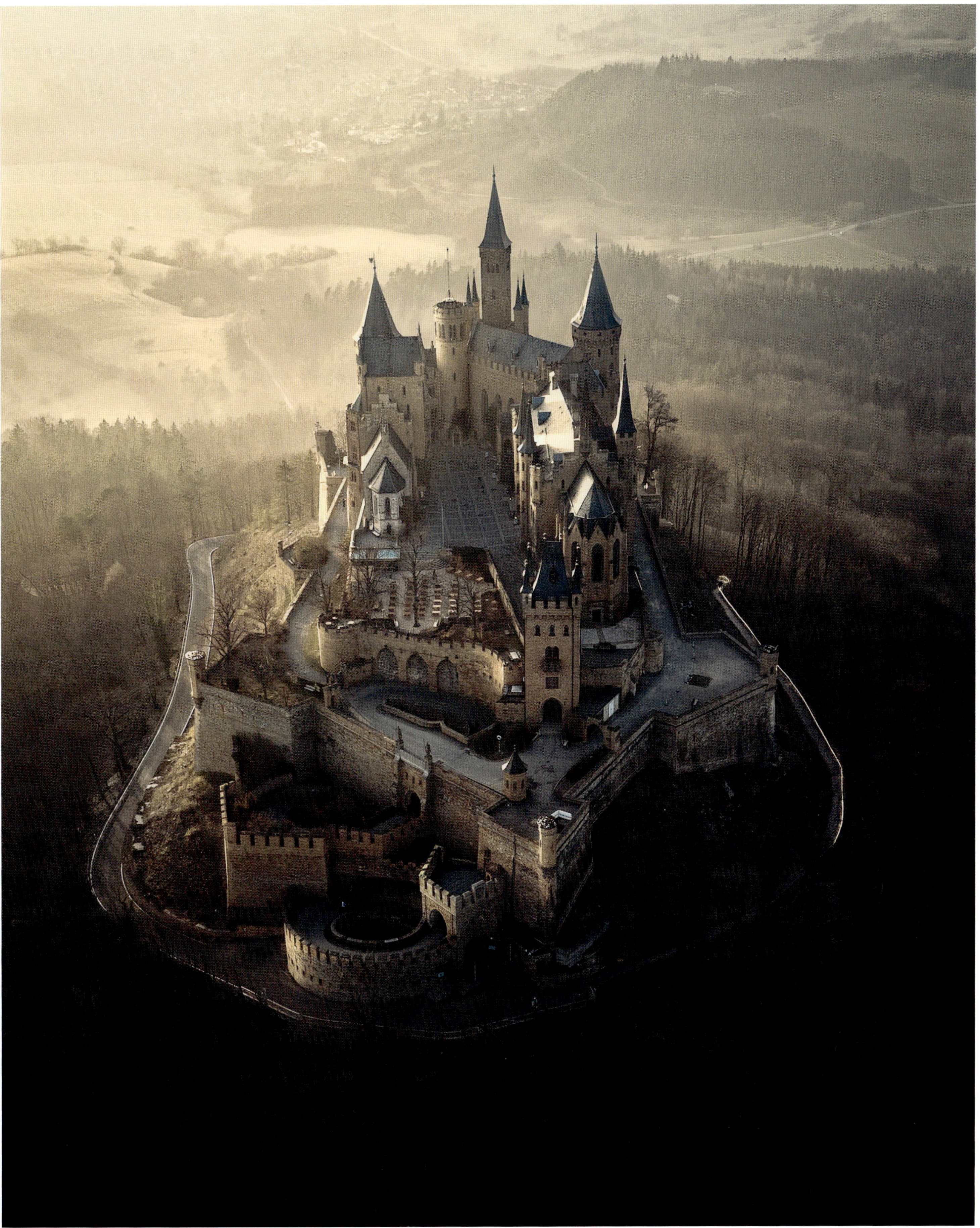

House of Hohenzollern, Germany

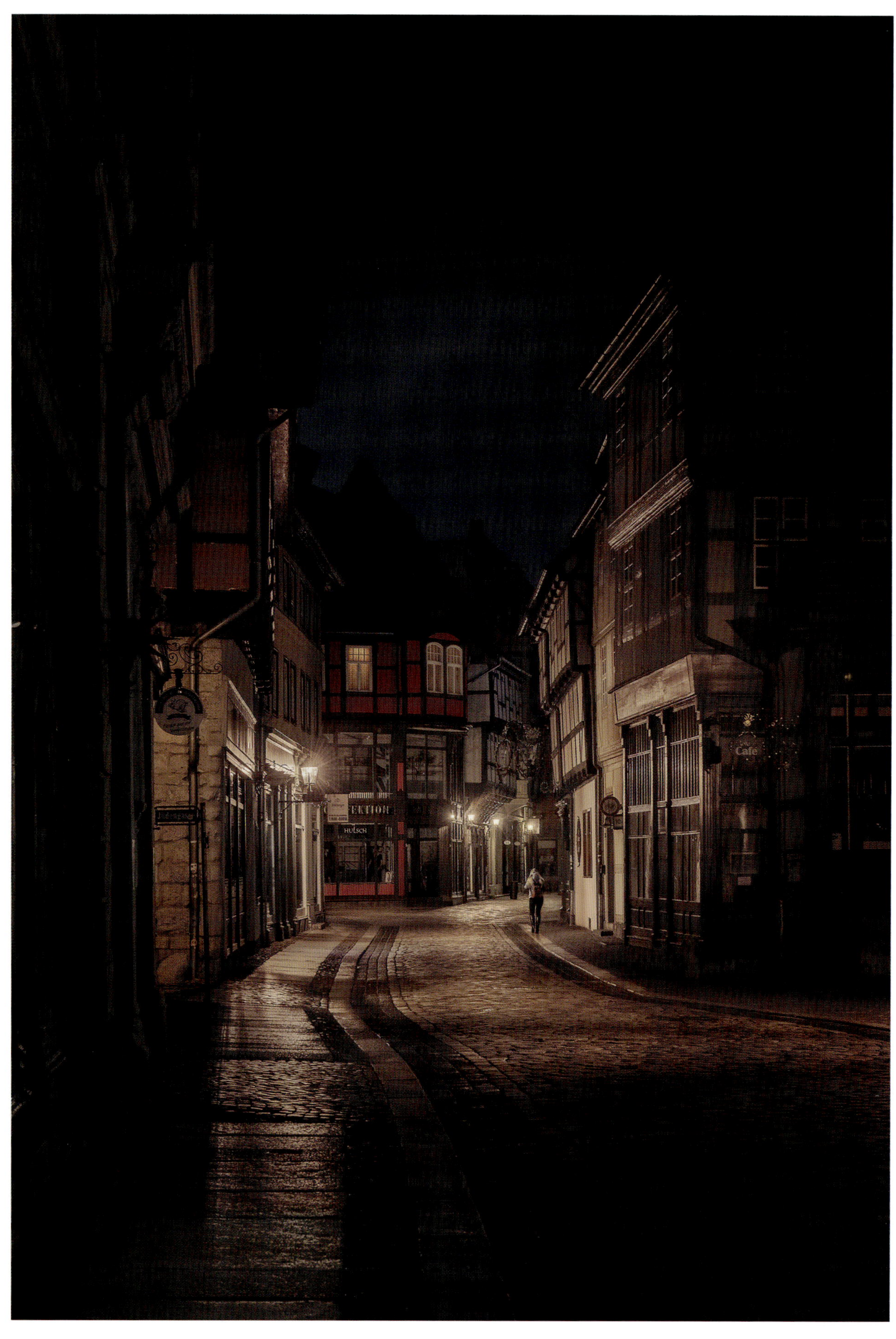

Quedlinburg, Germany

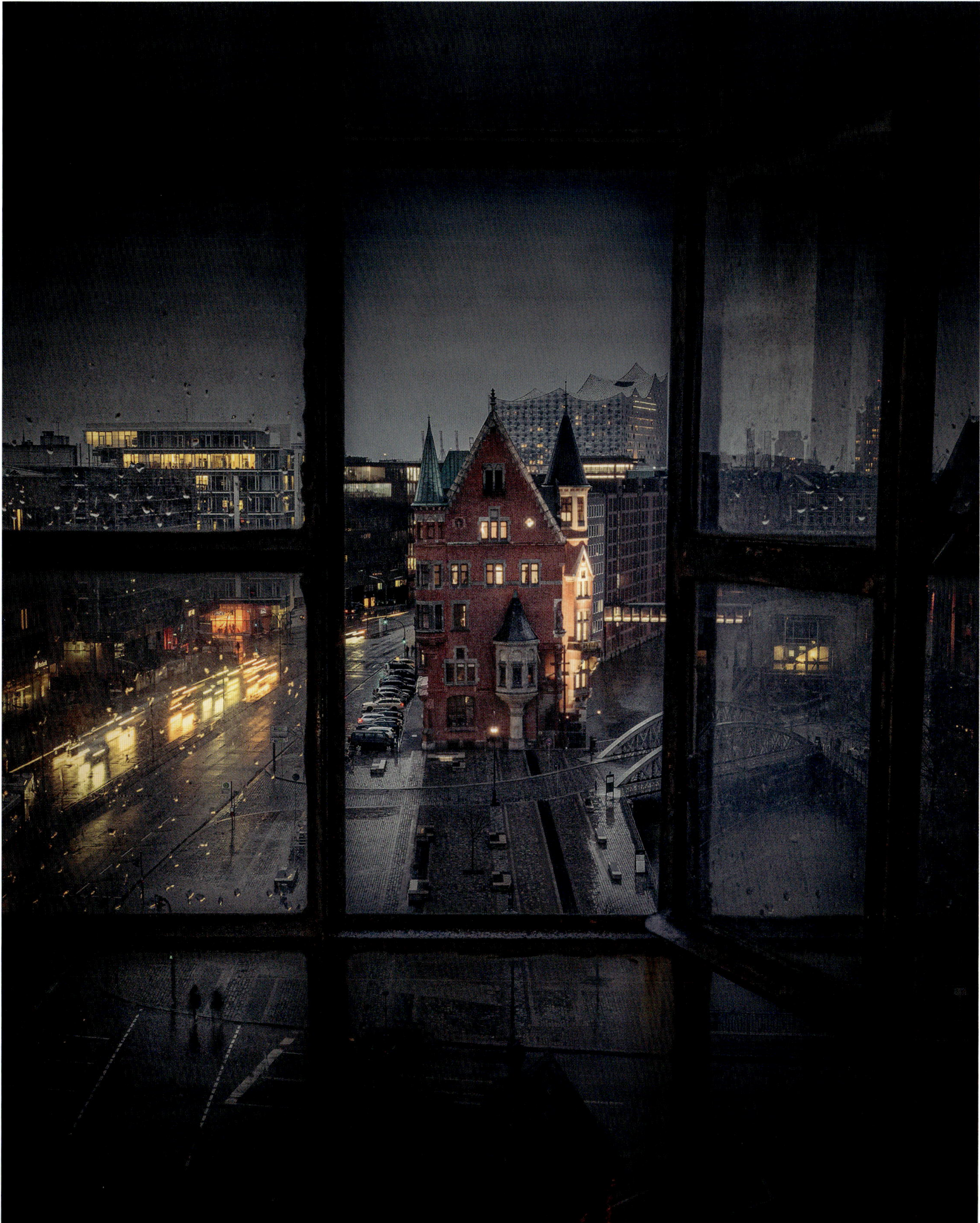

Hamburg, Germany

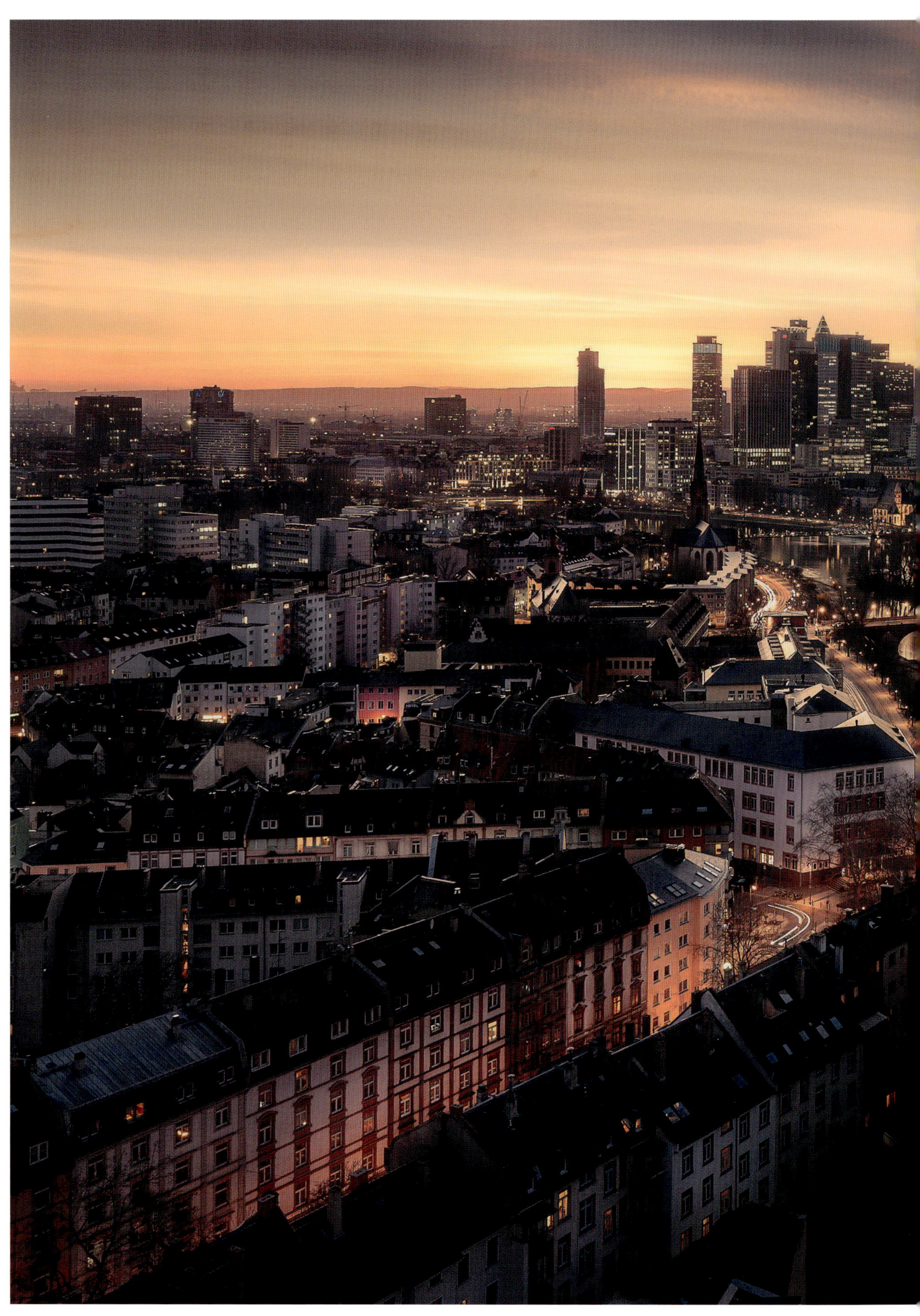

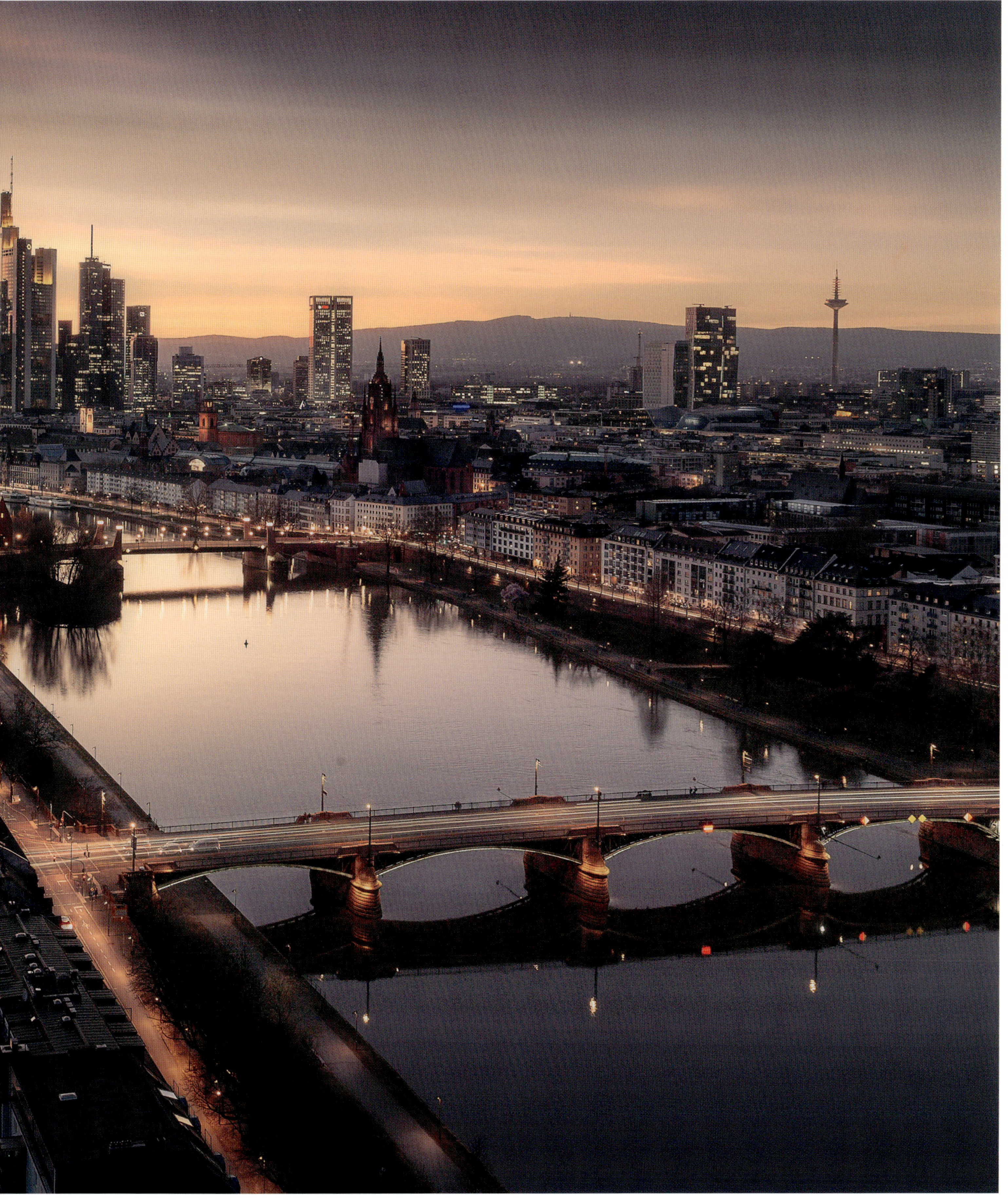

Frankfurt, Germany

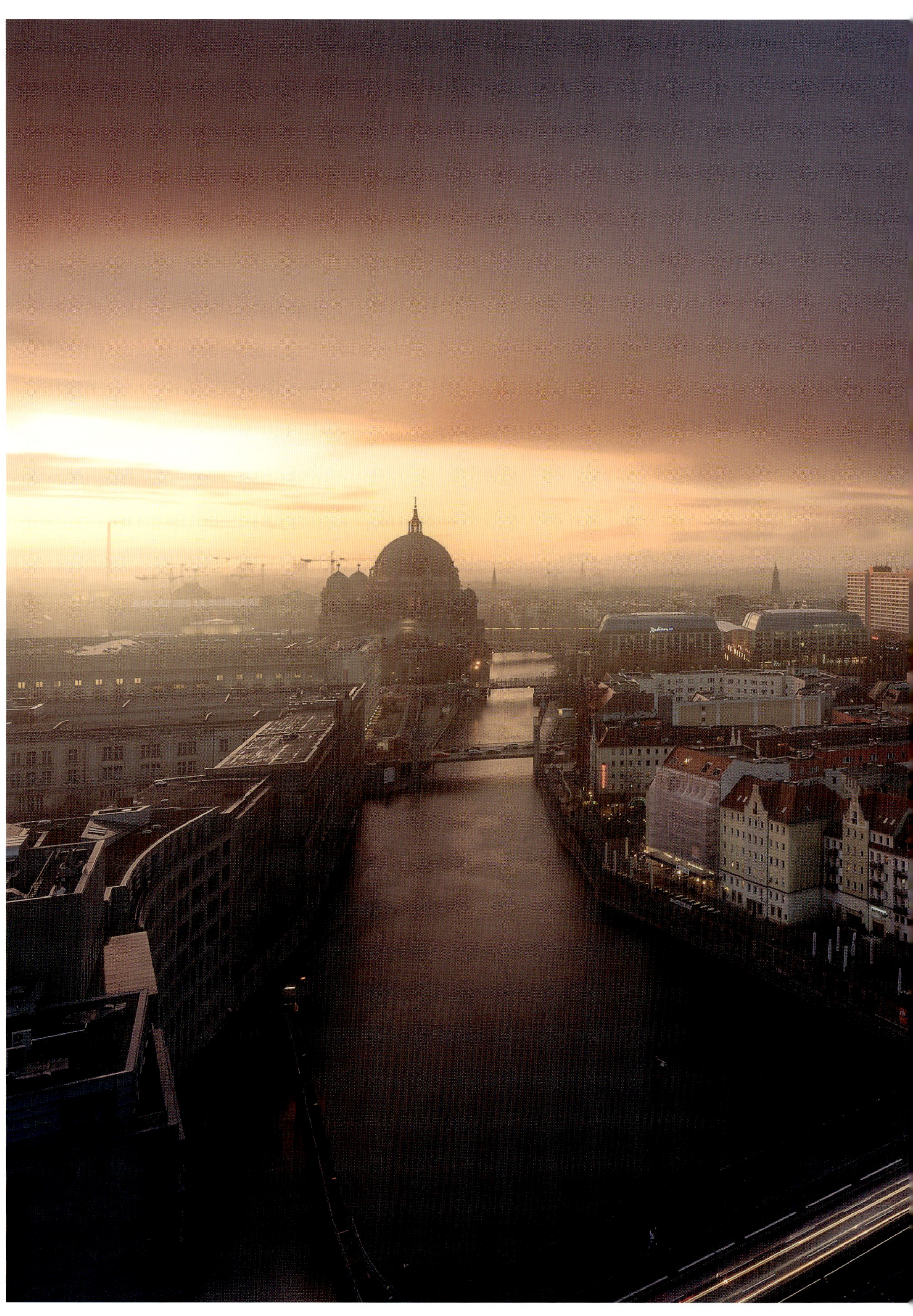

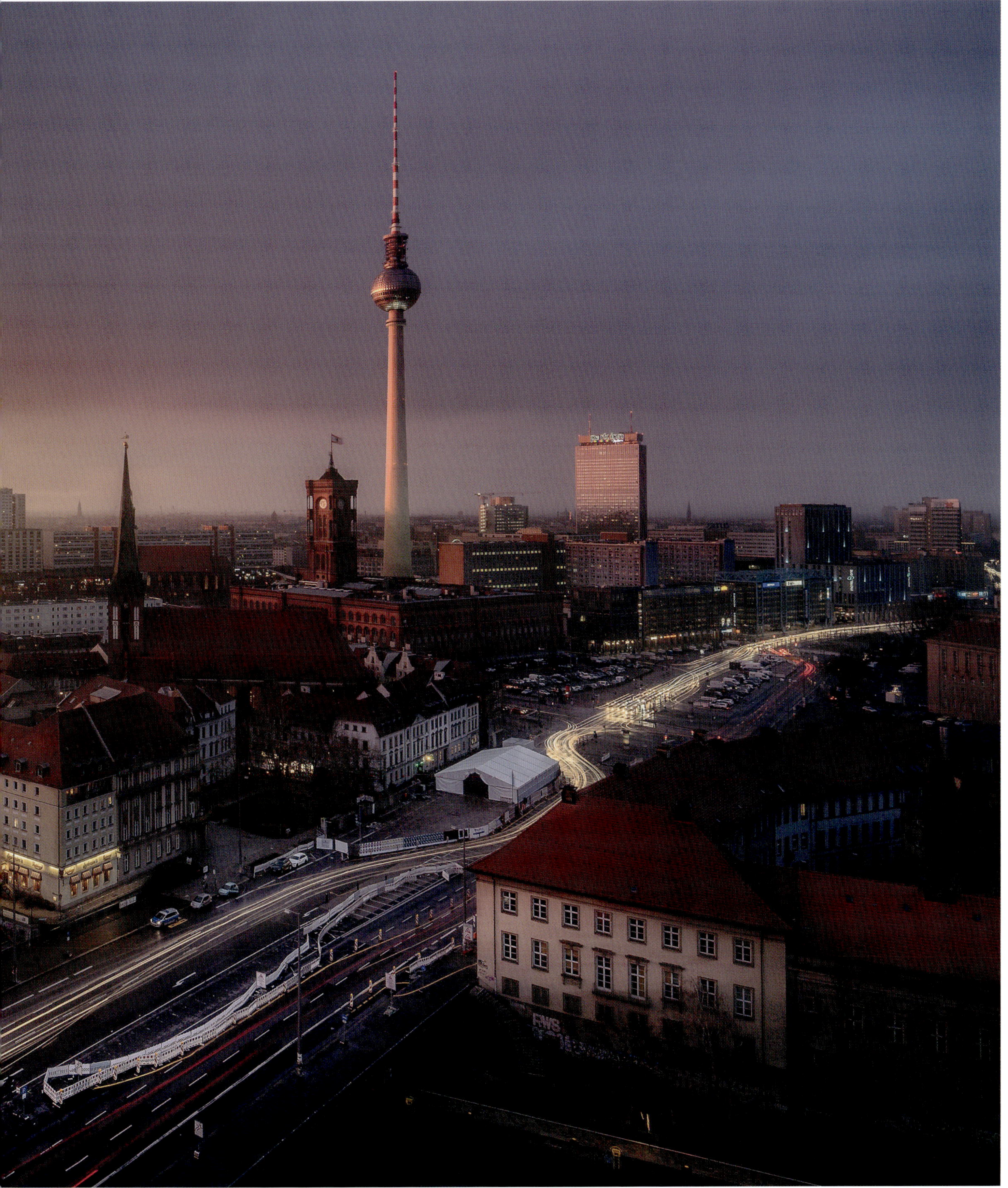

Berlin, Germany

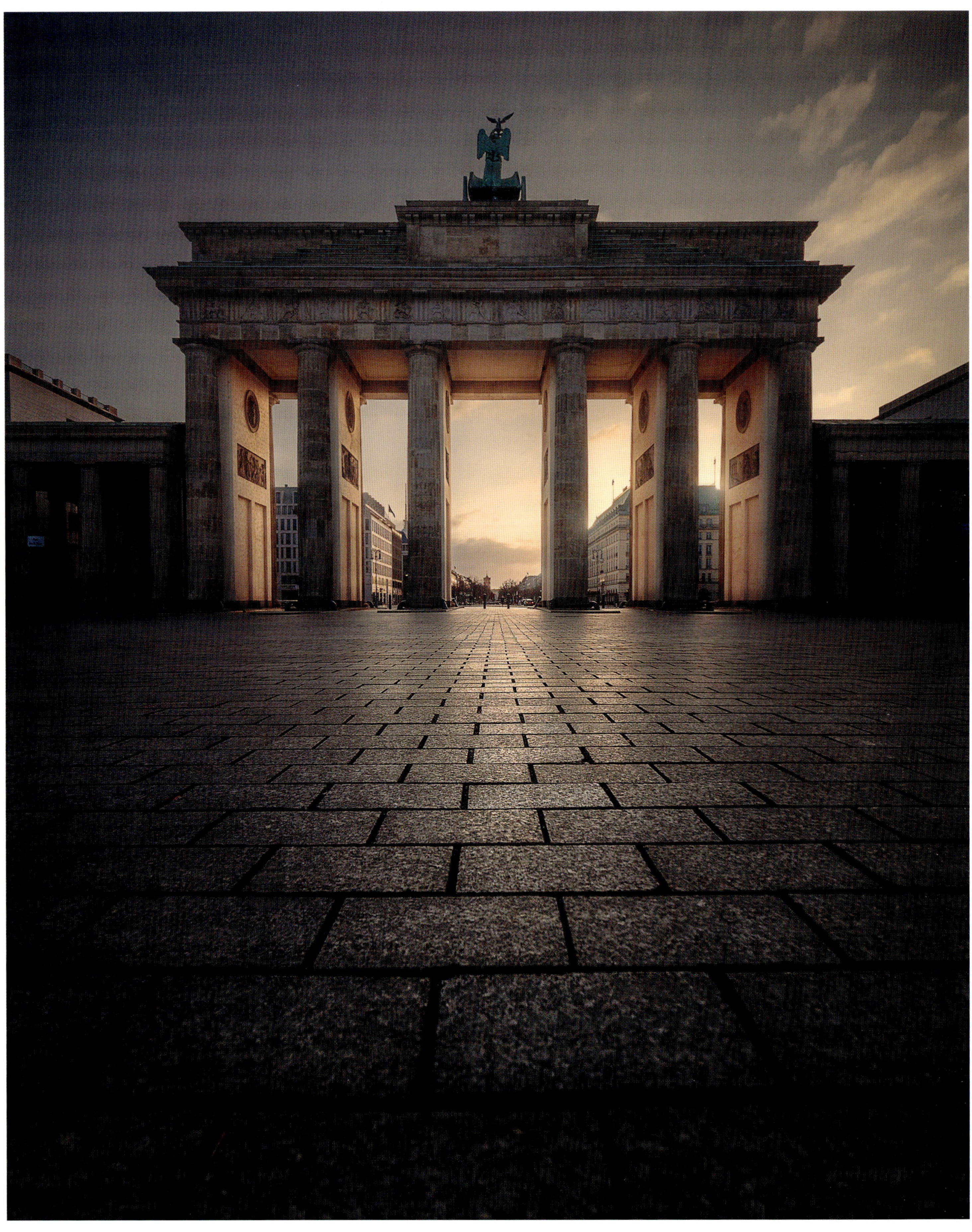

Berlin, Germany

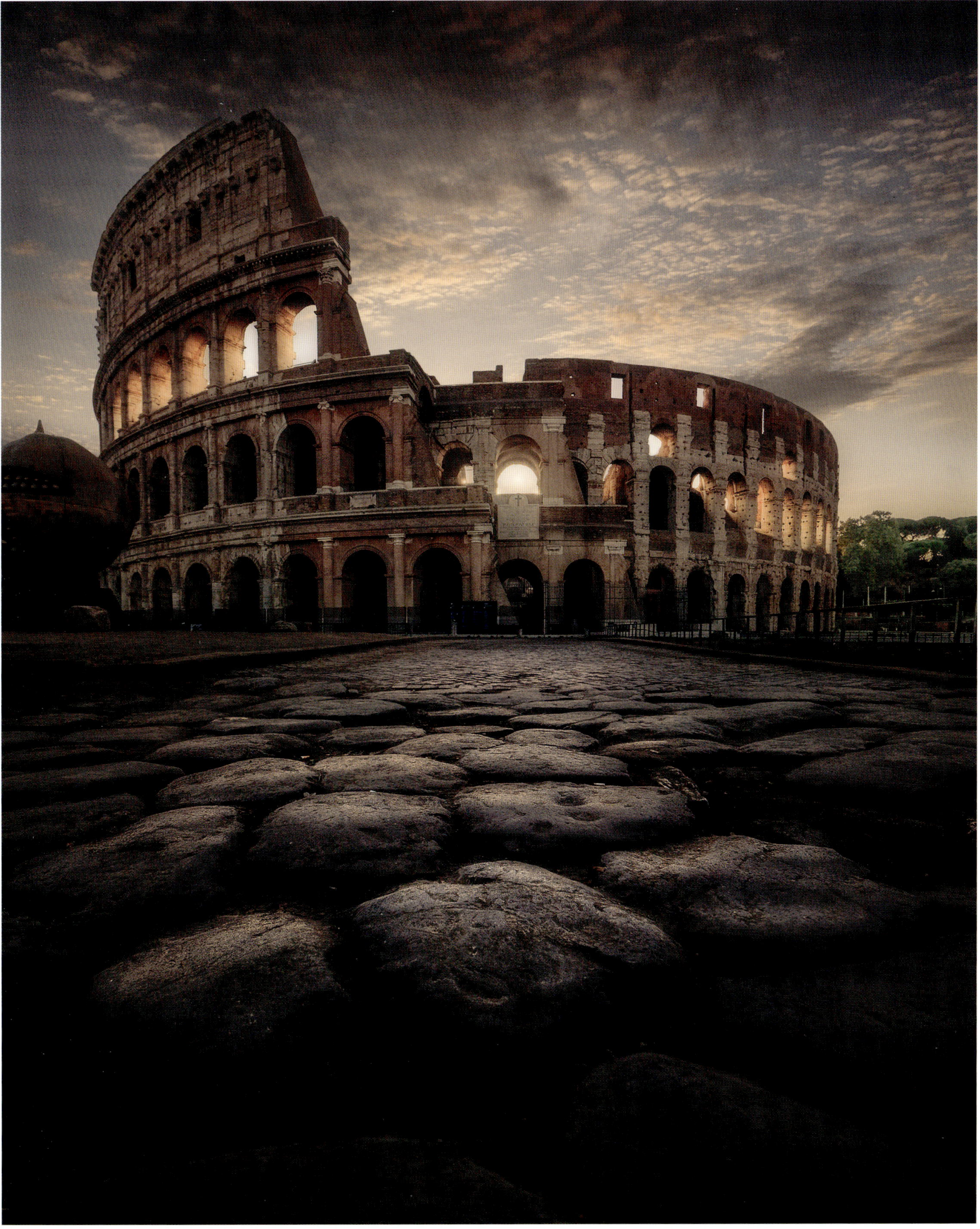

Rome, Italy

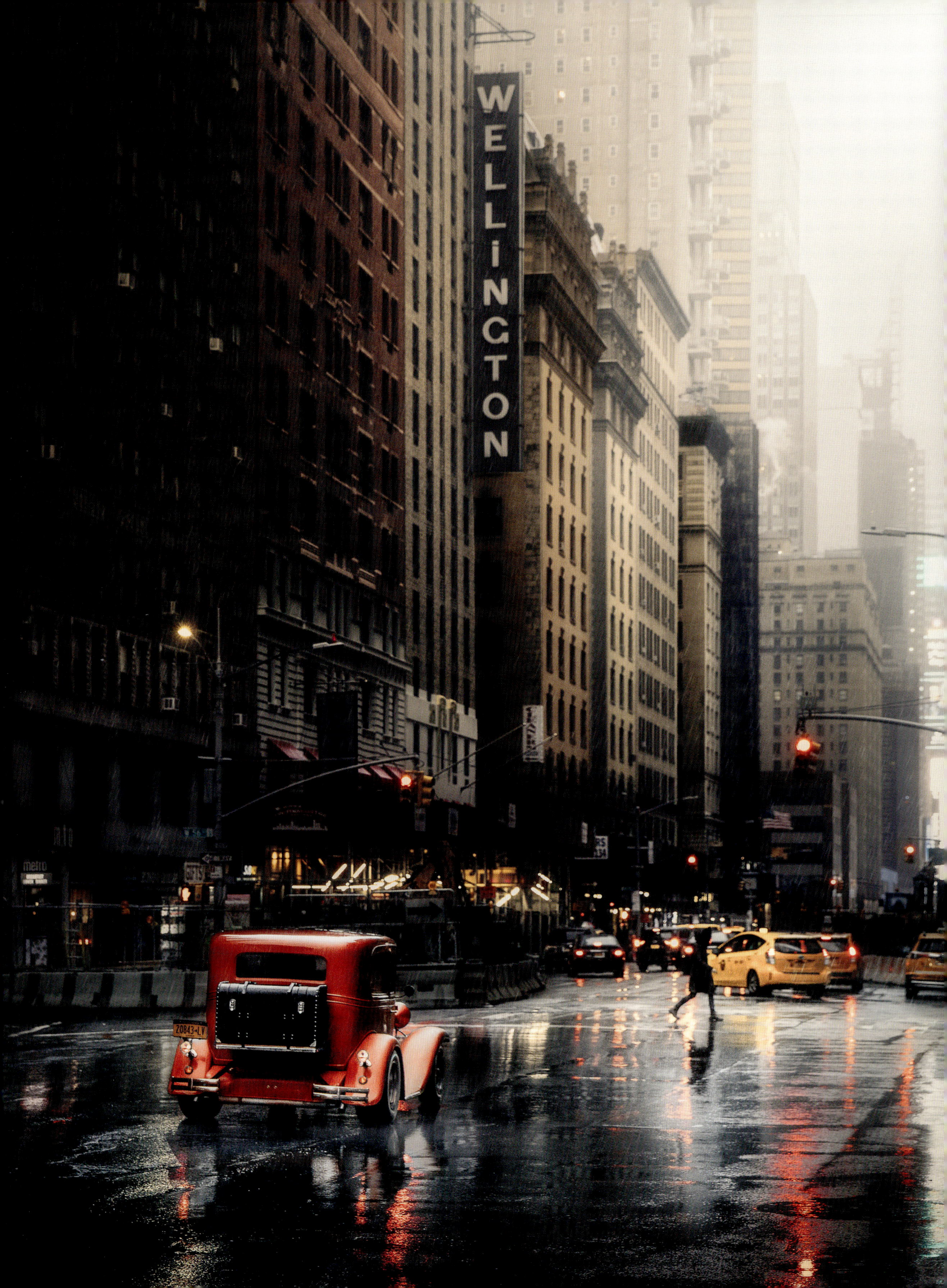

WELLiNGTON
Z0843-LV

WONDER
AROUND
EVERY
CORNER

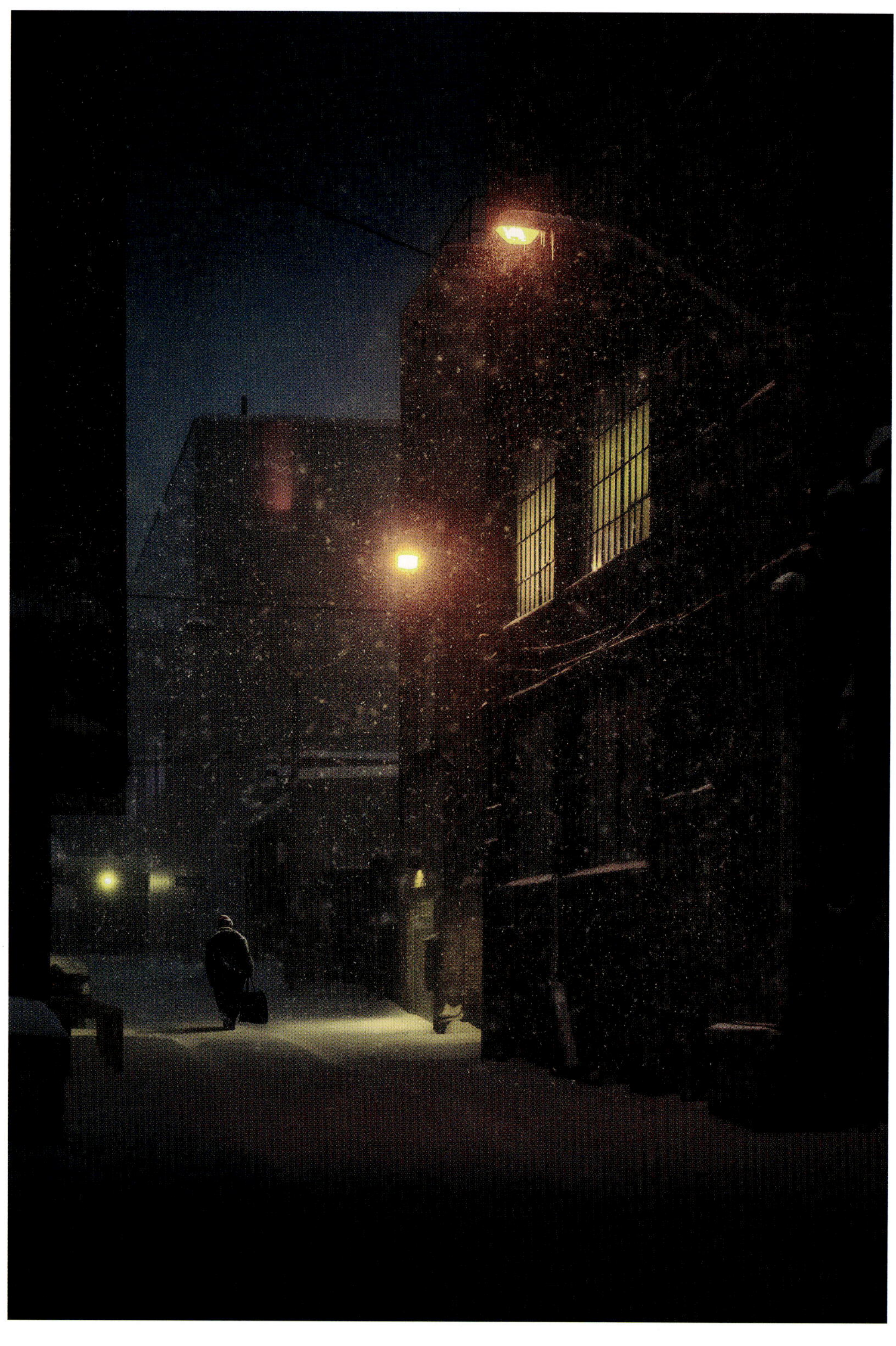

An Ode. They say inspiration comes in many forms and this piece is an ode to my late grandfather, Mickey Katz. He was an avid impressionist oil painter who had a keen eye for composition, color, and storytelling. His incredible and unique paintings adorned the walls of my childhood home and in many ways, though unbeknownst to me then, greatly influenced my style as an artist and photographer. Looking back, I found myself drawn to a specific painting he had created entitled "Chinatown by Night." It depicted a solitary figure walking down a dark alley lined by warehouses and buildings, some of which cast a soft glow of warm light. This particular piece always resonated, the contrast evoking a sense of loneliness, sadness, and despair—feelings I easily related to during an earlier time in my life. Since becoming a photographer, I have been in constant search for the composition and conditions that would conjure those same emotions I felt from viewing that painting. One could argue that a good portion of my photography reflected this quest, though I could never quite capture the essence of my grandfather's piece. Until that one snowy night in the streets of Toronto, I finally found it.

Michael Sidofsky is a professional photographer from Toronto, specializing in elevated travel photography. Being an avid traveler and photographer, his goal is to capture the essence of a destination through advanced techniques in photography and post-processing. His images aim to portray a unique perspective of places or things that may seem commonplace to the everyday eye, but which trigger some sort of emotional reaction. Whether he's shooting landscapes, cityscapes, streets or architecture, his goal is to always create a connection between the subject and the viewer. Michael has worked with notable brands including Samsung, Sony, Ford, Hilton Hotels, Air Canada, Scotiabank, and Fjallraven, as well as the tourism boards of Germany, Switzerland, Poland, Indonesia, the United States, and Dominica. His work has been sold as part of Sotheby's Modern & Contemporary Discoveries Sale. *Wonder Around Every Corner* is his first book.

LCCN: 2023905242
ISBN: 978-1-9519630-9-5

Printed and bound in China
First printing, 2023

Michael Sidofsky's photographs from
Wonder Around Every Corner can be
purchased as prints. For inquiries,
go to trope.com or email the gallery
at info@trope.com.

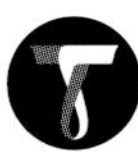

+ INFORMATION:
For additional information
on our books and prints,
visit trope.com

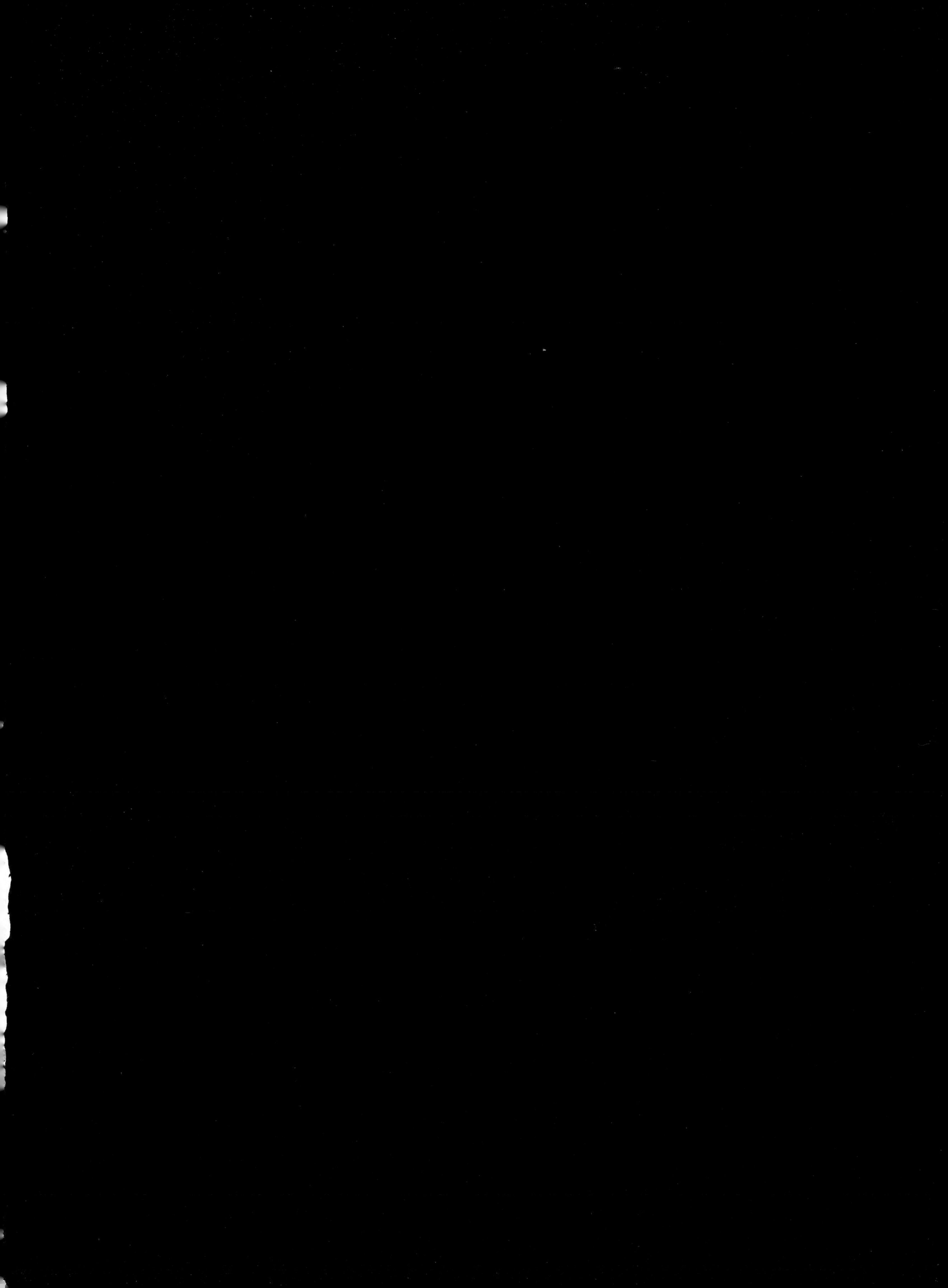